THE CHOICE
TO BE HUMAN

For my wife
Sara
and our friends
John and Adelaide Gallagher

THE CHOICE
TO BE HUMAN

Jesus Alive in the Gospel of Matthew

Eugene Kennedy

DOUBLEDAY & COMPANY, INC.
GARDEN CITY, NEW YORK
1985

Unless otherwise indicated, all scriptural citations are from *The Jerusalem Bible*, copyright © 1966 by Darton, Longman & Todd, Ltd., and
Doubleday & Company, Inc. Used by permission.

Library of Congress Cataloging in Publication Data
Kennedy, Eugene C.
    The choice to be human.
    1. Jesus Christ—Biography—Meditations.   2. Christian
biography—Palestine—Meditations.   3. Bible. N.T.
Matthew—Meditations.   I. Title.
BT306.4.K46   1985   226'.206

Library of Congress Catalog Card Number: 84–28694
ISBN: 0-385-19280-0

THE CHOICE
TO BE HUMAN

This book consists of a series of personal reflections on the Gospel of
Matthew. It does not pretend to be a commentary, although I turned
often to scripture scholars for help as I read and thought about this first
and longest Gospel account of the life of Jesus. These pages are essentially spontaneous, personal reflections; in short, meditations whose
metaphors and imaginative structure arose within me. They necessarily
reflect my own interests and experience as well as my conviction about
the choice to be human that is both our simplest definition of the
Incarnation and our essential task as believers.

I began these meditations several years ago as a feature in a newsletter, *You,* published by the Thomas More Association. The first few
chapters appeared in that publication in a different form. I stopped
writing that newsletter but I did not stop reading Matthew's account
of the life and preaching of Jesus. To read one Gospel intensely is an
experience that forces you to think deeply and freshly about people and
events with which you have been so familiar that you may have come
to take them for granted. Meditation offers us a way to rediscover this
profoundly human story and, as may happen in taking a new and slower
route into our native city, to enter it from an angle that gives us a fresh
vision of its energy and truth.

I recall the instructions given to the knights in the Arthurian legends
as they departed on their quests. They were to "enter the forest at its
darkest part," they were not, in other words, to follow somebody else's
path. The essential note of any authentic search for spiritual meaning is
that, enriched by our tradition, we must nonetheless find our way to
the Grail of spiritual understanding on our own. The path hacked by
another simply will not do.

These meditations will not fit everyone and they are not offered as
the only way in which the Gospel can be approached or entered freshly.
They may, however, serve as a stimulus for the reader's own meditative
powers. They will, I trust, reinforce people's confidence in their own
ability to find a path that matches their own life experience. Making

the choice to be human, we all enter the forest at its darkest part every day. That is the story of all our stories, the point of Matthew's carefully arranged narrative. Like the virgins in one of the parables, we must burn with our own oil, we cannot beg or borrow it from others at the last moment. If this book is not a detailed map through the murky woods, I hope it will encourage ordinary people to trust their own deepest human instincts and experience as they· reflect on the Gospel.

Many contemporary gurus advocate meditation as a means to inner peace, to controlling blood pressure, to securing a safe and warm haven in a boisterous and cold world. The root of meditate, *med*, means *to take appropriate measures*, and the whole word means *to think about*. Standing at this dimmest edge of forest, meditation invites us to take the measures that are appropriate for men and women, that is, to think for ourselves about our spiritual destiny, to find our way into life rather than out of it. Meditation may disturb us before it yields peace; it may stir our blood and consciences rather than relieve them of pressure; it will, in any case, demand that we examine our lives and beliefs deeply.

Each person who moves slowly through the Gospel of Matthew will be struck by something slightly different. I was impressed by the way in which the scriptures have been misused to blame the Jewish people for the death of Jesus. One cannot meditate on this Gospel without thinking again about the seeds of anti-semitism. Neither can one read this Gospel without sensing that what Jesus came to challenge was the superficial and manipulative use of religious faith and practice. He confronts the bias that seems so deeply a part of life: the hypocrisy, the making things look good, the settling for appearances, and the reliance on formulas that are well rationalized and readily incorporated into all human institutions.

Jesus repudiates all religions that accept the dead husks and throw the living fruit away. Religious institutions share the temptation to settle for control of people and events through the manipulation of surfaces; they are afraid of what bears life of itself and may, therefore, move and grow in unpredictable directions. The devil dwells in this urge to control rather than to liberate the human soul. One can hardly live in these closing years of the twentieth century without realizing again how the forces that want to control have gathered, like apocalyptic horsemen, to lead another charge against the camps of ordinary people who wish to live and believe freely. We do stand by a dark forest through which fearful religious and political leaders would force us to pass in single file through their exclusive pathway of righteousness. They want to intimidate us, make us afraid, and hand over our souls to them once more. Jesus saw such shadowed forces as the corrupters of the essential nature of religion in his time. They are no less so all these centuries later.

Meditation may be the only way that we can fortify ourselves for the daily struggle to be truly human that I believe is the core of the Gospel message. Being human is a choice and nobody else, no matter how vested with authority or gifted with ability to work wonders, can make it for us. I hope that this series of meditations will be a source of strength for men and women as they make the choices that define their true humanity.

Eugene Kennedy

MATTHEW

CHAPTER 1

Verses 1–25

A genealogy of Jesus Christ, son of David, son of Abraham:

Abraham was the father of Isaac,
Isaac the father of Jacob,
Jacob the father of Judah and his brothers,
Judah was the father of Perez and Zerah, Tamar being their mother,
Perez was the father of Hezron,
Hezron the father of Ram,
Ram was the father of Amminadab,
Amminadab the father of Nahshon,
Nahshon the father of Salmon,
Salmon was the father of Boaz, Rahab being his mother,
Boaz was the father of Obed, Ruth being his mother,
Obed was the father of Jesse;
and Jesse was the father of King David.

David was the father of Solomon, whose mother had been Uriah's wife,
Solomon was the father of Rehoboam,
Rehoboam the father of Abijah,
Abijah the father of Asa,
Asa was the father of Jehoshaphat,
Jehoshaphat the father of Joram,
Joram the father of Azariah,
Azariah was the father of Jotham,
Jotham the father of Ahaz,
Ahaz the father of Hezekiah,
Hezekiah was the father of Manasseh,
Manasseh the father of Amon,
Amon the father of Josiah;
and Josiah was the father of Jechoniah and his brothers.
Then the deportation to Babylon took place.

After the deportation to Babylon:
Jechoniah was the father of Shealtiel,
Shealtiel the father of Zerubbabel,
Zerubbabel was the father of Abiud,
Abiud the father of Eliakim,
Eliakim the father of Azor,
Azor was the father of Zadok,
Zadok the father of Achim,
Achim the father of Eliud,
Eliud was the father of Eleazar,
Eleazar the father of Matthan,
Matthan the father of Jacob;
and Jacob was the father of Joseph the husband of Mary;
of her was born Jesus who is called Christ.

The sum of generations is therefore: fourteen from Abraham to David; fourteen from David to the Babylonian deportation; and fourteen from the Babylonian deportation to Christ.

This is how Jesus Christ came to be born. His mother Mary was betrothed to Joseph; but before they came to live together she was found to be with child through the Holy Spirit. Her husband Joseph, being a man of honor and wanting to spare her publicity, decided to divorce her informally. He had made up his mind to do this when the angel of the Lord appeared to him in a dream and said, "Joseph son of David, do not be afraid to take Mary home as your wife, because she has conceived what is in her by the Holy Spirit. She will give birth to a son and you must name him Jesus, because he is the one who is to save his people from their sins." Now all this took place to fulfill the words spoken by the Lord through the prophet:

> The virgin will conceive and give birth to a son
> and they will call him Immanuel,

a name which means "God-is-with-us." When Joseph woke up he did what the angel of the Lord had told him to do: he took his wife to his home and, though he had not had intercourse with her, she gave birth to a son; and he named him Jesus.

Time is the silent sea we cross at the beginning of Matthew's Gospel. And Matthew, like a captain who wants his ship to lie steady at a precise latitude and longitude, throws as many anchors backward as he does forward. Here the tale begins, tied into the depths of times past but flowing also into the currents of the future.

The story of Jesus breaks into our history on our own terms; it is a commitment to our experience and its twin demons of time and change. The fire and light of the Spirit do not glow steadily in the closed vacuum of eternity; they rise and fall in a swaying lantern that hangs on a rib of time itself.

Matthew begins with a cadenced genealogy of Hebrew names that are like voices crying from a distant homeland. There is a pull in these strong, sweet names; something stirs in us about the land where our spiritual pilgrimage began. Something of it is in our souls no matter how far we have traveled, and it comes awake at the chanting of these names. It is the lineage of Jesus, the human roots that tie him into our experience, and its rhythm is irresistible.

Jesus is not a person out of time, a hero cleansed of his Jewishness, a blond WASP rising out of Nazareth. He is a Jew, a man in time and place and relationship, not a stranger but a friend. Jesus is born into the poverty not just of the stable but of specific human consciousness and feeling. He is one of us, more like us than different; that is the whole point of it.

We are caught up with him still in this mystery of time. Jesus is not a memory, not someone we mourn, but someone with whom we remain in living relationship. It is no accident that the gospel begins with a network of relationships nor that we are brought quickly to that between Mary and Joseph. For here is a central mystery filled with the power of man and woman, a relationship still at the heart of the world's agony and joy. Their relationship gives life and growth; it is webbed with mystery and wonder, with misunderstanding and the need for tenderness, but it is described in a few lean words that leave us on the outside, unsure and perplexed in the silence.

But this story is not old to any of us—the tale of a man and a woman struggling to understand their relationship, wanting to reach each other even as they are confronted with all that they do not know or cannot know about each other. They did not live in some distant silence, two figures waiting like plastic crèche pieces under a Christmas tree. Their anguish and uncertainty were as real as their love.

What, indeed, was happening to them, in this mystery of invitation by the Spirit that confounds us still? They worked their way through it, just as we do, by inches, by the insights love mines out of our hearts, by the trust we learn to give when things are beyond our grasp, when what we are asked to do seems beyond the farthest edge of possibility.

Our lives are in the ancient story; we find ourselves there face to face with the mysteries constantly lived out in our relationships with each other. The summons is to enter into relationship and to let mystery have its way with us, to say yes in a trembling voice to our lives with each other, and to find our way together to the source of the Spirit.

CHAPTER 2

Verses 1–23

After Jesus had been born at Bethlehem in Judaea during the reign of King Herod, some wise men came to Jerusalem from the east. "Where is the infant king of the Jews?" they asked. "We saw his star as it rose and have come to do him homage." When King Herod heard this he was perturbed, and so was the whole of Jerusalem. He called together all the chief priests and the scribes of the people, and inquired of them where the Christ was to be born. "At Bethlehem in Judaea," they told him, "for this is what the prophet wrote:

> And you, Bethlehem, in the land of Judah,
> you are by no means least among the leaders of Judah,
> for out of you will come a leader
> who will shepherd my people Israel."

Then Herod summoned the wise men to see him privately. He asked them the exact date on which the star had appeared, and sent them on to Bethlehem. "Go and find out all about the child," he said, "and when you have found him, let me know, so that I too may go and do him homage." Having listened to what the king had to say, they set out. And there in front of them was the star they had seen rising; it went forward and halted over the place where the child was. The sight of the star filled them with delight, and going into the house they saw the child with his mother Mary, and falling to their knees they did him homage. Then, opening their treasures, they offered him gifts of gold and frankincense and myrrh. But they were warned in a dream not to go back to Herod, and returned to their own country by a different way.

After they had left, the angel of the Lord appeared to Joseph in a dream and said, "Get up, take the child and his mother with you, and escape into Egypt, and stay there until I tell you, because Herod intends to search for the child and do away with him." So Joseph got up and, taking the child and his mother with him, left that night for

Egypt, where he stayed until Herod was dead. This was to fulfill what the Lord had spoken through the prophet:

I called my son out of Egypt.

Herod was furious when he realized that he had been outwitted by the wise men, and in Bethlehem and its surrounding district he had all the male children killed who were two years old or under, reckoning by the date he had been careful to ask the wise men. It was then that the words spoken through the prophet Jeremiah were fulfilled:

A voice was heard in Ramah,
sobbing and loudly lamenting:
it was Rachel weeping for her children,
refusing to be comforted
because they were no more.

After Herod's death, the angel of the Lord appeared in a dream to Joseph in Egypt and said, "Get up, take the child and his mother with you and go back to the land of Israel, for those who wanted to kill the child are dead." So Joseph got up and, taking the child and his mother with him, went back to the land of Israel. But when he learned that Archelaus had succeeded his father Herod as ruler of Judaea he was afraid to go there, and being warned in a dream he left for the region of Galilee. There he settled in a town called Nazareth. In this way the words spoken through the prophets were to be fulfilled:

He will be called a Nazarene.

———————⌘———————

How do we make our way to the truth if we stick only to numbers and facts? What happens to the kind of truth that was in last year's almanac? How fragile is the grasp of information, temporary by nature and quicksilver to the examiner's eye. The population of New York, the number of phones in Alaska, the average price of anything: How true can these facts ever be when their validity melts away like a snowflake on our outstretched palm? The truth needs a more lasting instrument of transmission; it needs something to preserve it from the acid bath of changing times. The truth demands a stronger container than yesterday's facts.

We are not surprised, then, to find the gospels filled with poetry and stories, with the metaphors that tell the truth about existence far better than computer printouts. We are coming once more to understand that imagination is not just the language of fancy but that it is the servant of the truths we never want to forget.

Yes, and that perennially confusing word *myth* that has frightened people, making them think that Bible scholars who employ it are saying that the scriptures are pleasant fables with no roots in human time or place. Myth is, however, that special language of faith that ties us to the ways of human understanding. How do we save the truth of life unless we put it in a story—unless, in other words, we use a language far more powerful and lasting than that of facts?

We are, after all, caught up in a story that is not easy to tell, and one that we may only begin to understand after a hundred and more times of hearing it. God became man, the Christmas story tells us, and made a lonely pilgrimage in a darkened and unfriendly world. We can only make our way to Nazareth—and feel the circle of prophecy drawn full —if we understand the poetic heart of the Incarnation. Everything we learn about life helps us to understand that mystery better; we are always journeying back to it, grasping it better because we understand ourselves more deeply. One needs a special language for such explorations.

Poetry is a creative language and it possesses unfolding layers of meaning. It is, then, the right language to describe the birth and infancy of Jesus. The birth of a boy. It is a common story and yet, as in our own lives, it changes everything. The balance that existed before can never be regained. Mother and father are no longer just husband and wife; they are implicated in a complex set of new relationships in which they must always re-create themselves.

So, too, the balance of the world is changed at the birth of Jesus, and the forces of good and evil, the human capacity to receive or to reject, to embrace or to pull away from—are unsettled for the rest of history. They must be spoken of in metaphor, in the story of the vengeful Herod and the vulnerable young family on a new flight into Egypt, in the terror of the homeless dark and the fulfillment of finding Nazareth. We read it for the truth rather than for the facts.

And we look back from what we have learned about the creative process for a better understanding of God's intervention in our human

16

story. Research has discovered, for example, that creative men and women, when confronted with a problem, do not stand outside of it trying to take its measure from a distance. Instead, they plunge into the problem situation, becoming part of it themselves in order to feel its power and direction. They work toward an understanding of it from the inside by bringing the force of their intuitions into play at the heart of the challenge.

So creation illumines Incarnation, where God does not take our measure from a distance but enters into our situation in the person of Jesus, permanently transforming history through the force of His presence. We are caught up in the mystery that is still working itself out, the mystery that could never be summed up in an exact birthdate, the mystery that needs wandering stars to underscore a New Creation.

CHAPTER 3

Verses 1–17

In due course John the Baptist appeared; he preached in the wilderness of Judaea and this was his message: "Repent, for the kingdom of heaven is close at hand." This was the man the prophet Isaiah spoke of when he said:

> A voice cries in the wilderness:
> prepare a way for the Lord,
> make his paths straight.

This man John wore a garment made of camel hair with a leather belt around his waist, and his food was locusts and wild honey. Then Jerusalem and all Judaea and the whole Jordan district made their way to him, and as they were baptized by him in the river Jordan they confessed their sins. But when he saw a number of Pharisees and Sadducees coming for baptism he said to them, "Brood of vipers, who warned you to fly from the retribution that is coming? But if you are repentant, produce the appropriate fruit, and do not presume to tell yourselves, 'We have Abraham for our father,' because, I tell you, God can raise children for Abraham from these stones. Even now the ax is laid to the roots of the trees, so that any tree which fails to produce good fruit will be cut down and thrown on the fire. I baptize you in water for repentance, but the one who follows me is more powerful than I am, and I am not fit to carry his sandals; he will baptize you with the Holy Spirit and fire. His winnowing fan is in his hand; he will clear his threshing floor and gather his wheat into the barn; but the chaff he will burn in a fire that will never go out."

Then Jesus appeared: he came from Galilee to the Jordan to be baptized by John. John tried to dissuade him. "It is I who need baptism from you," he said, "and yet you come to me!" But Jesus replied, "Leave it like this for the time being; it is fitting that we should, in this way, do all that righteousness demands." At this, John gave in to him.

As soon as Jesus was baptized he came up from the water, and suddenly the heavens opened and he saw the Spirit of God descending like a dove and coming down on him. And a voice spoke from heaven, "This is my Son, the Beloved; my favor rests on him."

————————⟋∞⟍————————

John the Baptist, one savage eye flashing out of his shadowed face, strides across the beginning of Matthew's gospel like a harsh poet out of patience both with himself and with the world. He seems to come straight at us still, an iron figure against the sky, a dust-caked pilgrim of the absolute. Have we always felt two ways about this mysterious man, both intimidated and attracted by the very same qualities in him?

The world is a patch of compromises and sometimes our lives, even at their best, are the same way. In John we feel the energies of commitment and single-mindedness, of a spiritual bet unhedged in the face of smugness and worldly power. The ground still trembles where he throws down the challenge to a generation of vipers; he remains a man to make us uncomfortable with our shortcuts and forgotten promises, with our failed aspirations and uncertain wills.

John is almost too stark for us as he proclaims the one who will come after him to baptize in the Holy Spirit and fire. John stands, as prophets do to this very day, as an unyielding presence unsettling us and leaving us not quite sure of how we feel about him.

The axe is indeed laid to the root of the tree. John's words ring as loud as the blade in the wood; he is a stormy figure against the weather fronts that cloud our passage from older times into new. Only such a fierce man could straddle the shifting ages, reminding us of our roots in the past and heralding our destiny in the one who would follow him. John helps us understand Jesus when he speaks later of coming not to destroy the law but to bring it to fulfillment.

And yet John seems hard to know, hard to like even though we stand back in admiration of him. We react the same way to most absolute figures, those who throw everything aside to pursue a simpler, sterner, and spiritually less mortgaged existence. Most ordinary people feel ambivalent about those who give themselves to a specialized form of life without compromise. We are moved by them; we admire them but we have doubts that we could ever live like them.

So the craggy shadow of John falls across our path in a hundred different ways, perhaps as some cosmic force that balances the universe

19

out so that we can find a place to live between the extremes of affirmation and negation. Hard enough, we say, to keep on our feet there without thinking that we are all called to climb hand over hand up the sharpest crags of our experience.

Jesus seems to say this in those incredible few moments when John, determined as ever, backs away, almost truculently refusing Jesus' request for baptism. Jesus is a gentler presence, a person with a sense of the times coming together, a man feeling what is right for this powerful moment of self-realization. "Give in for now," Jesus says, in another translation of this passage, to the gaunt prophet whose preaching has used few phrases with this human flavor.

Give in for now: what a strange thing for Jesus to say to a steadfast and protesting prophet. And yet what a comforting thing for us who cannot burn with an unwavering flame, what an understanding phrase for those of us who cannot live in fiercely absolute ways. But Jesus is the one to fulfill the law, to preach mercy rather than justice, to speak of forgiveness rather than revenge.

It is a moment of realization for us, a moment of fire and the Spirit, and of our seeing better who Jesus is and who we are. Jesus may, after all, be more like us than the herald who balks at baptizing him. There are traditions to be respected, things to be done, choices to be made, as our own consciousness of the meaning of our lives comes gradually clear to us.

Jesus chooses the world of ambivalence for his life and work with sinners and wine drinkers, the just and the unjust on every side. He dresses not in the skins of animals but in the ordinary clothes of the day; he eats not grasshoppers and wild honey but the food of everyman. Jesus the Lord enters our life as it is and calls us not away but more deeply into it.

CHAPTER 4

Verses 1–11

Then Jesus was led by the Spirit out into the wilderness to be tempted by the devil. He fasted for forty days and forty nights, after which he was very hungry, and the tempter came and said to him, "If you are the Son of God, tell these stones to turn into loaves." But he replied, "Scripture says:

> Man does not live on bread alone
> but on every word that comes from the mouth of God."

The devil then took him to the holy city and made him stand on the parapet of the Temple. "If you are the Son of God," he said, "throw yourself down; for Scripture says:

> He will put you in his angels' charge,
> and they will support you on their hands
> in case you hurt your foot against a stone."

Jesus said to him, "Scripture also says:

> You must not put the Lord your God to the test."

Next, taking him to a very high mountain, the devil showed him all the kingdoms of the world and their splendor. "I will give you all these," he said, "if you fall at my feet and worship me." Then Jesus replied, "Be off, Satan! For Scripture says:

> You must worship the Lord your God,
> and serve him alone."

Then the devil left him, and angels appeared and looked after him.

--------&--------

What is this wilderness or desert, this place out of time that ties the testaments together where we journey so often in the scriptures? A place of wandering as well as discovery—the air ablaze at noon but chill as moonlight when the sun has gone—the desert fills our dreams, stretching to the rim of our spiritual imagination. We are drawn to it as we are to the sea; something in us calls us over and over to the sand and stars. The desert has worked its way into our souls. We have been here before, we know the feel of the place and that we will return.

The desert is part of our pilgrim life, alternately a place of trial and a place of peace. Jesus comes here to rest or pray, but also to reveal to us a place of mystery and hidden springs in which we can feel our Jewish heritage. The desert is not just a background for biblical stories; neither is it a place to be challenged or conquered. How mixed are our feelings as we stand at its edge. It seems both inviting and forbidding, tender as its flowers and harsh as its storms, a mystery and more than that, but we all gather here. For what?

We can only listen to the desert, opening ourselves to the symbolism that is as deep as it is silent. The desert hands us back our chance to hear the Spirit just as it allows us to hear ourselves again. In its quiet we can hear the hollow sound of power, fame, and wonders sought only for themselves. In the desert light we can see again—both ourselves and our world. We do not hide in the desert; we go there so that we can leave it with a purified sense of purpose and a better understanding of ourselves as we go back to our regular lives. The desert is filled with unexpected gifts of fruit and shade and cold water, of cloud by day and flame by night, a place of testing and cleansing, a place to confront our good and evil, a feast for those who go there empty, a homeland for the believing heart.

Verses 12–25

Hearing that John had been arrested he went back to Galilee, and leaving Nazareth he went and settled in Capernaum, a lakeside town on the borders of Zebulun and Naphtali. In this way the prophecy of Isaiah was to be fulfilled:

> Land of Zebulun! Land of Naphtali!
> Way of the sea on the far side of Jordan,
> Galilee of the nations!
> The people that lived in darkness
> has seen a great light;

on those who dwell in the land and shadow of death
a light has dawned.

From that moment Jesus began his preaching with the message, "Repent, for the kingdom of heaven is close at hand."

As he was walking by the Sea of Galilee he saw two brothers, Simon, who was called Peter, and his brother Andrew; they were making a cast in the lake with their net, for they were fishermen. And he said to them, "Follow me and I will make you fishers of men." And they left their nets at once and followed him.

Going on from there he saw another pair of brothers, James son of Zebedee and his brother John; they were in their boat with their father Zebedee, mending their nets, and he called them. At once, leaving the boat and their father, they followed him.

He went around the whole of Galilee teaching in their synagogues, proclaiming the Good News of the kingdom and curing all kinds of diseases and sickness among the people. His fame spread throughout Syria, and those who were suffering from diseases and painful complaints of one kind or another, the possessed, epileptics, the paralyzed, were all brought to him, and he cured them. Large crowds followed him, coming from Galilee, the Decapolis, Jerusalem, Judaea and Transjordania.

———————— ✺ ————————

Dread hangs like fine mist over these plain words, and power rumbles like a distant storm through these quiet verses. John has been arrested and the beginning has come to an end. Terror dances like a flame across this intersection of time. Jesus turns his face full toward us. We can see him better in this moment of action; we can feel the swiftness of his decision, the edge of purpose in the tension of a journey that must be made out of Nazareth and toward Capernaum.

But how could Jesus escape what we have all come to know? The times are both unfolding and crying out for fulfillment. We taste these moments when, if ever we are to find our destiny, we must move forward into the places we have not yet been.

Jesus separates himself from his past; it is a choice we face with mixed feelings. Human life is a pilgrimage always away from the fires where we have warmed ourselves and into the windy dark on the other side of which we discover ourselves anew. Hard facts, these: We either separate ourselves from our past or we are, sooner or later, separated by forces or conditions we cannot predict or control. We break away, not out of resentment, but out of necessity. Whether or not we live fully hangs always in the balance.

Purpose is neither an accident nor a gift of the grinning gods; it grows into shape around our hard decisions to abandon our shelter and to challenge the night. It is a tale told here in a single line. Yet how complex this mystery is!

We journey to the strange and noisy place where the work of life awaits us but we trail the roots of our existence after us. We break loose and change the past that clings to our persons like a charged field. We are new and yet old, fresh but grown from an ancient tree, a mystery of past and present compounded as we move into the future.

So Jesus moves to Capernaum bearing in himself the history of the Jews, feeling in his soul the mixture of longing and exile, of prophets' cries and Rachel's mourning. He separates himself from Nazareth and moves into a new age; he leaves Nazareth as home behind him but takes Nazareth as history with him.

The ages merge in his person as he hurries toward the sea, to the teeming province of Galilee as eager for trade and new ideas as California two thousand years later. A new place indeed, and Josephus writes of its people: "They were ever fond of innovations and by nature disposed to changes, and delighted in seditions."

The time of quiet has ended and, for now, the desert is far behind. It is in the jangling noise of the city that Jesus proclaims the fulfillment of an ancient pledge. The Kingdom of God is at hand.

The public life of Jesus begins and yet it seems hard to see his face. He marches across the countryside and we follow behind, catching our best sense of him in the faces of those before him. There is a different rhythm in the verses and one hurries to keep up with Jesus as he calls out in a new way to the men he has known before.

The shore is in counterpoint to the desert all through the gospels. It is the place of tumult, the city of man, filled with shouting voices, the cries of gulls, and water lapping against the boats. If the desert is a place of separation and prayers, the teeming shore is the place for milling crowds and a call to action.

And the fishermen? How can one see them afresh, these men we have seen in our imaginations put aside their broken nets a thousand times? Matthew tells us all too little of this moment when the fishermen join themselves to Jesus. He will let it go in order to accomplish a larger purpose; we only stand in thought beside their boat as they follow Jesus down the shore.

It is too much like life to be magic, too plain to be a moment of first meeting. It is more a mood of truths and purpose crystallizing; it is the way we all finally do things we have been thinking about for a long time. All the talk they must have exchanged about Jesus is now ended and, facing him again, they know they must choose once and for all. This is a moment the fishermen knew would come, as we ourselves sense a consciousness of our own challenges building within us, a moment, indeed, that waits for all of us. It is the beginning of something new, but it is also the end of a long preparation.

But we are also caught in Matthew's summary of Jesus' mission as the word trails like a sputtering fuse across all Galilee. The shorthand account is powdery dry and does not turn Jesus' face any more fully toward us. Is Jesus, we wonder, of two minds about the fame he must confront whether he seeks it or not?

We hear the echoes of Jesus' telling people at one time not to talk and at others to go and tell what they have seen and heard to everyone. Does he sense the destructive possibilities of celebrity, the hook sunk deep in the notoriety that is not a goal but a condition of his preaching? Perhaps that is why it is still hard to see his face and why Matthew will let the preaching and healing speak for themselves.

His eyes do not sparkle like those of a leader gathering loyalists to himself; they are filled with tenderness, the eyes of a strong man with feelings for human weakness. Many go unhealed, but life can be redeemed. There is a promise in all this, a pledge against the tragic darkness, a hint that we are not without hope in finding the outlines of our experience. A light has indeed begun to shine. We see Jesus' face better because he has turned it fully toward the weak and the sinners; he is looking right at us.

CHAPTER 5

Verses 1–12

When he saw the crowds he went up on the mountainside. After he had sat down his disciples gathered around him, and he began to teach them:

"How blest are the poor in spirit: the reign of God is theirs. Blest too are the sorrowing; they shall be consoled. [Blest are the lowly; they shall inherit the land.] Blest are they who hunger and thirst for holiness; they shall have their fill. Blest are they who show mercy; mercy shall be theirs. Blest are the single-hearted for they shall see God. Blest too the peacemakers; they shall be called sons of God. Blest are those persecuted for holiness' sake; the reign of God is theirs. Blest are you when they insult you and persecute you and utter every kind of slander against you because of me. Be glad and rejoice, for your reward is great in heaven; they persecuted the prophets before you in the very same way." (NAB)

Where else could Jesus speak from? The mountains abide, now rock sharp in outline, now gone blue in haze, but enduring witnesses to history surviving it as a landfall survives the hungry sea. The mountains brood in silence or ring with song; they seem close enough to fall on us at one moment and distant beyond any climb in the next. The mountains outlast our vanities, always ancient and always young, a place to stand for a frozen moment on the edge of time itself and, animal-like, to paw the ground sensing that we stand at a joint in the universe unsure of what would happen to us if we stepped completely across.

The sermon is a thousand echoes collapsing on each other and bouncing endlessly off the hillside. We have heard it before and lived in its welling sounds but we have neither fully understood nor tired of it. Words from a mountainside translated from one language to another, each one siphoning off some of the primal energy of the original, and yet they are still filled with lingering power. We must hear them again and again, for this is the core of Jesus' message, dense and rich, compacted and arranged by Matthew so that we can hear the whole of it. Where else could we listen except on a green slope of the lasting hills?

And yet what can we now make of it, this message that promises so much to our longing hearts? It gives no sign, points to no wonder, gives us nothing, not a scrap of ritual, to carry out. What price must we pay for the self-possession of this blessedness? How do we lay hold of this joy of which Jesus speaks? He is the prophet of a mystery as old as the mount on which we stand. We are already in the place of pilgrimage; the journey is done for those who can look deeply within themselves. Our blessedness is not to be found outside of our experience; joy is ours when we embrace rather than attempt to escape our lives.

Happiness is a word that reveals itself in its structure; *hap,* its root, comes from the word for *by chance* or *by accident.* Joy does not arrive through luck; the blessedness that Jesus speaks of is not the outcome of a cruel lottery that delivers prizes to some while it denies them to others. This joy is available to all, to the lame and the blind, the oppressed and the luckless, to the poor and, miracle beyond telling, to the rich as well. It depends on opening ourselves to life rather than closing ourselves off.

We have to stand on the mountainside, on that perilous line where we can feel the pull of time and yet want to reach across to eternity; that is the line that runs through all of our days. Joy comes not as a blessing of rest but as the crown of creating and re-creating ourselves in life itself. We must stand on the mountain and feel the winds and grow dizzy with the sight of the stars. There is no pointing to the place of joy; we are standing there already, clustered joyfully in the kingdom within ourselves where we find again everything life seems to ask us to give away.

And now the words that sweep down the years like a wind that sometimes grinds the soul with the teeth of winter and at other times heals it with the scented oils of spring. A paradox and more than that. Discovering our poverty we find that we are already rich, in letting go of everything we get the best of it all back, heaped up and overflowing, the staggering bounty that is the inheritance of the true believer. The lock on the Christian treasure is here and the key is in it. How do we grasp and turn this key so that the treasure may fall open?

The most dizzying paradox of the gospel is connected with this, for we must open it ourselves. Nor is it as difficult as some alchemists of the Spirit make the secrets of religion seem. We can open it only if we give up complications and the air-scratching rituals of magic. That is the whole point of what Jesus teaches. It is as simple as saying, "Follow me," and as hard as breaking our hearts open to life all around us.

How blest are the poor in spirit: the reign of God is theirs.

Poverty of spirit is a theme that has been chewed white by the jaws of preaching. It is not really something that can be talked about. Poverty of spirit is one of those deep understandings that can be appreciated only by persons who have given themselves over to the experience of life. You are poor—and blessed—if you do this. Poverty of spirit is not something that can be sought.

Poverty of spirit does not come by itself; it is the gift that accompanies and is indivisible from a loving life. It resembles the peacefulness of an autumn morning or the easy atmosphere of trust between two genuine friends. There is no way to buy or earn what is essentially a gift. Not all the earnest predawn prayers or the most harrowing self-denial can make purchase of something so rare and rich.

That is why these sayings of Jesus celebrate what believers already possess; these are not gifts to come, not promises over the horizon, but the wealth we already possess if we have entered into life with each other. How else could we expect to find the meaning of our existence? And where else are we challenged to die the death to ourselves that makes life to the full available to us? The answer, if it is to be found at all for most ordinary people, is in our relationships with each other. The heart is harrowed by loving, but like the field split open by the farmer it suffers not unto death but unto new life. The Kingdom of God belongs to those who love others enough to let them be separate, to let them have their own lives.

Lovers understand poverty of spirit, and because they know each other they understand something more about our relationship with God. We cannot demand His regard or claim it for fulfilling certain promises. We can only let go, trusting wholly in Him, knowing that each surrender is not passive resignation, but a positive gift, seeking no return—the kind of gift lovers poor in spirit make of themselves all the time.

Blest too are the sorrowing; they shall be consoled . . .

But who can hear the words, much less believe them wholeheartedly? Of suffering the world has known enough; it has stumbled under the burden, risen dazed like a man under a midsummer sun and, unsure of the right direction, has bloodied itself on the sharp rocks of a hundred wrong paths. Suffering unsettles human beings, we say in protest, it scars and cripples them, destroying their chance at beauty and peace. It is the sentence of a raving blind judge passed all too often on the innocent. Who can count it a blessing?

And we are right in a way and wrong in a way. Suffering is a mystery not easily solved; there is really no good answer to the age-old question of the mocking skeptic, "How can a loving God permit so much pain and cruelty?" And who has ever been convinced, much less consoled, by the variety of answers, smooth and fragile as eggs in a box, that have been manufactured over the centuries?

In the long run we do not understand and we cannot explain the powerful and central role of suffering in our lives. We can only enter, as Jesus did, into the human condition where suffering abides, all of us innocents at first until we gradually build our consciousness of right and wrong, of good and evil, of the justices and injustices that pile up swiftly even in a young life.

We cannot successfully flee pain, we cannot turn our gaze away from it without running the risk of missing what we must inevitably endure if we are to grasp the meaning of life itself. Trying to escape suffering—ignoring it, refusing to react to it, wishing it dreamily away—is the curse that blights the harvest and leaves us dumb and hungry.

And here is a clue for us to ponder: only suffering breaks us open; only suffering, whether it is in the midst of love or tragedy, shatters the thick stone walls of our self-concern. We cannot understand it and we remain pledged to eliminating all unnecessary suffering. And yet we are humanized by suffering; we do not comprehend it fully, but when we can accept the pain that is part of any worthwhile human activity we come more fully alive. We are different afterwards; suffering opens something in our souls to deepen us as human beings.

The Spirit hovers not over dead low tides in the psyche but over the waters churned by our reaching out toward the brokenhearted and the abandoned; we are saved by responding to the pain-racked world. We are reborn by being forced to enter into our own suffering, into the

29

dark mysteries of misunderstanding and separation that are part of love itself. Suffering breaks us open so that the waters of life can wash through us and make us clean. We are blessed when we say yes to our continuing inheritance of pain because this frees us from the prison of ourselves. It enables us to lay hold of the joy that others can only dream about.

Blest are the lowly; they shall inherit the land . . .

Where lies this power in weakness, where do we find this strength to lay claim to the land? What can we make of these words when those other words, fiercer by far, about the Kingdom being borne away by the violent still ring in our ears? Who are these poor and meek persons in our midst who so quietly cup the fire and light of the Spirit in their hands? How can we find them and learn even a little of their secret?

These are not the grovelers of life, not the fearful or those whose meekness involves them in the desperate effort to win mercy and affection by pleasing everyone. The lowly already possess the land because they already possess themselves. They are that secure tribe who live by truth rather than artifice, those vulnerable people who are in touch with their own spirits and who, lacking all defenses, are defended against the worst that life can offer. Blessed already are those who love inwardly because they are truly related to everything that is outside them. Their secret is that there is no secret, that a person armed with the truth of the self can go unarmed into life.

With how many scrolls and seals we still bind the agreements about the sale or transfer of land! And in what strongboxes do we lodge these records to save them from loss and destruction! Still the land passes from hand to hand and each of us, no matter how many acres we may count, must at last let go of them. Yet the lowly possess the land in an unfearful way; they cannot lose it because they understand something of the freedom to live fully that is their inheritance. They can enjoy the land, exult in it, and sing of its beauty; no one can deprive them of God's universe and its seasons. They possess the land because they have a vision of the Kingdom of peace and love that Jesus proclaims. They are not worried about losing everything because they are not holding tightly to everything; they spend life rather than hoard it. Blest indeed because theirs is the joy of the loving-hearted persons who give all of themselves to life and find the gift returned twice over every day.

And such people have a blessing for us too. We know who they are because we find that we need not impress them and yet that their truth is richly available to us. Blest are the unselfconsciously real people of this world, because the Spirit shines through them to enlighten us all. Blest are they because they bless us by their presence, making us more at home with ourselves and with the green and fruitful world in which we celebrate the Kingdom by sharing what we truly possess of ourselves.

Blest are they who hunger and thirst for holiness; they shall have their fill.

A sentence that drops into the heart like a hand grenade into a cushioned room. One hardly notices or even hears the noise of entry; everything seems familiar, just as it has always been. And then the words explode and we can never be quite the same again. Are we dulled to their meaning or have we heard them so often that we just nod our heads as automatically as peasants passing the church in the town square? Have we ever heard the challenge and the promise put with such simple power before?

We cannot think about the words and fail to ask ourselves just what it is that we do want out of life. It is an inquiry that unsettles the heart because it puts our distractions to flight and forces us to look hard at what we are doing and why. We don't ask for much, we say modestly, but that may be because we settle for so little.

What is it that we could do—and what would we be like—if we had a ravenous hunger, hunger enough to make us steal, and thirst enough to make us claw at the stony earth for water, for goodness, for wholeness and holiness, for living out the full truth of our possibilities? We all want to be good, but the feast in the Kingdom is prepared for those who want it desperately.

What have we here, a call to become zealots who cast away all their concerns in a forced march, eyes looking neither right nor left, toward holiness? Are we all to be prophets of this insistent imperative? We are ambivalent at the prospect and yet our spirits are stirred deeply at the same time. It makes us return to that question: What are we seeking in life and how are we going about it? Is there anything we give most of ourselves to, and what does it say about our values?

Blest are those who don't wait around for something to happen but actively do something to bring the goodness in themselves and others to life. This is not a summons to a wild-eyed rejection of our mostly ordinary lives, but an invitation to live them with a feeling for existence, a passion for the gift of life. A hunger and thirst for wholeness means that we do not hide away from life, but that we take it on almost fiercely.

We need a taste for the joys of life but we have to harvest these for ourselves, battling for them sometimes, exhausting ourselves as we do, but laying hold of the mystery a little more as we recommit our energies to life every day. The believer does not stand passively before the Lord, twisting his hat timidly in his hands as he hopes for a look of favor, a good harvest, or fair weather. He struggles with the gift of existence, working out the meaning of its majestic imperfection.

Blest are you who risk everything to find your right place at the banquet, for you are already inside the Kingdom. Blest are you, for the scrolled invitations are out and the best of the calves have been killed. The Kingdom of God is a banquet, but only if you are truly hungry and thirsty for life will you have your fill.

Blest are they who show mercy; mercy shall be theirs.

The hillside is quiet now, heavy with the silence of people who are absorbed in the words of Jesus, words that touch their simplest yet most telling experiences. And we are silent, too, before the phrases we have heard all our lives but perhaps never heard quite clearly until we wrestled enough with life to understand them.

Matthew gives us a dense paragraph, a final potent distillation—boiled and cooled and boiled down again—of what Jesus said at greater length and in different ways in his preaching. But the power is there, the force of truths that cannot be resisted by anyone who has ever felt the leverage that existence puts on our souls. If we have hurried by these notions the way we go down a familiar street, it is time to find a quiet place to wait while their meaning sinks in again.

Mercy challenges us in a world that has grown cynical about its possibilities. Mercy is fine, everyone says, but power settles the issues and is the decisive weight on the creaking scale pan in which peace and war are absurd. Mercy is better than sacrifice, but there are many who sniff the air inquiringly for the smell of gunpowder as the best evidence of justice done. We are still invested in the shoot-out and the put-down as sources of deliverance from the abrasions and annoyances of life. Mercy still seems weak, a wraith of a virtue, something second-best in a he-man world where it finds little respect in either sport or war.

And yet it takes strength of character rather than force of arms to look mercifully at humankind in a consistent manner. Pity can rise and fall as easily as a breaking wave across our psyches, but mercy is something different; it is a permanent way of regarding the world around us, a set of the mind and heart that does not waver. We may feel sorry for the world and look away; we feel mercy only when we are ready to live in and with its struggles and sufferings.

Mercy is from the Hebrew *Hesed*, a concept as rich and self-renewing as black farmland; there is nourishment for a lifetime and more in its meanings of loving kindness and convenant fidelity, in its echoes of forgiveness and understanding. It is not a notion to pass by quickly; mercy arrests us because it forces us to look at all of life, deeper into ourselves and into each other. The molten core of this loving kindness is understanding, that capacity to empty ourselves of our own concerns and view things from inside someone else. This is an extension of incarnation, this virtue that exists only if we can take on the flesh of others and know their experience not with the wise judgments of outsiders, but with the very taste of their lives in our mouths and the feel of their sufferings in our bones. This sensitive pilgrimage into the soul of another depends on surrendering our own distractions and feelings, on giving rather than taking.

Mercy is a source of life because we breathe our own spirits through it into the lives of others. Mercy is a long journey that begins with putting ourselves aside by allowing our own concerns to die, but it leads us to an enlarged sense of life and the promise of compassion as well.

Blest are the single-hearted for they shall see God.

The grace is not for innocence of life but for knowledge of the self; the blessing belongs not to those who are strangers to evil but to those who face it honestly and find themselves purified in the process. The single-hearted are not the naïve but the knowing, the persons whose respect for life is not wide-eyed but measured, like the respect of a wise old fighter for a resourceful opponent, or the respect of survivors for the sea.

The match tests us thoroughly and we do not engage in it absent-mindedly. Our wholeness is an outcome, a gradual rather than an overnight conversion. We are winnowed by the steadily blowing winds of existence as we make the decisions that define us as human beings. We establish a moral presence that is stable and compact, the fluids and fats of our own evil possibilities drained or burned away by the brightening fires of our own integrity. Blest are those who know the ill that they can do and do it not.

And yet it is a phrase to make us feel bad because we know the foreign particles that float like motes in the sunlight through our own motivations. So we long for the sheltered innocence of the very young or for what seems to us the uncomplicated faith of the peasant or for the grateful and untainted beliefs of the very old. We are far from single-minded; we know this even when others do not. We have looked on the line of our judgments as arced and whorled as a monitored heartbeat. We are familiar with ourselves and long to be rid of our uncertainties and our ambivalence. Who would call us pure of heart?

But wholeness is not incompatible with such complexity. We can see God when we can see ourselves, when our eyes are not shaded by obstacles in ourselves that we deny or disguise or pretend are not there. The sight of God is delivered to those who refuse to be blinded by their own conflicts. They see God because the ledges and defiles of their inner selves afford them a perspective on life; they find their way with the sureness of blind persons who sense the things around them even in a strange room.

Such is this blessing for the scarred and the lame, for those with eyes that sprout wrinkles from looking steadily toward the truth, a blessing for those whose special peace is as deep as their own commitment to fullness of life.

Blest too the peacemakers; they shall be called the sons of God.

Even the youngest of us have had nightmares of war and dreams about peace. The flares of war have burned late into our century, edging with light the corpses beyond counting—the memory of which, although a weight in our souls, does not stop the killing. It is a strange half-light in which the dead stare dumbly, in wonder, at a world in which a dynamite maker endowed a prize for peacemakers.

Peacemaker, a word that occurs only once in the scriptures, is a word Jesus uses, one feels, more in compassion than judgment, a word spoken softly by one who knows how hard it would be for the world to grasp its meaning.

Peace is sacred for the Jews, who understand *shalom* to be a word as filled as a harvest with the best of human purpose; it is a greeting and a prayer, not just that life should be free of evil but that it should overflow with everything that is good. A multiplied blessing rewards those who bring this gift to others. But there is a clear emphasis on making peace rather than on just liking it or even praying for it. An ancient truth is entwined in this saying, for God's grace goes to those who work actively for peace rather than those who merely wait or yearn for its coming.

Passivity is not a virtue to open the gates of the Kingdom. It is a form of death, the kind of withdrawal from existence that paradoxically destroys peace anyway. Passive people—those who settle for any of the strange varieties of peace that have brought so much woe to this century; peace at any price, with honor, as a cold form of war—draw violence finally to themselves. Peace is something positive; it is not a cease-fire nor, in personal matters, just an avoidance of disagreement. Peace is not lapsing into silence in the face of the complexities and cruelties of human relationships. It is never really found by those who "don't want to get hurt." Peace is delivered, as the nodding rabbis always taught, to those who face rather than evade the troubles of building good relationships between human beings. Peace is not the inheritance of those who don't want to be bothered, but of those who seek it honestly and consistently in their own lives.

God blesses those who celebrate life together rather than those who hide from it. Who is this God who turns us always back toward each other to discover his will? He is not a jealous God breathing fire if we look away from his face; he does not devour us or make us enter his temple single file and afraid of taking a sideways glance at each other or his universe. What a strange and loving God to bless those who do his own work by helping persons to find the right relationship with each other. "The Creator has made the world," the American Indians pray, "come and take a look at it." Yes, and live in it together as those who make peace because they understand something about love.

Blest are those persecuted for holiness' sake; the reign of God is theirs. Blest are you when they insult you and persecute you and utter

every kind of slander against you because of me. Be glad and rejoice, for
your reward is great in heaven; they persecuted the prophets before you in
the very same way.

Something rumbles under our feet as troubling as the ground moving
on the hillside where these words were pronounced. They are sentences
filled with almost forgotten power of unyielding moral commitment;
they offer a confrontation with what seems to the modern world an
ancient and naïve certainty of belief. Such fidelity is like a storm blown
long ago out to sea. We must nurse the faintly glowing embers of
memory to light the scene once more.

For we have grown wise about the world and we celebrate daily its
fine-webbed complexity more than we do a simple faith. We understand that our homeland is a gray area, that cliché for the wasteland
where every sign points both ways and where moral vacillation no
longer shames us. Who can blame us for hesitating to speak *yes* or *no*
too loudly or too distinctly on the question that tests our allegiance to
this Kingdom of which Jesus speaks? Who can accuse us because we no
longer offer our necks cheerfully to the hangman to defend a principle
of faith? Yes, and most issues have sides enough to shame a polyhedron.
See them all and say nothing into the atmosphere that is so heavy with
ambivalence.

We are, in fact, uneasy with the figures, saints and heroes, whose
single-mindedness once inspired us. Let them go quietly into the shadows, these giants from another age like the steely-eyed Mindszenty
whose refusal to bend to his shadowy old persecutors made him in his
old age an embarrassment to a church seeking détente. A man out of
due time, indeed, who stared us down to the very end, troubling our
qualified hearts. It is not so simple anymore, we say, but we are still
disturbed by those, whether they are princes of the church or peace
marchers, who live in our midst responding to and suffering for an
absolute voice of conscience.

The words still confound us although we have traveled a long way
from the martyrs and we understand the complicated psychology that
explains away some of the fierce prophets of the kingdom. And yet
. . . The words are clear enough: if we try to live as Jesus told us we
will not have an easy time of it. We may no longer have to face a
jeering crowd of unbelievers but we will have to face ourselves every

36

day. Our contemporary determination to live by faith is tested more quietly and privately than in the early days of Christianity.

Jesus speaks of something we feel in our own lives if we try to follow him. The gift of life is never at rest, saving and nourishing only itself. We are called to share our lives and that cannot be accomplished unless we die to the selfishness that turns us back always on ourselves. We suffer the private deaths of overcoming our own capacity for evil and we rise again with the expanded gifts of the Spirit that beggar such showy ones as praying in tongues.

We need not look or long for persecution to validate our life in the Lord. Most of us have a simpler calling through which in undramatic ways we discover the suffering for our beliefs that Jesus promised for those who hear his words. The martyrs and the saints stir us not to yearn for their seemingly more simply defined moral challenges, but to give ourselves in faith to a way of living that gives happiness beyond measure to those who accept the daily deaths of giving themselves away.

Verses 13–16

"You are the salt of the earth. But if salt becomes tasteless, what can make it salty again? It is good for nothing, and can only be thrown out to be trampled underfoot by men.

"You are the light of the world. A city built on a hilltop cannot be hidden. No one lights a lamp to put it under a tub; they put it on the lampstand where it shines for everyone in the house. In the same way your light must shine in the sight of men, so that, seeing your good works, they may give the praise to your Father in heaven."

There is more to hear, pointed reminders about the life Jesus wants those around him to understand. Does he look steadily into our eyes still, binding us down to earth rather than letting us soar toward the skies? Jesus seems to anticipate the temptations that will dazzle the spiritually minded throughout history and to call them back to a more basic order of things, to life as elemental and plain as salt and light. For the world will be filled with prophets calling people to a more complicated life, to special heights to be scaled hand over hand by the chosen who willingly leave the world far behind.

If the crowd has been stirred by the blessings Jesus has pronounced on the poor and the suffering, it is suddenly stilled by the bedrock simplicity of what he now says. The words still slice through the air of dreamy spiritual ambition, confronting those who savor divine election as a birthright for an elite few, with fundamentals about the kingdom that can be entered by everybody. The words are not harsh but neither are they subtle; they are spoken in celebration of life itself and of the manner, fresh and mysterious as dawn, in which believers are meant to extend the celebration in their own lives.

Believers are not called to be hooded pilgrims uneasy at the feel of the earth beneath their feet. They are not to be timid about life, for it is like a river of the old law in which the unclean may bathe, the rushing currents of the Jordan that wash away our sins, the place of the living water that rises up to eternal life. Christians are meant to be as much a part of life as salt and light and simple goodness; believing in God implies believing in his universe, sealing it with the blessing of lives fully lived.

Salt, gift of the water and the earth, speaks to us with the compressed power of simple things. Salt takes on its meaning always in relationship to something else. As it brings out the flavor of food, so believers are called to season existence, revealing the dimensions that might otherwise be hidden. Salt and light are elements of revelation that enable us to see life as a prize rather than a burden, as a place for a feast rather than an endless rite of mourning. What can sad and self-centered believers tell a world about the promise of joy when they cannot look tenderly at life itself?

These are not hard sayings that Jesus speaks, but they rob us of romantic illusions about a life of the Spirit above and beyond the sprawl of homely realities that rise up before us every day. Here is our homeland, back in the place where there is daily need for light and salt and unselfconscious goodness; this is the kingdom where the plain things wait for the blessing of believers who have a consuming passion for existence.

"Do not imagine that I have come to abolish the Law or the Prophets. I have come not to abolish but to complete them. I tell you solemnly, till heaven and earth disappear, not one dot, not one little stroke, shall disappear from the Law until its purpose is achieved. Therefore, the man who infringes even one of the least of these commandments and teaches others to do the same will be considered the least in the kingdom of heaven; but the man who keeps them and teaches them will be considered great in the kingdom of heaven.

"For I tell you, if your virtue goes no deeper than that of the scribes and Pharisees, you will never get into the kingdom of heaven."

"You have learned how it was said to our ancestors: *You must not kill*, and if anyone does kill he must answer for it before the court. But I say this to you: anyone who is angry with his brother will answer for it before the court; if a man calls his brother 'Fool' he will answer for it before the Sanhedrin; and if a man calls him 'Renegade' he will answer for it in hell fire. So then, if you are bringing your offering to the altar and there remember that your brother has something against you, leave your offering there before the altar, go and be reconciled with your brother first, and then come back and present your offering. Come to terms with your opponent in good time while you are still on the way to the court with him, or he may hand you over to the judge and the judge to the officer, and you will be thrown into prison. I tell you solemnly, you will not get out till you have paid the last penny."

Belief is not a dream, nor is Jesus merely a dreamer. When he speaks this way we sense the steel webbing that gives shape to his message; there is nothing wistful or fanatical here, nothing of nebulous promise, nothing glowing palely in these words. They are iron-scraped sparks, the hard-edged phrases of somebody who knows exactly what he is about. Jesus draws intersecting lines across religious history and invites us to inspect the place where we stand.

The mystery of newness is here because Jesus speaks always of rebirth and of a new world coming into being. And yet the old world is never destroyed; it is not torn down like the sets from a closed play, nor is it impotent or unrelated to our lives. The ancient order of things is mysteriously linked with everything new. It is the source of the cycle of rebirths that brings us to this moment, an old world made ever young, achieving a more complex and yet simpler sense of itself every morning. History is a strange overlapping mystery and the power of a thousand previous springtimes is still felt in our souls.

Our religious growth is an elusive but cumulative reality and it cannot be hacked into sections without destroying its total meaning. Our believing past stretches on into the present, an inheritance that cannot be disowned any more than our genetic endowment can. Our future is processed from the same nerve fibers and blood of time itself; we ride a living religious history and we misunderstand everything if we deny or ignore this.

Jesus would have us look backward so that we can look forward with a deep sense of our religious identity. We are brothers and sisters to the past just as our spiritual ancestors are to us, and the present is a place big enough for all of us to stand together. Yet what a startling paragraph to comprehend, for we live in a world that despises yesterday as the price of being modern. And Jesus' words strike home forcefully; what indeed does it mean to be modern, either religiously or in any other way? Is the past just an attic we visit once in a while to discover its antiques, a panorama purged of its pain by the softening lens of nostalgia? For many, being modern means being separated from every root and anchor of time, committing themselves to everything that is novel in order to break free from the long shadows of times gone by.

But Christians cannot easily do this without losing far more than they gain in the process. And Jesus underscores this, not to tempt us back to primitive magic but to alert us to the depths and riches of the Spirit's action all through time. Our religious pilgrimage begins in the Old Testament, and our own life stories can be read there still. The old law is not all to be crossed out or regretted; it is a journey to be completed in and through the life of Jesus. This is an instant of consolidation in religious history, of the forces of time playing like lightning around the figure of Jesus, a moment in which we can feel the power of the Spirit running dramatically through the length of history itself.

Jesus forges a bond between past and present; and then his life, like a swiftly striking hammer, seems to sunder the links of the old law, scattering rather than gathering them, and leaving us to wonder what it means for Jesus to fulfill the law. He has spoken of it as something lasting, a mountain of stone rising above the smoke of history, and yet Jesus breaks it deliberately time after time, to the astonishment of those who observed him then and of us who reflect on it now.

For Jesus does not worry about the ceremonial handwashing on the Sabbath; there is a quality of conscious choice in these decisions whose power we feel still. They are not accidents, not the stuff of oversight or forgetfulness. Jesus does not pluck the corn or cure the sick absent-mindedly on the Sabbath. He will be condemned finally as a law-breaker. What, then, is he talking about when he exalts the law?

Jesus is clearing our heads of easy religious visions, shattering in his time the crystal maze of regulations constructed by the scribes as God's wishes for the lives of men and women. These laws are not the Law, Jesus says, and they can only mislead you. The law is lessened by those who believe that it can be spun into a glistening web of details; God's will for us does not lead us into a delicate structure through which we must pass on tiptoe, holding our breath lest it collapse and engulf us. Jesus gives a sign, a strong and masculine symbol, in breaking these regulations himself. He is one with his words as he tells us that the law abides but that it has nothing to do with such matters. The law abides precisely because it has nothing to do with the tiny details of living; the living law is richer and deeper and reaches into a person's heart. That is the Law of which Jesus is the fulfillment, and in its living expectations it asks far more of us than the multiplied regulations drawn with a fine stylus by the squinting and cramped-spirited scribes.

Jesus invites people to live rather than to try to a trap life in a master plan of regulations. The latter is as perennial a temptation as the human race has ever known and it returns in every generation to offer us its spurious promises of security. There is no end of preachers with detailed plans for our salvation, blind guides making us blind to both the wonder and the challenge of a life based on the utterly simple law of love. This is the power that Jesus proclaims, the power of the Spirit that does not grow old, the power of love that fuses the ages into one because it is strong enough to defy both time and death.

Jesus is not raising an army of dreamers or romantics to follow him; he is not raising an army at all. Rather he speaks to the very hearts of persons, making them feel the demands of a Law beyond law, of the kind of life that must shame the righteousness of the scribes and Pharisees. Life proceeds from the inside out; it is the discovery and the prize of those who commit themselves to the special discipline of responding with respect and reverence to God's universe and people.

There is no way we can guarantee our religious practice by pointing to rules kept and regulations observed; salvation belongs not to bookkeepers of the Spirit but to those who love by the power of the Spirit. We break the bonds of time when we break the bonds of the dead regulations that kill rather than enlarge life. We do not find ourselves when we try desperately to save ourselves by pointing to how good we are, but rather when we forget ourselves in the kind of loving that opens us to eternal life.

It seems hard, almost impossible, after twenty centuries to work our way around the edge of the crowd for a better look at Jesus. The compact art of Matthew leaves us with paragraphs that are stunning but difficult to absorb; they have been baffled, like an electric coil bound a dozen times over with insulation, by the translations and re-translations of history. And yet the energy still crackles at the core of the message, cutting through the padding of time and translation to touch us still.

Jesus speaks directly to us; we are indeed on the hillside, as struck by these words as their first hearers were. Why is it, then, that we cannot see the man Jesus more clearly? For here is a moment of immediacy in which his words are not disembodied echoes from a thousand pulpits nor flecks of colored ink on a copyist's parchment, but living words addressed directly to each one of us. Jesus of history has been frozen in paintings and statues, each reflecting a different culture's special view, and it is hard to shake our imagination free of their claims. But in this moment Jesus speaks to us; if we listen quietly we can see him more clearly, not as a vision for the fervent nor a dream for the mad, but as a man, as a presence commanding our attention and response.

Jesus quotes the law only to contradict it. He speaks, Matthew tells us later, "as one having authority." He does not make claims for his interpretation of the law nor for his vision of religious experience. Jesus speaks calmly and deliberately and not, like the religious teachers of his time and of ours, with constant recourse to outside authority. Jesus is not the father of footnotes for a world that will look for centuries for rational proofs about theological truth. He speaks directly to human experience and he does so on his own. If Jesus does not pile citation upon citation from the rabbis, neither does he wildly stir the pools of human emotion. Jesus does not manipulate us. He speaks with powerful simplicity to the basic human experience of men and women. Perhaps that is why we have not been able to see him clearly. He is looking so directly at us that we find it hard to look directly back at him.

The test of his authority, of whether Jesus can speak on his own about the defining moral experiences of our lives, is not whether he can shake the raveled scrolls of the scribes at us but whether he speaks about us so that we recognize ourselves in what he has to say. We, the hearers on the edge of the silent crowd, are the only valid test of whether Jesus knows our life or only knows about it. Is he speaking on the basis of some abstraction, in a thin voice, about what somebody else said about what somebody else said was important to God and persons? Or does he arrest our attention precisely because he knows for himself about the inner surface of the human condition?

The human Jesus stands revealed before us, not as an audacious claimant to authority that is not his, but as someone whose authority is an aspect of his intensely real presence to all of us. We may wish to turn away, preferring sentimental versions of Jesus looking like a moonstruck shepherd or of an historical Jesus sealed off in a dry recess of time long gone. Jesus is a strong but not harsh presence who knows what he sees as he looks into our eyes. It is not a moment to tremble and to throw ourselves on the ground, pawing the earth for mercy. This is a very different kind of experience because we are invited through it to place ourselves in relationship to Jesus, who demands that we find more of life by going more deeply into it.

Jesus offers an example about killing to tell us something about life, hurling the words at the gathering of listeners tiered on the hillside around him. He does not shred the ancient law so that it is lifted away like straw on the wind. He heads single-eyed to the very heart of it, plucking out the core that was first dulled and then left for dead by the fibrous growth of legal prescriptions. Jesus, with the intensity of a person who has waited for the right moment to speak about a problem he understood long ago, proclaims the fulfillment of the ancient commandments like a man who is finally able to unroll God's scrolls completely. Here, he says, here is where life is to be found, in the fullness of existence that I announce to you.

The seed of the Old Testament Law flowers in the life Jesus describes; the external observance of commandments is organically one with our inner selves, or we are estranged both from life and from morality. We do not save ourselves from the sword of judgment by merely pleading our case like a surveyor who holds his measurements to the surface of things. The unseen realm of personality bears the stamp of our souls and it cannot be forged or disguised. We tell the story of our lives in our hearts, in the reality, hard as a diamond, of our intentions, in the patterns of choice through which, no matter what we look like outside, we shape our lasting moral presences.

What, then, is murder? The simplest questions become awesome if we are sensitive to the powers of life and death we hold over each other. We are all involved in the rise and fall of many, in enlarging or diminishing the chance people have to drink deeply from the sweet waters of life. We can breathe our own spirit on others or we can let them choke to death, saving ourselves and feeling safe under a cover of piety that hides our inner selfishness. Murderers may roam the earth looking like holy people because we cannot see the dry and deadly patches of their souls. But appearance does not bring justification, and all the doors that have closed on the smug and self-satisfied who have plundered the innocent of their earth will one day be reopened. The world is filled with quiet murderers, the subtle killers of dreams and hopes and others' reputations. See to it, Jesus thunders, because the measure of our righteousness is taken on our inner selves.

Jesus speaks vividly of another abiding dimension of our existence, the mystery of time in which our moral lives are set. It is not something to be savored like a passing season; time is all we have in which to look deeply into ourselves, and against the background of its relentless passage we must discover the inner balance of true justice. Time does not allow striking hard bargains or exacting everything the law allows from our fellows. Settle, Jesus says to his stirring listeners, on the way to court. Get things straight while the light lasts or find yourself in an eerie half-darkness of judgment that you choose for yourself. Are the crowds less than astonished at this new vision of holiness? Or are they now ready for it, hungry for it the way people hunger for justice, and ready to respond as good people always do to words that speak to their own experience?

Verses 27–38

"You have learned how it was said: *You must not commit adultery.* But I say this to you: if a man looks at a woman lustfully, he has already committed adultery with her in his heart. If your right eye should cause you to sin, tear it out and throw it away; for it will do you less harm to lose one part of you than to have your whole body thrown into hell. And if your right hand should cause you to sin, cut it off and throw it away; for it will do you less harm to lose one part of you than to have your whole body go to hell."

"It has also been said: *Anyone who divorces his wife must give her a writ of dismissal.* But I say this to you: everyone who divorces his wife, except for the case of fornication, makes her an adulteress; and anyone who marries a divorced woman commits adultery.

"Again, you have learned how it was said to our ancestors: *You must not break your oath, but must fulfill your oaths to the Lord.* But I say this to you: do not swear at all, either by *heaven,* since that is God's throne; or by *the earth,* since that is *his footstool;* or by Jerusalem, since that is *the city of the great king.* Do not swear by your own head either, since you cannot turn a single hair white or black. All you need say is 'Yes' if you mean yes, 'No' if you mean no; anything more than this comes from the evil one.

"You have learned how it was said: *Eye for eye and tooth for tooth.*"

———◆———

The words of Jesus still charge the air with that strange freshness that is the work of lightning. This metaphor is a sharp sword cutting through our easy dreams and illusions about life, a stinging slap not to punish but to awaken us to the moral edges of our existence. For we are not human if we sleep our years away without knowing what is happening to us; we are estranged from ourselves if we do not understand that we shape our lives more or less every day, that with our own hands we draw the lines of our meaning, that there is more to life than going through the motions, righteous though these may seem. The life Jesus speaks of is interior, in the world of motivation and intention, in that realm which is invisible, except to ourselves, where the real structure of our identity stands free of disguise and distortion. We finally face ourselves in that place, so different from outward appearances at times, at the core of ego where the energies of choice either make us morally whole or leave us as scattered and dead as dry leaves after the harvest.

History has swarmed with pilgrims of the literal absolute, almost feverishly anxious to brand the iron form of Jesus' words into humanity while they throw their substance away. They have severed limbs and plucked out eyes, innocent victims of a fervor gone wrong, or fought long vigils against their own dreams in the desert, flailing themselves and wearing hairshirts in a battle to purge themselves of the last winking coals of a contrary humanity. Yes, and there is still a harsh appeal in this savage and romantic asceticism that tries to wrest freedom for the spirit from the smudged weight of our flesh. Is it only the passion of the rationalizer that seeks another meaning in Jesus' words?

Or can we possibly hear him unless we understand his emphasis on our being whole if we are going to be moral at all? It would be far easier to flog our way to supposed holiness by accepting the simple notion that the body and soul are antagonists in the tale of our personal salvation. There is something more tempting than our wildest images in the confinement of our ethical choices to the small but fiery war that seems kindled between flesh and spirit. But there is not room enough here for Jesus' more penetrating vision of us as persons whose wholeness is built on a fundamentally interior morality. We are called to treat ourselves as full persons rather than to chop ourselves up into parts, to stay in the midst of a world where we make a difference in the balance between good and evil rather than to wage a war with the demons of our own imagining in the desert.

To be one, that is the invitation Jesus offers, and to achieve this goal by being willing to live in the midst of many. Holiness is not a gift to those who remain untouched by the world but the accomplishment of those who walk its jumbled streets and embrace the shadowed mystery of humanity. Wholeness comes to those unafraid to love; for love, rather than blind denial, cleanses our motives and brings peace to our dreams. We find the fundamental asceticism of the gospel in the dying and rising of meeting and living with others—but we find our wholeness there as well, the wholeness that makes us citizens of the Kingdom.

46

The gospel writer knows something about effects; he has a feel for weights and measures, a tax collector's acquired gift for hefting a sack of coins and judging their number without counting them. Is it something of this art—this subtle knowledge passed down through the tribe of bookkeepers that enables them to summarize the stand or fall, the drama of all the passionate calculating of a business, the agony of things gone right and others gone wrong, and to get all this into a single bunched line of figures—is this what Matthew employs in massing the final paragraphs of Jesus' sermon? Everything unnecessary is pruned away and what is left is as simple and powerful as the account's linear statement of the hopes and fortunes of an anguished merchant. It is no accident that we use a bookkeeper's term, that we speak of "summing up" to describe what the writer does with the thoughts of Jesus that take away our breath like a succession of blows from a fighter.

The medium fits the mood: even if Jesus did not say these things quite as tersely as in Matthew's account, the hairs must still have prickled on his hearers' necks even as they do on ours. Jesus himself is speaking with a passion that breathes in the astounding words, these descendants of the Aramaic phrases, born full-bodied for the explosive occasion of confronting his hearers with the truths of marriage, the taking of oaths, and the pledging of one's word. It is impossible to imagine that Jesus uttered these words in the cadences of deadly piety or in the sonorous tones of the preacher with a bag of oratorical tricks. These are urgent words about important things, and Jesus' eyes sparkle in the manner of convinced men who have no secret places in their personalities. He cannot dissemble or strive for effect, and what is left in his hearers' hearts afterward is a sense of his strong and uncompromised presence, the outline left by a man revealing himself as rooted in the ground of truth itself.

So the accountant, crowding his paragraphs like columns of figures on a finely lined sheet, makes us feel the strength of Jesus; there is nothing here of the softness, nothing of the man always on the edge of mourning painted in by the lesser artists of history. These are not sentimental words and they are certainly not political words. They can only be spoken by a man who looks deeply into life and tells us exactly what he sees.

So the words astound us still because they focus us, as a burning point of truth always does, on the things that count, on the realities we may disown but cannot change—on what we are like in life. We find our measure in what we deliver of ourselves to each other in the relationships, like marriage, that are not merely contracts or social conveniences but perhaps our best chance to push aside the veils of mystery and draw close to the meaning we seek. Can the world, still caught in the coils of so many confusions, shake its head clear and understand this clue to its real possibilities?

What could be more closely linked to this than a call for truth, for oaths without conditions, and yeses and noes that are untinctured by ambiguity? Perhaps it takes the tax collector, who has looked long and hard at men, to draw a simple and clear picture of Jesus standing for the truth he embodies and underscores as the abiding moral energy of life.

Verses 38–48

"You have learned how it was said: *Eye for eye and tooth for tooth.* But I say this to you: offer the wicked man no resistance. On the contrary, if anyone hits you on the right cheek, offer him the other as well; if a man takes you to law and would have your tunic, let him have your cloak as well. And if anyone orders you to go one mile, go two miles with him. Give to anyone who asks, and if anyone wants to borrow, do not turn away.

"You have learned how it was said: *You must love your neighbor* and hate your enemy. But I say this to you: love your enemies and pray for those who persecute you; in this way you will be sons of your Father in heaven, for he causes his sun to rise on bad men as well as good, and his rain to fall on honest and dishonest men alike. For if you love those who love you, what right have you to claim any credit? Even the tax collectors do as much, do they not? And if you save your greetings for your brothers, are you doing anything exceptional? Even the pagans do as much, do they not? You must therefore be perfect just as your heavenly Father is perfect."

———————

A passage well lit by the attention of time; and yet it has the feeling of being both familiar and unfamiliar. We have made a pilgrimage to these words many times over as we might to a fork in a great river, where the white water divides to slice in an entirely new direction through the black land. Such places are filled with mystery, and no geologist weighed down with printouts on the rise and fall of the land can fully explain the way a river seems to have a mind of its own. Something decisive happens at the fork in a river, just as Jesus' words are now decisive, sweeping with all the power of tumbling water in a new direction.

Yes, we have stood at this fork before, in wonder at what Jesus proclaims as the new direction for his followers. And like a father of powerful waters, like a Mississippi before it splits across the land, the ancient law of retaliation still rumbles past with fury enough to make us step back from it. One can see the savage gesture of revenge that plucks out the eyeball and rips out the tooth. It is a law that still has the strength of absolute things, of orders uttered without ambivalence and without counting the dead in the morning. It seems a proper law for everyone caught up with impacted hostility at life and its frustrating jumble of injustice.

In truth, the commentators tell us that the law was an effort to limit vengeance rather than to let it proceed unchecked. It resonates familiarily, however, with the possibilities of our own fury. Part of the power we feel in it springs from the feelings we breathe into it ourselves. But here, too, there is something unfamiliar. Here the river turns—because Jesus asks us to surrender our feelings of resentment and retaliation rather than attempt to carry them out even in a moderated form. In these words Jesus does not ask us to look back at an older, superseded morality; he bids us to look into ourselves, at the harvest of hurts that every day we pull out of the waters of our existence. Some are as big as lobsters and some are as tiny as scallops, yet their weight on the soul is suffocating. We can forgive, we say, but we cannot forget.

Yet Jesus says that believers empty themselves of their poisoned moods, including the thought of exacting a final revenge. Believers die in surrendering the desire to nurse wounds and to right wrongs; as they die to these inclinations they are filled with a new life. So the followers of Jesus do not insist on their rights, nor, when pressed into unpleasant service, carry them out with one eye to the chance to strike back at the oppressor: images, all of them, from life in an occupied land in which affronts and injustices to the citizens could barely be counted.

Believers must do more than not complain; Jesus does not offer an invitation to a passive stoicism. Believers are asked for something positive; they are invited to transform themselves through a redemption of what we understand as natural feelings. The principal asceticism of the Christian always takes place on an inner stage, where no one can see the sacrifices that are made in the name of growing in the Spirit. What counts is whether we possess ourselves internally, and whether we can become obedient to a law of love, obedient as servants who empty themselves of what they might make a case for clinging to. For this is the obedience of Jesus-become-man, the mysterious emptying in which we are filled beyond measure.

Here are things simple and yet central to Jesus' way of speaking about the Old Law and its new life in the Kingdom. But metaphor still bewilders the children of democracy. Are we not well rid of kingdoms, purged forever of any need for sovereigns, put off by imagery that seems ancient and uncomfortable to us? We shake our heads to clear them, groping for the meaning behind the idea of a Kingdom, wondering what it could be like and whether it is different from the sunlit places in our children's stories or the burnt-out lineages of the world's empires. "Kingdom" is a foreign but a familiar notion, part of our history and part of our prayers, a word that is a confusing alloy of the sacred and the profane. What can we understand about this Kingdom to which we are called?

The Kingdom, of course, is a place of realized values in which we will find the fullness of our human possibilities—not in the exaggerated and enthusiastic sensuality of twentieth-century "fulfillment trips" with bubbling baths and nodding gurus, but in a richer, a deeper, yes, and a more lasting sense. The Kingdom is a place in which we will find ourselves without the burden of all our incomplete and half-spoken longings; a place of celebration, for we will know ourselves even as we are known. A Kingdom for persons, then, in which all those denied a feeling for the wonder of their humanity or who only had a hint of it in their best moments—yes, and the lame and the lonely and those out of love—will find it all without the haunting feeling that it is already slipping away in the first moments of its being experienced. It is a Kingdom of wedding feasts and banquets, of celebrations held because of homecomings, of friends gathering with the wounds of estrangement and alienation healed forever. The scars will show—the places in our spirits that are stronger for being tested every day—but they will not ache anymore.

We will feel throughout ourselves that we are *striving* in reaching out toward each other all through our lives. The shadows will be gone, however, just as the struggle against our own contrariness—our need to let them die out like old fires—will also be at an end. We will be filled because we were willing to be emptied of the corroding acids of revenge and recrimination. We will be at home in our own personalities because the places in our hearts that we yielded to our enemies were filled with God himself. Jesus asks us to face our humanity in this life and transform it rather than run away from it; he asks us to confront our finely honed capacity to reject relationship and to overcome it by breaking free of ourselves. Then we become fit for the Kingdom in which relationship with each other is our great opening to relationship with God. The Kingdom Jesus proclaims is uniquely human and we enter it not by becoming angels but, in the best sense, by becoming ourselves.

The Kingdom of which Jesus speaks is not far away; it has no sheer walls climbing into the clouds, nor a thousand drawbridges to cross before we get there. No, it is a moveable feast, a journey and goal, movement and rest, a great arc that loops out across space and time to lead us back to where we are. The Kingdom, Jesus tells us, is in our very midst, in the mystery of our relationships with each other. We are within its gates when we draw close to one another with the love that is fired by the Spirit. We are already on the sacred ground when we reach out to understand rather than condemn, when we forgive rather than seek revenge, when as unarmed pilgrims we are ready to meet our enemies. We are citizens of the Kingdom not when we stand in the isolation of heroic detachment from all that is human but rather when we accept it, as the Lord did, as the basic condition for our citizenship, when, in other words, we make the choice to be human.

It is a Kingdom not of the smugly saved who keep their spiritual secrets clutched in a miser's grasp, but of the openhanded and the openhearted who make room for newcomers all the time. It is a Kingdom that reminds us of a simple rather than a royal family, for it has the ordinary wonder of a family whose members love each other even though they know each other very well. In an ordinary family it often looks as though nothing is going on but, in fact, everything that is of importance to Jesus' Kingdom is taking place—people believe in and love each other, they trust and forgive each other, they hope and stand by each other. Here is the action of grace, the superabounding evidence of the Spirit in the simplest and yet most profound signs of life.

If the Kingdom is not far away we can enter it more fully at any time by becoming more human with each other. This is the task, but how long-neglected and misunderstood it has been. What a far journey— farther than that of the Prodigal Son—have the seekers of the Kingdom made across history, seeking in the dark and the cold for the holiness that could only be found at home. Perfection has claimed its victims, generations of people obsessed with rather than drawn gently to holiness, good people misled by the minor gods of ascetic competition throwing themselves on the wheel to break and purge themselves of the last of their human sighs and longings. Perfection came icy out of the night like a floating white island in the North Sea, silent and sharp-edged and without hospitality, a glacial kingdom for those who believed in holiness as a condition of personhood chilled down, pulse and blood flow quieted, as in a patient prepared for surgery. This is the god who is dead, the estranging majesty of alienated perfection totally unrelated to human possibilities.

Yet the sentence persists—"Be perfect just as your heavenly Father is perfect"—and it is still invoked to support a spirituality that turns people away from themselves and each other, pointing to holiness that can only be approached individually by those who find the world that Jesus freely entered "too human" for them. A mystery of misunderstanding that even the scholars cannot quite clear away; it will take time for all the seekers of the Kingdom to find their way home again.

The notion of perfection spoken of by Jesus is powerfully human, the scholars tell us, because it refers to growth toward genuine fullness as it is felt in a mature adult rather than in an adolescent, or as we sense its fullness in a master teacher and only its beginnings in a young student. The Greek word is *teleos* and signifies a functional perfection, the realization of the purpose for which anything is made. We are perfect when we realize the purpose of our lives and become as profoundly and truly human as we can. We become like God when we become fully ourselves.

CHAPTER 6

Verses 1–5

"Be careful not to parade your good deeds before men to attract their notice; by doing this you will lose all reward from your Father in heaven. So when you give alms, do not have it trumpeted before you; this is what the hypocrites do in the synagogues and in the streets to win men's admiration. I tell you solemnly, they have had their reward. But when you give alms, your left hand must not know what your right is doing; your almsgiving must be secret, and your Father who sees all that is done in secret will reward you.

"And when you pray, do not imitate the hypocrites: they love to say their prayers standing up in the synagogues and at the street corners for people to see them. I tell you solemnly, they have had their reward."

———————⚬———————

Here are words for our human experience, the sentiments that underscore the sacredness of Jewish giving and yet seem to be spoken freshly rather than cited from ancient texts or practices. Jesus speaks as one who knows what is in our hearts; the tone is that of a man who has been to the well of our petty vanities and back again, of a man who still hopes in us even though his view of us is de-romanticized. This paragraph rises out of the pages to shift our vision the way a rock side does in cutting a sharp turn into what had been a die-straight road. We see ourselves in these words and with a wry smile of recognition we know that the reflection is true. Jesus speaks directly to the inner world of our motivation, to that area we do not light up fully even when no one else is looking.

A curse lies curled in our thinking too often about who is looking, that sets our sense of ourselves rising and falling like a sailing ship on the winds of another's approval or disapproval. We are a long time cleansing ourselves of the subtlest of our urges to be admired for our studied goodness; we can ride the tides, catching their ebb and flow throughout a lifetime, never missing the chance, main always to our

53

inner eye, of appearing graceful and good to other persons. Yes, Jesus says, you can do that very successfully in giving alms, but the applause you hear will be payment in full for your efforts. Self-consciousness, not virtue, is its own reward. But, Jesus says starkly, you commit yourself to a self-contained system that recycles itself like a plaza fountain caught up in its own never-ending gush. It does not break out to water the parched land; it feeds only its own stone imagery.

But who can escape watching oneself do good in a world in which even the churches that worship Jesus have mastered the techniques of embarrassing people into charitable giving? How can free giving, blind as Justice balancing the scales, survive the pastor's printed list of donors, the intricacies of charity for tax purposes, booster ads and testimonial tickets wheedled out of us with the sly pressures of shame and guilt? Our fund-raising mechanisms are built on an appraisal of our motives that is as clear and uncluttered as that of Jesus; they are engineered to our hearts like bionic devices and they reveal a mixed rather than a totally crass picture of our impulses for giving.

We grow in giving when these pressures are no longer the decisive reason for our generosity. But we all heed to grow if we are to cut free the mooring lines of selfishness from our gifts and thus liberate them from our own claims to recognition or gratitude. That is a task we may have to work at most of our lives, getting better but falling back now and then as well. Our gifts are freer as we become more loving. For then we forget ourselves and do not even notice ourselves when we respond generously to the needy all around us. We focus more on them and are trapped less in the ticket window of our own souls; our gifts are free because we are freed of the need for records and accounts, for applause and appreciation. We let go and find that we have received more than we give away. All the best gifts come from the loving hearts of men and women who have won an easy freedom precisely because they have stopped trying to trap life into paying them back for goodness. That is the freedom of the Godlike that marks those who understand what Jesus is talking about.

There is paradox enough for all history in the fact that people have never had much trouble doing what is bad but that problems beyond numbering have always attended their efforts to do what is good. Evil does not demand nearly the effort that has been systematically associated with doing good, with humanity's often strained expectations about what doing good entails. We have continually complicated the works of charity and benevolence, making virtue a mountain rising above Everest and the good life a long and exhausting climb to its summit. Everywhere in history we find experts, like artists retouching spring, improving on the simplicity that, over and over again, Jesus proclaims as the heart of his teaching.

Prayer has been no exception, and to this very day we find people, anxious about their final station in heaven, worrying about prayer, straining for the achievement of techniques that may not fit them at all. Some people feel a duty to invest prayer with a muscular grandeur; they are sincere and determined crusaders mounting an assault on the interior castle. Prayer remains, however, a pearl of great price; and now, as when Jesus spoke these words, it needs to be cut free of the encrustations of ornate settings that have hidden it from view. A spirit needs to be exorcised: not a traditional evil spirit, but an old spirit that rises out of our flawed situation, the spirit of complication, the ghost of never enough, the restless soul of bureaucracy and red tape, the viruslike motive for making the smooth paths rough in preparing the way of the Lord.

Jesus hacks away at the tangle of temptations that destroy the power and meaning of simple prayer. He would return us to the fundamental Jewish instinct, pure as a spring bird's song, that responds to the richness and wonder of God's creation and is only choked by dead ritualization, repetition, and the use of prayer to impress others rather than to express ourselves. The Jewish people prayed at the coming of the light and knew that prayers were the right response to the wonders of fire and lightning, the seeing of the new moon and the coming of the rain, the sight of the sea or the beginning and ending of a journey. Here was a clear and penetrating vision of prayer as poetic language for a sacramental universe. And, Jesus notes, it remains so, despite the needless complications made by human beings anxious for the formula that will trap God into dispensing his grace.

Jesus says that it is not hard to pray but that it is impossible to pray when we turn it into a difficult exercise. The snares are set by ourselves; we are like hunters anxious to be caught in our own traps, relishers of our unworthiness more than free children of a loving God. And Jesus points to the temptations to real evil: we can pray to impress ourselves and other people, and we are as caught up in this difficulty as the hearers grouped around Jesus. But prayer, spontaneous and unmort-gaged by side bets, is as plain and simple as the language of friends, rising as clearly from the heart as the pledge of lovers. The best and most honest things in life need no decoration; they have power in and of themselves. We can be ourselves with God, and when we realize this we are already praying; we have found the secret that is no secret at all, the secret made so by the veils thrown over it by generations of people who have felt that God's gift of humanity is not pleasing enough in which to stand before him.

Verses 6–18

". . . when you pray, *go to your private room and, when you have shut your door, pray* to your Father who is in that secret place, and your Father who sees all that is done in secret will reward you.

"In your prayers do not babble as the pagans do, for they think that by using many words they will make themselves heard. Do not be like them; your Father knows what you need before you ask him. So you should pray like this:

> "Our Father in heaven,
> may your name be held holy,
> your kingdom come,
> your will be done,
> on earth as in heaven.
> Give us today our daily bread.
> And forgive us our debts,
> as we have forgiven those who are in debt to us.
> And do not put us to the test,
> but save us from the evil one."

Yes, if you forgive others their failings, your heavenly Father will for-give you yours; but if you do not forgive others, your Father will not forgive your failings either.

"When you fast do not put on a gloomy look as the hypocrites do: they pull long faces to let men know they are fasting. I tell you solemnly, they have had their reward. But when you fast, put oil on your head

56

and wash your face, so that no one will know you are fasting except your Father who sees all that is done in secret; and your Father who sees all that is done in secret will reward you."

———————⟨∞⟩———————

Here is a prayer that echoes in the consciousness of Western man, a prayer spiked with the sounds and smells of our lifetime, a prayer whose varied translations have flown the battle flags of religious prejudice but have also been kneaded with the oil of healing for people broken by life. Yes, a prayer droned into the dull air above banquet tables and uttered from terrified hearts under the exploding stars of battle. Is it a prayer we have heard so often that we do not hear it clearly anymore? Its utterance by Jesus should make us pause and look up from the void of our distractions and the tangle of our resolutions about improving our prayer.

It is too utterly simple for a generation that works hard at prayer, groping in the dark for its mystic edges, and choosing to define its spirituality through its prayerful achievements; the castle of perfection is as much under siege as it was in the time of the Old Testament pursuit of the exact scheme of prayer, and hordes of the devout throw themselves at its ramparts every day. We have never been cleansed of a suspicion about the gods that was born on the rough plains where the earliest men and women struggled for survival. It was then that the first wagers with the Deity were made, the first tentative agreements were laid on the altars of sacrifice to the gods of the sun and the rain and the winds.

But Jesus, knowing the uneasiness generated by these distant and oh so silent gods, speaks in a new way about prayer. His statement, according to Luke, is a response to a question from a disciple; it is certainly directed to those who would follow him, and its essence is simplicity. Jesus proclaims a style, an attitude of prayer, rather than words to be fused into an automatic formula; he offers us a setting in time, coupling the simple staples of a believer's life with the phases of our passage. We need bread for the present, forgiveness for the past, and the strength of grace to find our way through the uncharted tests of the future.

The very essence of our relationship to God has been robbed of the attribute humans can grasp, and, in fact, can feel as right and fitting throughout their beings. We have been left orphans by the stainless steel and aluminum God who is secure against the rust and change of time and chance, the God who cannot alter no matter what the fortunes of his children. And if God cannot change, how, we wonder, knowing that change is the wavering base line of affection, can God love us in a way that we can possibly understand? How can our destinies be intertwined, how can we work out his glory in time if there is no vital connection, no relationship that makes a dramatic difference both to him and to us?

It is to these questions beyond the question of prayer that Jesus addresses his answer. God is in relationship to us as a father; what else can we know of him except what we know from the richest and least exhaustible of our human experiences? Jesus' prayer says that we establish a living relationship with God as growing children do with a loving father; we are not unknowing children protected by a benevolent paternal figure watching us play in his garden; no, we can sense that we are in an adult relationship to a Father who understands and does not abandon us but who wants us to be responsible—a Father who knows we are his, a Father with a feeling for us.

Jesus says that if we are human we begin to glimpse the dimensions of our relationship with the God we can, in realism rather than sentiment, address as Our Father.

We have lived all our lives with these words. They have been a presence and a mystery, for they say something to us and for us about our experience, they stand like a grove of great trees that has sheltered and absorbed all of history. If one knew their secret one might strike them and release the captured breath of ten thousand springs, because everything that has occurred in their presence has been recorded in some fashion deep in their ringed hearts. Knowing trees, then, with the wisdom of all our suffering and joy encoded within them—yet symbols, too, signs of life and its power in the daily struggle with time and death, trees that might just match the shape of our days and the depth of all our human longing.

This prayer, *the* prayer Jesus speaks for us, has lived with us just as we have lived with it; it swells with our earliest memories and, although said and muttered in every key of human fervor and distraction over the years, it retains the majesty of all great things, the strength to outlast our every neglect or disservice. It is a prayer of life that could never be offered to the multiplied principalities of paganism, a prayer too human and too relevant to ordinary existence to be recited to a court of indifferent deities rolling dice about our fate.

No, it is not a prayer for the superstitious or for those anxious to placate laughing gods in the darkness in order to coax unearned blessings out of them. It is too much filled with the simplicities of existence, with the God who is a Father to his sons and daughters and who can understand the needs of every day, a God to whom we can dare to ascribe a feeling for our least remarkable moments as well as our most profound needs, a prayer, indeed, like those knowing trees, bowed down with wisdom about us.

How far we travel from the lesson Jesus teaches here! For we have never given up our efforts to improve on what he said: we have made prayers fancier, longer, yes, and sometimes more dramatic, but we have never made them deeper than this. We still look beyond our human experience for mystical enlightenment; where people once fasted and kept vigil in hopes of trapping the Spirit we now hold workshops and teach courses in the same quest. We never have done with the search for something more than the staples of life that Jesus underscores in the prayer to our Father.

For we need this day, and we need to count it as God's gift just as we need to inhabit these moments fully, taking our simple share in working out God's will on this earth. And we need bread, a just share of it for everyone, the right view of our gifts and our responsibilities in this world. Where else would we need to forgive and be forgiven except in the close quarters of trying to reach and understand each other? What blessing fits our needs for and failures at love better than this reciprocal grace of healing and being healed?

The tests come every day, the tests of all our resolve and promise; there is nothing dramatic, no great scene of temptation staged at one crossroad of existence. The tests are seeded into the ordinary experiences of our pilgrimage, in the simple choices and decisions through which we enlarge or cut off life for ourselves and others. Life is the test that confirms our strength and sharpens our sense of how everything that is important is at stake in the simplest moments of existence. Our deliverance is from the evil that blinds us to the reality in which our lives are set and deceives us with the dream that life lies somewhere else.

The words of Jesus are not the phrases of a religious demagogue skilled at manipulating us into spiritual subservience. No, not the sayings of a savage messiah, eyes like summer fires, making us cringe at impending vengeance. These are more the words of a man who understands us well and gently. Is there a tracing of a smile on Jesus' face as he identifies the small vanities of the crafty soul and urges us to grow out of them? Who has not felt at least the impulse to let others in on our spiritual strivings?

Here surely is one common temptation for the weary believer, the slightest of gratifications and no more to be measured and stored in the records than a passing spring shower is to be included in the year's rainfall. Letting one's piety show, at least on occasion, has been the only sweet to save out of a long, bad day. Jesus does not sound wrathful, not ready to order us out of the garden for our self-consciousness; he sounds understanding, the way a man might who sees deeply into us. Jesus forgives us while he calls us forward, in the manner of a wise man who knows we are capable of more than the gratification of a minor pride.

Fasting is too serious to be solemn about it. When we grasp something of life and the world we have a new freedom in the wisdom that is a gift of the Spirit. When we see clearly we are liberated from lesser concerns; they fall away, habits disintegrated not so much by acts of the will as by the power of a new focus in our lives. When we see deeply into existence we are freed from worrying about the impression we are making, cleansed of the vanities, sticky as a spider's web, that reduce our concerns to their own gossamer texture and dimensions. When we have grown out of ourselves we are in the clear at last, not because we have forged into the lead in some ascetic race but because we have a different goal from winning.

So it is with the fasting that is inevitably a part of our passage toward greater fullness in the Spirit. Fasting and its effects are no longer sought as the lesser emblems of our dedication to God; fasting and self-discipline—only some of the faces of dying to ourselves—are conditions for living a loving life, sought not in themselves but present because we reach out beyond ourselves, as essential and as much a part of ourselves as the effort to stretch our arms toward others, as important and yet as incidental as the energy expended in a comforting embrace. The core of the action is also its center of gravity, the point that draws everything else into perspective around it.

So the life of a true lover is filled with sacrifice, with the endless round of giving that does not register a count of its every act of surrender and self-discipline. When we fast, Jesus says, it should be more like the fasting of people who are too caught up in life to settle for the smattering of applause that is reserved for watchful piety. The best of our fasting is in secret, hidden even from much attention from ourselves. Such fasting—in giving up meals and time and personal convenience, in letting go of our own way, and in making a present of the first fruits of our work to those we love—fills the lives of believers who have left the surface of existence far behind them. These are the lovers who take love seriously and who are therefore never again tempted to take themselves solemnly. Who can count the willing deaths for love in their every day? They are secret, unsuspected even, because the faces of such persons shine with joy.

Verses 19–23

"Do not store up treasures for yourselves on earth, where moths and woodworms destroy them and thieves can break in and steal. But store up treasures for yourselves in heaven, where neither moth nor woodworms destroy them and thieves cannot break in and steal. For where your treasure is, there will your heart be also."

"The lamp of the body is the eye. It follows that if your eye is sound, your whole body will be filled with light. But if your eye is diseased, your whole body will be all darkness. If then, the light inside you is darkness, what darkness that will be!"

———◦∞◦———

Jesus speaks here like a clear-eyed poet, a man of the spirit with a sense of metaphor for things of the earth, an easiness with what is familiar to the people crowded close to him, a pastoral feeling for the world of their daily pilgrimages. Are the sources of the metaphors at hand? One cannot doubt it, for some of the crowd finger fine garments even as they listen; in the half-distance stand the houses and barns offering their illusion of security. Yes, and eyes, eyes everywhere, the flashing links of the listeners' humanity, the eyes that can be filled with light or dark and whose self-revelation can no more be hidden than fire in the night.

A special silence holds the crowd still; it is the quiet that trembles on the surface of energies coiled for attention. For Jesus is speaking about things we all understand, about the needs and drives that hold our lives together. He invites us to look at what we wager on, to inspect the existential bets we make with life and fate. The words are strong still, although they have been painted over by a dozen translators, and they still arrest our attention. We are part of the crowd and cannot look away.

There is a flavor of irony for us in the realization that built-in obsolescence bedevilled the ancient world as much as it does ours. Even the finest garments finally wear out; is there anything more melancholy than a closet of once splendid clothes choking in the must of out of fashion exile? Where do we invest ourselves, Jesus asks? In the things that go out of style or slowly disintegrate; in the harvests that are not safe from consuming rats even in the stoutest silo; or in the well-guarded homes that almost invite burglary? Where is the security for persons made anxious by the ever-present possibility that they can lose everything? Where, Jesus asks, is the center of a well-lived life?

A question still to puzzle, if not to astonish us! Is Jesus telling us to shun the world, to arm ourselves against the fear of loss by possessing nothing? Holy people have done exactly this in different centuries. But fleeing the world is not the course that Jesus himself takes; it cannot be the only way for us. We are too familiar with those who have put the world behind only to anguish narcissistically over the state of their own souls. There is a distinction between fear of loss and vulnerability, for the latter is the very condition of blessedness. Fear of loss closes us off from ever even seeing the fullness of God's good earth. Vulnerability urges us to open our arms to it, to run the risk of hurt in our passage into its mystery and beauty.

It is no wonder that Jesus speaks of eyes, because it is a way of seeing that we need, a vision that places things and people in perspective and makes us strong in our weakness. The eyes of faith permit us to see things as they are, to see, in fact, into things so that we may live deeply and truly at the root of real experience. The problem is not with the world or things; it is with the way we tag them in our personal inventory of values. What do we live for? It shows in our eyes, yes, and in the rhythm of our pulse, in the way we hold things—in whether we clutch them or are openhanded with them. It is the way we stand in life that reveals what we stand on and what we stand for. It is a story we tell every moment, a message we can read, if we care to, in every movement and attitude of our hearts.

Verse 24

"No one can be the slave of two masters: he will either hate the first and love the second, or treat the first with respect and the second with scorn. You cannot be the slave both of God and of money."

———————∞———————

Jesus will not lose our attention now. He must feel, as has any speaker who has ever said anything worthwhile, that he has forged a bond with his hearers and that its heaviness and depth are measured in the weight of the silence in which they stand together. People grow quiet when someone touches the inner vault of their souls. Something changes about the nature of the space they inhabit; it is pulled together, compressed with time itself into a third thing, a new mystery of being, a vale of awareness in which the texture of existence becomes more clear. When truth is spoken we are suddenly hushed in its resonations, caught on an outcropping of eternity, suspended in contemplation between ticks of the clock.

So are we now as Jesus says that we cannot be slaves to two owners, that we will never get the hours or the bookkeeping right, that we will lose more than we can save in trying to balance allegiances. Preachers have embroidered the sentence for centuries, adding filigrees of rhetorical dread and solemnity, but they have never improved on it. It is too powerful in and of itself for commentary or for qualification. But what a passion we have had for distinguishing and subdividing the simplest and deepest of religious truths! We either catch the idea or we miss it completely. We belong to God; it is as plain and demanding as that.

This truth resembles an earth tremor that collapses the once energetically assembled structures, built on the supposition that we could live somehow outside his presence and had need of spiritualized visas and proper appointments to contact him. How strange are all the ruminations—they continue until this day—about finding God only if we escape the world that is also his. The theology is as thin and haggard as some of the prophets who emphasize this way or that as the sole mode of passage to the sight of the Lord. One may cast away worldly cares and be no closer to God; every vow of poverty is, after all, subsidized by somebody, and it has never of itself guaranteed an openhanded attitude toward people or possessions. Piety, like everything simple, has suffered from bureaucratization over the centuries.

It is a time for quiet, for thinking deeply about whether we sense our place in God's good gifts of creation. Are we alive to the mystery of his hand involved somehow in all of history; do we sense that we are not merely children set like windup toys on the plain of time? Is God without regard for our presence or our suffering even though we are in some way his agents of consciousness on earth?

Is it possible that the vision of our link to God is too terrible for us to face, finally too splendid but also too demanding on the way we live out our lives? Suppose the story of salvation, of whether creation goes this way or that, depends on our clear *yes* to God, on our commitment to living out rather than escaping his gift of life? It is not just the dream of secularism that vanishes but also the dried bones of legalized spirituality, of God's kingdom subdivided according to our ambition or taste for perfection. No, there is something grander in Jesus' words, something we have to think about and begin to feel about the shape of our own existence. And we can only do that in the silence that his compelling remark has cast like a net over us.

Verses 25–34

"That is why I am telling you not to worry about your life and what you are to eat, nor about your body and how you are to clothe it. Surely life means more than food, and the body more than clothing! Look at the birds in the sky. They do not sow or reap or gather into barns; yet your heavenly Father feeds them. Are you not worth much more than they are? Can any of you, for all his worrying, add one single cubit to his span of life? And why worry about clothing? Think of the flowers growing in the fields; they never have to work or spin; yet I assure you that not even Solomon in all his regalia was robed like one of these. Now if that is how God clothes the grass in the field which is there today and thrown into the furnace tomorrow, will he not much more

64

look after you, you men of little faith? So do not worry; do not say, 'What are we to eat? What are we to drink? How are we to be clothed?' It is the pagans who set their hearts on all these things. Your heavenly Father knows you need them all. Set your hearts on his kingdom first, and on his righteousness, and all these other things will be given you as well. So do not worry about tomorrow: tomorrow will take care of itself. Each day has enough trouble of its own."

And what are we, rueful inhabitants of the age of anxiety, to make of what Jesus says here, filling the air with metaphors as gracefully as a magician fills it with snow-white doves? Jesus does not want us to take him wrong, for he is talking about the finest ore in the deepest mine of faith. Belief is to living as trust is to love; they are, indeed, all part of the single mystery of existence, the gift of life that is rich in steadily unfolding promises. If we take a step in faith the ground will hold beneath our feet, the darkness will be lighted for us, and we will lack neither clothes nor food. The journey, Jesus says, can be made without worry, without that killing anxiety through which we deprive ourselves of joy by trying to make ourselves completely secure against fear.

It is religious poetry of the most irresistible kind: God will take care of us like a good father. There are subtleties here, however, that we must ponder—for, despite the undoubted providence of God as Father, there is no justification for our remaining children who can surrender to play in the certainty that someone else is minding the universe. And whose are the faces of the hungry, their great round eyes floating in uncomprehending longing above bloated bellies and sores that will not heal? Are these faithless children who merely lacked trust in their creator and who now suffer the consequences? And what of the lands blown into deserts by the savage winds out of hell itself, the lands clotted with the stick-limbed corpses of animals and people? Are we to count these as the unbelievers who lacked trust?

No, we say, because depending on God involves depending on ourselves as well. We must plan with an eye to the good of the community of the world as well as to our own concerns. The theme is familiar and we are reminded of it times beyond counting. There is world population and food to plan for, yes, and the conserving of our sources of energy. Are there any who do not hear these entreaties in their dreams?

Have people ever lived in an environment more aware of planning, of pension plans and social security, of a thousand remedies for our fear of insecurity later on?

What then is Jesus talking about? It is some balance, some blend that gives life and tone to the dry sound of prudence, freedom to enliven a puritan soul, a mood perhaps of the spirit that is committed to the right values and so finds deliverance from fear. For it is the killing fear, the obsessive drive to nail down the last flapping edge of tent so that there is neither exit or entrance, that takes life away and betrays the excessively anxious. A margin must be left, a space large enough to admit the demons of mistake, for it is that distance—wide as the measure of our best efforts—that God does not leave empty.

God attends persons who live with integrity, who do what they can do with an awareness that this binds them to God and God to them. This is not, however, a guarantee that such persons will not suffer, not even that they will be spared the normal anxieties that are part of a deeply lived life. Jesus does not urge us to live numbly in our trust in God; we are rather to live easily, redeemed from the corroding power of fear that is out of control. Men and women who trust in God have deep and pervasive feelings; but they are about the right things, about the issues and values of substance rather than about trivial and passing matters. They may weep and they may tremble, but this is because they have loved deeply, because, in other words, they have already overcome the deadliest of fears.

CHAPTER 7

Verses 1–5

"If you want to avoid judgment, stop passing judgment. Your verdict on others will be the verdict passed on you. The measure with which you measure will be used to measure you. Why look at the speck in your brother's eye when you miss the plank in your own? How can you say to your brother, 'Let me take that speck out of your eye,' while all the time the plank remains in your own? You hypocrite! Remove the plank from your own eye first; then you will see clearly to take the speck from your brother's eyes."(NAB)

--------⚬--------

Why does a paragraph as compassionate as this sound stern and reproachful? How, indeed, can humans, lovers of gossip throughout history, escape the judgment that here falls open like a hangman's trap beneath us? Is the harshness in our hearing? Do the words seem to have scythe-like edges because of the hardened hearts on which they fall?

We are startled still by this confrontation, by this direct assault on an ancient and twisted growth in our hearts. Jesus speaks in the tradition of the rabbis but his words carry across the centuries as clearly as a radio signal on a clear cold midnight. The message is for us and its seeming harshness is a function of its clarity; it has the power of compelling truth but its core is a gentle understanding of the human situation.

This may be why Jesus' metaphor is that of eyes. He speaks of eyes many times—more often perhaps than of minds or wills—as much, it seems, as he speaks of hearts. Judgment depends on what we see, on how deeply we can look into other persons and the unique circumstances of our lives. And seeing depends on our eyes, which, clouded or clear, filled with light or darkness, represent our whole personalities.

Our eyes, mysteries of mysteries, not only trap and bend light and color for the tapestries of sight, but they reveal our souls, whether they are spacious or cramped, stale as sealed attics or fresh as spring gardens

—our eyes, better than anything else, make clear the breadth and depth of our spirit's vision. What can we see of others or of the tumbling wonder of life which works out for so few according to either their plans or their best hopes? How can we look at most men and women—few, if any, purposely cruel; none, one can be certain, wanting darkness more than light—and not feel for their failed plans and uncertain loves? When we see clearly we are drained of wrath for we see enough of others to stay our judgment on them.

Such compassion is not a simple virtue. It does not arise from the easy choice of looking away but from the much more trying experience of looking deeply into reality. Compassion does not distort the truth as much as it seeks it in all its complexity. Compassion does not oversimplify; it takes on the spiritually profound task of understanding when quick judgments—how rapidly we construct our heroes and villains— are so popular. The mines of truth are deep but the mills of visionless judgment grind away at every creek and stream.

Judgments without compassion are deadly both to those who make them and to those who suffer them. Jesus cuts through to the nerve and bone of this truth; that is why we still jump at his pronouncement. But he speaks clearly because his own vision is unclouded and because he has a tender feeling for our human problems. Here we find words that challenge us but which also provide a steady and deep comfort for all those who struggle to do their best in the human condition.

Verse 6

"Do not give what is holy to dogs or toss your pearls before swine. They will trample them under foot, at best, and perhaps even tear you to shreds."(NAB)

Has there ever been a phrase with a guttier resonance than this one about pearls thrown before swine? It has sent scholars fluttering like stone-scattered doves in search of smoother terrain. It cannot quite mean what it says, they tell us, finding reasons to round off the words that remain jagged rocks in spite of them. It is, nonetheless, a splendid phrase, ranking in its startling qualities with the verse about the Kingdom being borne away by the violent—words that, no matter what the authorities say, are very hard to understand.

So the biblical experts tell us that it had a "temporary" meaning in Jesus' time and a "lasting" meaning for our own, or, hold on, there is a mistranslation at the root of it all. The Hebrew words for "holy" *(kadosh)* and "earring" *(kadasha)* have the same consonants, look exactly the same, and may have been mixed up here. The Hebrew parallelism is preserved if we are not to give earrings to dogs or pearls to swine, but are we really any more satisfied? The phrases still bite the tongues that pronounce them; there is energy in these words for which scholarship can give no helpful account.

This verse has been interpreted as offering spiritual advice and worldly counsel at the same time, a hybrid of the secular and the sacred, porcupine words difficult to grasp. But what is wrong with an errant phrase, one strong enough to brand itself into our consciousness despite the reassuring translators and apologists? We may be reassured by our puzzlement, comforted that the years have not refined away all the mysterious clumps in the ore of scripture.

Perhaps that is what these words describe—the strange, often muddled and uncertain background for even our deepest experiences. There are differences in our human transactions and we cannot blink them away, there are moments that are right and others that are wrong, there are shifts subtle as the turn of the wind, in the persons, places, and times of our lives. The world people count on rumbles and may split open even for lovers. Risk attends our best moments—one of the cruelest of truths—and there is no easy balance for anyone who would take life and other persons seriously.

It is almost too easy to lose one's balance, to do or say the thing that is out of place, to offend when one wishes to soothe, to miss the moment for reaching another and to purchase estrangement instead of joy. Yes, the human situation is filled with good things trampled underfoot, with our souls torn to shreds by misunderstandings that should never have occurred, with the pearls of the spirit scattered beneath the blind and unknowing scavengers of existence. Life can be filled with out-of-place things, with events hurting and separating people in an almost random way.

We are the bearers of this desolating power, the agents of indifference that is not intended, of forgetfulness that is not willed, speakers of the careless, rocklike words that smash the windows of others' souls. It is power to be pondered, and it is well symbolized in a scripture verse that cannot be quite toned down or talked away. We must, as we read in other places, be on watch lest we scatter where we should gather or extinguish the guttering candle or set the placid sheep to flight. Is it too much to imagine that Jesus is reminding us of the qualities of tenderness and sensitivity in a world that is coarsely scarred by those who have neither?

Verses 7–11

"Ask, and you will receive. Seek, and you will find. Knock, and it will be opened to you. For the one who asks, receives. The one who seeks, finds. The one who knocks, enters. Would one of you hand his son a stone when he asks for a loaf, or a poisonous snake when he asks for a fish? If you, with all your sins, know how to give your children what is good, how much more will your heavenly Father give good things to anyone who asks him!" (NAB)

———∞———

This is one of the most reassuring of Jesus' sayings for, despite the blanket of time that has covered it, something of its tone, vibrant and enthusiastic, still reaches us. The words embrace us, welcoming us as though we were prodigal children, inviting us closer in the manner of a campfire on the shore of our arrival. These seem to be the kind of words we have been waiting for. Were they left until now by Matthew, a man careful of balance, according to his own tax-collector's wisdom? Might not this and the following paragraphs be the things Jesus spoke of first, the things that he wanted people to know right away about their relationship to God, the truths that flowed so naturally from the Jewish notion of Yahweh? Did Matthew have reasons like those of a modern theoretician of religious education for placing them here? It may be that, presuming his readers had this idea already, he would place it, artfully in his judgment, deep in his narrative.

But for us this passage remains salient because while it urgently tells us how we should feel toward God it also lets us know how God feels toward us. It is a section that has often been explained as though our relationship with God was that of very young and unknowing children with an all-provident father. Yet there is more truth if we understand it as something slightly different, for it has a deeper sense of something emergent about all of us, something God recognizes as the truest thing about our relationship with him. It is what any good father appreciates about his children, that they are growing, and that his expectations and responses are constantly modified because of this. God is trustworthy not because he remains rigidly the same in our regard but because he recognizes that he made us in order to change through growth and that we can count on his help if we accept our responsibility for becoming adults.

So the notion of prayer is twice seeded with promise, that God hears if we are open, almost insistent, with him. What of the explanations for the prayers which, despite this pledge, seem to go unanswered or are answered in ways that surprise and sometimes distress us? Preachers and spiritual writers have explained them according to the paternalistic rather than the paternal notion of God. He knows, we are told, what we really need better than we do and, although he asks us to say our prayers in our way, he answers them in his own way. Yes, yes, that could be it but it leaves one uneasy. Why would God urge us to pray, to keep after him in fact, and commit himself to giving us what we want if, in the end, this is not what he meant? He begins to sound like a parent who has decided to give a child something but insists, out of some minor vanity, that the child ask for it first.

No, the message must have a deeper significance, a hint of the power we are meant to experience as we acquire moral presence and maturity. God will not fail us or hold gifts behind his back; he tells us that it is our responsibility to understand what we really need, to make the decisions that reflect our developing sense of personhood and our appreciation of the things that come first in the Kingdom. God will not refuse us when we make the choices that match an honest and therefore humble sense of ourselves. God says that he remains in relationship to us as we learn what is best for ourselves and that he never fails to grant our petitions for these things. The prayers forged in the hearth of maturity ring true but their making is our highest responsibility.

Verse 12

"Treat others the way you would have them treat you: this sums up the law and the prophets." (NAB)

⎯⎯⎯∾⎯⎯⎯

The sentence proves the metaphors that are used in other places. Here is the pearl of great price, the precious stone found in a field, the sentence that rises out of the sermon like a fiery beacon out of the heart of the sea. It is like a sudden plateau of land from which we can see the path of our journey across the valley, the road which, in its twistings and turnings and thickly hedged sides, was so hard to follow until now. This sentence rises like a bright new moon over the geography of our lives. There is now light enough to finish the journey; it is affirmation from the mystical depths of God that religion is simpler and grander than the commentators—yes, and a great many theologians—have made it out to be.

The phrase is filled with echoes, of course, voices like those of Hillel and Tobias who spoke of the notion in a negative form, of not doing what you didn't like to have happen to you. But this is something new, an insight that is positive and almost dazzlingly simple, yet filled with power at the same time. Perhaps we have never meditated enough on what it means to treat others as we ourselves would be treated. That may be because we treat ourselves so badly at times that we have only a blurred vision of the reciprocity of grace. We don't know how to treat ourselves so we have a difficult time understanding how we should act toward other persons.

Our understanding of Christ's saying has been enormously complicated by the dehydrated observers who substituted some kind of justice, with its connotations about treating everybody the same, for a loving and self-forgetful address of oneself to humankind. But this is to endorse good manners in place of affectionate regard, to rank being correct about things above being passionate about our gift of life. Such viewpoints even mortgage our sinfulness, keeping us from seeing deeply into ourselves and denying us the full opportunity of being compassionate and forgiving of ourselves that does not close us off in airless vanity but breaks us open to our brothers and sisters and allows us to share with them the understanding we must first allow ourselves. The difficulty is that such virtue is not a practiced thing; practice does not make perfect; only self-forgetfulness does. We are stuck in the gooey mass of our own narcissism mainly because we don't like the sight of ourselves as we really are and because we prefer makeup, the right light, and the proper accessories to develop an acceptable image of ourselves.

The golden rule, as it has been named, is not built on more freshly pumped-in guilt because of our failures to do more for our neighbor, but on the hard truth that we turn so quickly away from the task of loving and forgiving ourselves. Trying to make the self absolutely perfect, whether in prayer or behavior, has always been an enemy of the truths preached by Jesus. The first discovery, the enormous opening to God's grace, is through treating ourselves better, through doing right by ourselves so that we automatically do right by those around us. It is only in loving ourselves as we are that we can love others as they are; when we understand this, the details, like the rest of the law, take care of themselves.

Verses 13–14

"Enter by the narrow gate, since the road that leads to perdition is wide and spacious, and many take it; but it is a narrow gate and a hard road that leads to life, and only a few find it."

These sentences sound across history like iron gates clanging shut on a winter morning. Even the echo has a shiver in it as it travels away from us and we, unexpectedly barred from continuing our journey, huddle together like peeved children looking for comfort after unjust punishment.

But the road we had counted on remains closed off, and if the pilgrimage is to be finished before dark it will have to be made across the countryside where no mark has been cut or light hung for us. It is not, we are suddenly reminded, a journey to be taken for granted, not a passage for the spiritually naïve or unseasoned. Has an Old Testament Yahweh, stern as the sourest of his prophets, suddenly reasserted himself to set our confidence to flight like a cloud of pigeons rising from a park?

73

Is God insisting on terror as a basic spiritual instinct? The words make us wonder and shift uneasily. But this dearest quote of old-fashioned revivalists and retreat masters is not meant to paralyze us in craven fear as much as it is to alert us to our own responsibility for the pace and direction of our lives. We are comforted by Jesus only so that we may summon up the reserves of faith and spirit we need to move forward on our own.

Jesus is the way; we know this. And following him—yes, making a clear choice to follow him—involves us in the same kind of pilgrimage that he makes. The way is not a broad, easy road; it is not in fact a road at all, but a call to live our lives as truly and deeply as Jesus lives his. The way for him was to take on our flesh and to exempt himself from none of the thousand tests that humanity knows. Is it a surprise that we are called not to become gods or angels but fully incarnate men and women, that the quest is coiled in all the tasks and tests of growing mature?

We need a reminder of how narrow is the way to becoming real men and women, for the world offers a carnival thoroughfare of easy ways, each one as tenuous as it is attractive, each one finally as filled with deadness as a short-seasoned fad. Was it ever easier to buy the look of adulthood or the invalid passports of pseudomaturity? Was it ever easier to pass for being spiritually grown-up, to turn away from the uncharted and demanding path, that narrow way to our true selves?

Jesus will call us back from our easier dreams, from our readiness to pursue a road that demands so little of us and that leads neither through real life nor to the fullness of life. What this comes to, Jesus says, is a choice that only we can make for that hard but right journey toward his Kingdom. There is no other way to get there.

Verses 15–23

"Beware of false prophets who come to you disguised as sheep but underneath are ravenous wolves. You will be able to tell them by their fruits. Can people pick grapes from thorns, or figs from thistles? In the same way, a sound tree produces good fruit but a rotten tree bad fruit. A sound tree cannot bear bad fruit, nor a rotten tree bear good fruit. Any tree that does not produce good fruit is cut down and thrown on the fire. I repeat, you will be able to tell them by their fruits."

"It is not those who say to me, 'Lord, Lord,' who will enter the kingdom of heaven, but the person who does the will of my Father in heaven. When the day comes many will say to me, 'Lord, Lord, did we not prophesy in your name, cast out demons in your name, work many miracles in your name?' Then I shall tell them to their faces: I have never known you; *away from me, you evil men!*"

These are the words of a man who knows the weather and the fields, the scriptures and the hearts of human beings, words trailing fire after being freshly branded into our souls. Who can speak of Jesus as a dreamer or, as is now the fashion, just a political leader, after reading this paragraph? This is not the stuff of politics, which to this day is bloated by the very things which Jesus here condemns.

There is no room left for life by mere appearances or manipulative persuasions, nor a way wider than a strand of hair for the passage of the thundering and self-righteous seekers of power over other people. Love is not something abstract or filled with the vague half-light of a dying day, not something elusive that can only be lunged for and missed. No, love is as strong as these words are clear; it is, in fact, illustrated for us in the condemnations of everything pretentious that are found in these phrases of Jesus.

Jesus literally says that there is no place in the Kingdom for those who use religion to deceive, to cheat, or to mislead, no admission even for those who seem to work wonders or seem to pray fervently, or seem to work cures or set demons to flight. The Kingdom is not an exclusive place, resembling, say, a well-trimmed suburb with snobbish rules about who can live there. The way, Jesus says, is not wide enough for false prophets and their bands of self-congratulating followers who look down at other people, at the ordinary people who are, in fact, the Kingdom's inheritors. The path is narrow because its paving is truth and sincerity; there is no way in which we can manufacture credentials or claim first-row seats except through lives that are genuinely loving, simple, and true.

This is a message that the posturing ignore and that the true believers do not need to hear except as an encouragement for them to have confidence in their basic spiritual instincts. Religions abound that victimize ordinary people, that grow fat and influential by feeding off their daily distress, misleading them about the nature of true religious faith. There are as many versions as there are false prophets; but their views, like the eyes of these prophets, are full of shrewdness, of guile that could be bottled, of a commitment to externals that destroys the heart and soul of belief.

False prophets trample on what is sacred in human possibilities, turning people away from an understanding of themselves and God, and involving them often enough in ways of life and styles of religious belief that visit hatred and division rather than peace and love on the world. Count the wars—are their dead at rest yet?—inspired by such prophets; count the torture and killing inspired by wild-eyed religious leaders sick in their need for power. Have we not had enough of it yet? Is there something in our vitals, something more powerful even than lust, that drives us back to magic, that groups us willingly at the feet of false prophets in every generation?

People who follow Jesus do it simply if they are going to do it at all; they can feel lonely or wonder if they have not somehow missed something as they hear the echoes of false prophets proclaiming new and exotic belief styles. This is a passage for all those who understand, as Jesus has said, that belief in him is proved in ordinary life rather than in extraordinary practices, and that the good shepherd, whose simple garb matches his mission, stands at the center of the true Kingdom.

Verses 24–29

"Therefore, everyone who listens to these words of mine and acts on them will be like a sensible man who built his house on rock. Rain came down, floods rose, gales blew and hurled themselves against that house, and it did not fall: it was founded on rock. But everyone who listens to these words of mine and does not act on them will be like a stupid man who built his house on sand. Rain came down, floods rose, gales blew and struck that house, and it fell; and what a fall it had!"

Jesus had now finished what he wanted to say, and his teaching made a deep impression on the people because he taught them with authority, and not like their own scribes.

76

It is a carpenter's metaphor, this swiftly drawn picture of two houses in a howling storm, their fates written long before, in fair weather, when the plans were drawn and the foundations laid. And it is a good one, a sharp and clear image to carry away from this far-ranging sermon. It is a conclusion that is also a summation, for the story of the windblown houses is directed at those who have a choice about whether they will listen to and do anything about Jesus' words. You have to hear, Jesus reminds the crowd, and that is not a small or passive effort.

Hearing mysteries in the commonplace is suggested many times in the scriptures; we learn later, for example, that faith comes through hearing, and we know that there is a special blessing for all those who hear the word of God and keep it. Hearing bears the same relationship to physical listening that truth bears to facts or wisdom does to information. Just as we can be someplace without being present, so we can listen, as we so often do, and not hear a thing. The effort to hear actively—that willingness to put aside one's fuzzy distractions or other interests in order to explore a deeper territory of truth—involves a kind of death, smaller or larger according to the moment, that makes a new birth of oneself possible. We cannot actively listen to another without hearing something richer about ourselves; it is a mystery, this price we pay for revelation, this yielding up the edge of our reverie to make room for the Spirit.

So it is not enough to know the content of Jesus' sermon. No, it requires an incarnation of our attention, a gathering together of ourselves to deal with the personal meaning of the words in our own lives. Listening is indeed like building a deep and strong foundation; it is not something merely of the surface, not something for the hasty check mark or the nod of the head, for faith regresses into superstition when it tries to live by external signs. It is a larger mystery than we at first thought, for what Jesus says demands the attentive presence of people ready to reorder their lives in order to make their foundation in Jesus' teaching deeper and more sure.

A speaker who only manipulates his hearers is not so concerned with their listening in such a deep and penetrating way; he is more comfortable if they do not probe to the core of his message, for it may be a dark void where the creaking and groaning of the speaker's artifice can be heard quite clearly. The persuader, the evangelical salesman—the false prophet in any age—is terrified that his tricks may be examined too closely. Listeners who give only the surface of their attention are well suited to manipulators, for in this setting their colorful magic works to its best effect. And thoughtful people turn away from such gimmickry, such shallow sacrilege in the name of faith all of it built anew in each generation on the sand, on the dry floodplain where the sound of the coming waters can already be heard.

Something different happens here. Jesus emphasizes the need to listen deeply and carefully, to bring oneself into relationship to him and his words. That is why he sounds different to the crowd and why their attention is not the cheap and passing surrender to the manipulator but the rapt concern of those who have listened with the fullness of themselves. Jesus does not speak like one of the scribes; his authority arises from his whole manner of revealing his truth in himself; his authority arises from touching and illuminating our innermost human experience.

CHAPTER 8

Verses 1–4

After he had come down from the mountain large crowds followed him. A leper now came up and bowed low in front of him. "Sir," he said, "if you want to, you can cure me." Jesus stretched out his hand, touched him and said, "Of course I want to! Be cured!" And his leprosy was cured at once. Then Jesus said to him, "Mind you do not tell anyone, but go and show yourself to the priest and make the offering prescribed by Moses, as evidence for them."

————————⧉————————

We now enter into another chamber of Matthew's artfully drawn Gospel, and it is a familiar room, crowded with faces that we recognize and with the stories not worn out by two thousand years of telling. It is a place of wonders, of miraculous events and encounters that retain their mystery even as we witness them again. The stories have lost none of their strength; they have, it would seem, gained force because they are narrated so swiftly and directly. The wasted word was long ago gleaned from the simple harvest of wonders. It is a chapter of Hemingway-like rhythm, of movement against the light and dark of ancient dawns and evenings, of energies of the spirit transmitted between Jesus and the variously bedevilled—of impressions still swimming like after-images of lightning across our eyes. Jesus is here revealed as a man sure of himself and of his strength. He does not search his soul or anguish about his powers or destiny. Instead he acts with great directness and moves on, never looking back at those freed of demons or cleansed of illness; he is moving out beyond these events, and even Matthew's clustering of them for effect does not lessen the sense of Jesus' healing, almost before the incidents are fully told, toward some greater purpose.

Indeed, Jesus does not make much of the miracles. We have nothing here of the evangelist's preparing for the dramatic moment of healing with extravagant gestures and loud prayers. The chapter may be read for the miracles but it may also be read for a message about Jesus' way of doing things, almost his refusal to allow the complications of men to interfere with the loving work of God.

The leper and his sores have been described in grisly detail often enough. Yes, and we know that contact with a leper was for the believing Jew a defilement second only to that of contact with a dead body. What strikes us as we view the scene once more is the simplicity of the communication between the leper and Jesus. They recognize something about each other, they sense something deep and reliable in each other, a shared truth that undergirds the cleansing itself. Have we missed the point that is to be discovered in what they are able to share in a few phrases with each other?

The spirit of truth and the spirit of healing are already alive in the exchange between the leper, who knows what Jesus can do for him, and Jesus, who understands the way the diseased man commits himself to Jesus in his confident request. This is not a favor granted to a stranger; the healer and the healed touch each other spiritually in this brief incident and they are both different because of it.

This is not a media event; it is a personal experience, and the leper is told, in the phrase that Jesus will use again and once again afterward, that he is not to talk about what happened, that he is, in effect, to minimize the wonder by returning to the ordinary rituals, to the slaughter of offerings prescribed in the law of Moses. The proof they need, Jesus says, will be found here, in the ordinary rather than the extraordinary, in disappearing back into history rather than becoming a celebrity. One wonders still at the cleanness of the incident, so unlike the labored efforts to cure that can still be found in the groaning of indecipherable prayers and the imposition of multiplied hands on the willing and unwilling of the world. God's spirit hovers now, as it always has, over simpler scenes; He is found directly, more often in truthful human exchanges than in convoluted efforts to escape humanity.

Verses 14–17

And going into Peter's house Jesus found Peter's mother-in-law in bed with fever. He touched her hand and the fever left her, and she got up and began to wait on him.

That evening they brought him many who were possessed by devils. He cast out the spirits with a word and cured all who were sick. This was to fulfill the prophecy of Isaiah:

He took our sicknesses away and carried our diseases for us.

The spiritual traces of all that has been left out to get this much in can be felt throughout this chapter. For the editing of the verses down to a spare tautness continues the sense of movement and energy; it is as if we were following Jesus with a cameraman's eye, for he is framed simply, and the jostling crowd is always around him, all but obscuring the scene while injecting excitement into it. So the individual moments of healing are highlighted as we travel swiftly from one wondrous encounter to another.

What pervades, of course, flows from the person of Jesus himself. It is his character that joins the verses together, it is his spirit that binds the day into a unity. The tale presses us to see the world through his eyes and to feel with him the rhythm of demand and responses, the tension of expectation that now fill his days. For the needy crowds are always waiting; they wear the wounds of all of humanity and live intimately with death and fever and demons. This is the homely heart of Incarnation, this meeting of God in man with men and women, this simple face of divine graciousness in ordinary life rather than in the hymns of church fathers or in the dry elaborations of theologians.

Sample here the experience of taking on the flesh of the human race. It is raucous, disordered, yes, and crowded with the enterprising and the curious as well as the meek and lowly of heart. Is everyday experience for Jesus like the tumult of a food giveaway after facing the devouring crowd, in part genuine and in some part phony, afflicted with every curse and every dream of greatness, with every human fault and possibility? Is this the tide of seekers rising with every sun and waiting till the first stars are lighted? Is God's entering our history robbed of grandeur by such surging crowds which, intent on securing their needs, displace the choirs of angels?

Is his life finally as unsentimental as duty and as steadily demanding as love? Jesus, we read in another place, knew what was in man; how could he help but learn it well, and wonder at times in his own heart

81

about these human beings whom he loved so deeply? One feels that the demands from the needy never let up and that as Jesus looks into the faces of the crowd he feels ever more intensely for them, crippled sometimes in spirit, blinded and driven, seeded with lusts and angers, yet more like lost sheep than bands of sinners, in need of being found and gently blessed rather than preached at or condemned.

The measure of being human is the one that we ourselves discover in the long passage of adulthood, at every turn of which someone in need waits for us. And to believe in Jesus means that we live as he did, always ready to give of ourselves in response to the spouses and children and students, to the strangers and even the enemies who want something, sometimes only a moment of attention, from us. To be human is nothing less than to be caught in the great congested pilgrimage of existence and to join ourselves freely to it in the face of the evidence of its never-ending troubles.

The story of Chapter 8 in Matthew is that of Jesus' healing, but it is also that of Jesus' own life and of his growing realization that the crowds would always be there, that the power of their need, like a suction on his spirit, would drain him finally of everything. This is the deeper sense Jesus carried as he touched the sick and healed the oppressed, this is his consciousness, ever more finely developed, of his servant's mission.

Verses 18–22

When Jesus saw the great crowds all about him he gave orders to leave for the other side. One of the scribes then came up and said to him, "Master, I will follow you wherever you go." Jesus replied, "Foxes have holes and the birds of the air have nests, but the Son of Man has nowhere to lay his head."

Another man, one of his disciples, said to him, "Sir, let me go and bury my father first." But Jesus replied, "Follow me, and leave the dead to bury their dead."

Jesus the man can be seen here as clearly as he is to be glimpsed in any of the gospel stories. He is not the disembodied preacher, the figure lost in the blinding glare of light, but the man on the edge of his mission, neither untroubled nor untried by these contacts with the crowds that now surround him, drawing him into the rhythms of their own ambivalence. Jesus can see nothing but the faces of those who press in on him —is there a demand for a new wonder in each of these glances? Or does he see dumb curiosity, like that of animals alerted by a sound in the forest, or that impersonality that settles on crowds at scenes of tragedy? He needs the simple blessings of fresh air and sunlight on the water and a clear place where he can stand.

One cannot ignore the press of human need in Jesus' clear decision —he "gave orders," we read—to cross to the opposite shore. It is a mood the commentators, anxious to track the names of places and parse the ancient verbs, ignore; they are more interested in where Jesus is going than in the fatigue and the hints of restlessness—Jesus will, after all, fall into the deepest of sleeps in the boat just a short time later —that prompt him to choose some privacy and a saving distance from the beseeching crowds. Have we ever seen the human Jesus at closer range?

We would be numb to the core if we could not feel something of Jesus' searching heart as he speaks of lacking any place to lay his head, and no clear recognition yet of his place in Israel. And what of his pulling away from the crowd? Is the desire to be away from its pressure also, in part, his way of stirring its members by turning away from them almost abruptly to let them think about what he has said and done? Is this, in other words, part of Jesus' style and one that is appropriate to the use of symbol and metaphor, to words and signs that trail mystery after them? Or is it something subtler than style, something basic about the nature of revelation in the human mode? For we have encountered here a powerful metaphor, one that still makes us uneasy despite the varied scholarly explanations that would temper its impact on us.

To say, in a country rich in commitment to family obligations, that the dead can bury the dead is to slash through the most tender of pieties and to leave his hearers, as he leaves us, uncertain of what it means. But we cannot be surprised that Jesus, drained by the intensity of the day, might speak tersely as he walks toward the boat. He has spoken of the Kingdom and he has spent himself with the crowds; what he says—and what he asks—is simple because he is contemplating the same absolute that he speaks of mysteriously to us. There is no way to reduce the tension generated by his statement; it is meant to be eternally disturbing, a current to rile the souls of those who claim to follow Jesus throughout all of history.

Verses 23–27

Then he got into the boat followed by his disciples. Without warning a storm broke over the lake, so violent that the waves were breaking right over the boat. But he was asleep. So they went to him and woke him saying, "Save us, Lord, we are going down!" And he said to them, "Why are you so frightened, you men of little faith?" And with that he stood up and rebuked the winds and the sea; and all was calm again. The men were astounded and said, "Whatever kind of man is this? Even the winds and the sea obey him."

───────────◇───────────

Here is the ancient dream of kings, to stay the tide and calm the storm, to work a regal will on the stubborn forces curling up in invisible winds from the deepest core of the universe. This story of Jesus in the boat from which he had just preached to the pressing crowds on the far shore has been unfurled by preachers as if it were a banner of power triumphant. In the long run, in a strategy to outwait doubters, the power of Jesus, restrained in public or used almost reluctantly, would flash forth in an unmistakable revelation of divinity. Such signs have always been trump cards for the apologists of Christianity, decisively thrust forward to demonstrate that Jesus is not a mere man but God himself.

And yet one wonders if this is the point of the incident after all. God has no need to prove himself Lord of the universe, no plan, one is sure, to establish a covenant with human beings that must constantly be validated with wonders. No, the faith he expects from his creatures would be as thin as mountain air if it depended on miracles ever fresh and increasingly intricate. The point lies not in the power of God that breaks or bends the laws of nature but in something simpler and finally more awesome.

For this is the story of God vesting Himself in human nature, accepting its every limitation and the discipline that is woven into each day of growth as a man. It is not a story of divine power exploding in starbursts about our history, but of divine power forsaken in the mystery of Incarnation, of God's speaking to us on our own terms, in our own language. The wonder here is not so much that a storm should subside as quickly as it arose—which of us has not been through a similar experience?—but that God should give Himself so totally to the human way of things that Jesus would lie in exhausted sleep, drained by the intense contact with the imploring crowds, with a weariness to the very bone that we all recognize.

The wonder of this tale lies in the Lord asleep beneath the rage of wind and water, of an exhausted Jesus drawing on no divine reserves to remain alert. It is a small story, no larger than the eye of the storm itself, but one in which we can see ourselves and can glimpse the Incarnation's deepest meaning.

The point has more to do with self-possession and human identity—with the roots of the peace that Jesus preaches—than with God's energies pitted against a lake squall. There is a deeper message for those with Jesus, for if they give themselves as totally as he does they will make purchase of a kind of peace that cannot be taken away. The wonder resides in the measure of God's taking on a body in Jesus and in exempting him from none of the experiences—some so small we cannot name them and some so great we spend a lifetime trying to understand them, some conscious, some unconscious, some affected by inheritance and some by social conditioning—none of the ordinary events that go into the making of a human being.

Verses 28–34

When he reached the country of the Gadarenes on the other side, two demoniacs came toward him out of the tombs—creatures so fierce that no one could pass that way. They stood there shouting, "What do you want with us, Son of God? Have you come here to torture us before the time?" Now some distance away there was a large herd of pigs feeding, and the devils pleaded with Jesus, "If you cast us out, send us into the herd of pigs." And he said to them, "Go then," and they came out and made for the pigs; and at that the whole herd charged down the cliff into the lake and perished in the water. The swineherds ran off and made for the town, where they told the whole story, including what had happened to the demoniacs. At this the whole town set out to meet Jesus; and as soon as they saw him they implored him to leave the neighborhood.

Jesus can now go few places without notice, few places in which he will not be forced into some confrontation with those who would extract something from him—a word, a gesture, a wondrous sign, or perhaps a judgment on the finest point of the law. One senses that there is no place to go now that the word has spread about him. Something will be made of whatever he does or says.

The world is lovable but it is a box too, with stuffy corners where the wondering and the needy are always waiting. What else could be said of the insane in a harsh, ancient landscape except that demons had seized them? How long the world would wait for a simple, more human explanation, that the lonely and the mad were those who bore the failures of our love, that the infecting evil was something we communicated across the wreckage of every trust and intimacy.

So we have here no simple passage; it is a difficult one for us because there is a lingering fascination—part attraction and part repulsion—in the evil spirits scattered at Jesus' word into the herd that thrashes to death in the now contaminated lake. We do not want to explain it away fully, despite the commentators. Perhaps we nourish an almost desperate wish that even our smallest impulses to evil—our bad tempers and selfishness, our capacity to hurt unnecessarily—could be explained as visitations by evil spirits and that these too could be cast out of us by a spiritual command.

But perhaps the point beneath whatever occurred is that Jesus, in a reaction greater in its way than the wonder we remember, did not shun the shambling men who had been made into exiles by their fellows. The wonder lies in Jesus' power to reach the outcasts, to touch them with hope and call them back to life, to deal with them humanly again after their long years of rejection. It is a challenge to a magical way of interpreting the world, an operational way of relocating responsibility within persons, of demonstrating that good and evil lie in our power, that we can give life or take it away from each other.

The crowd is disturbed; are we surprised that the animals are too? How could they miss the power of Jesus, in its impact on the howling men and the curious crowd, in the changed mood that settles on the human bystanders? So the word again spreads swiftly, rumors and stories run ahead of this Jesus who is so startlingly different from other teachers. Threatened religious leaders do not want him around; there is too much trouble, too much wonder in him. That is the melancholy point of the whole passage.

Gospel of Matthew, CHAPTER 9

Matthew's gospel is not a rambling tale told by an old man over a sputtering campfire, not a narrative in which stories are linked uncertainly on a swaying strand of association. No, Matthew's gospel is arranged with the discipline of art and a keen sense of a plot building in meaning and tension until it explodes in the violence of Calvary.

So Chapter 9 presents us with a turning point, one for which we have been prepared by the reactions of the crowds, that configuration of faith and curiosity, wonder and fear, approach and withdrawal, that delivers to us the living face of revelation, the human aura of reaction around the powerful presence of Jesus. We know him in what he says and in the way his listeners respond to him. By the mystery of Incarnation, Jesus' words cannot be uttered on a mountain top to the beckoning heavens but must be spoken on shorelines and in marketplaces to shifting crowds, now with him and now against him, of the human family.

Now everything has been risked; Jesus has spoken and worked openly, and the crowds, unsure of what to make of him, are everywhere. Word of him has flashed—have human beings in small villages changed at all?—to elders and religious leaders, to the keepers of the traditions which Jesus challenges. Matthew arranges his story so that we cannot miss the mood of mounting suspicion, of forces in outline beginning to array themselves against Jesus, of the avalanche of rocklike tradition beginning to tremble above the place where Jesus teaches something new.

The teachers of the law, which Jesus would bring to fuller growth, accuse him of blasphemy when he cures a paralytic, of immorality when he eats with sinners and tax collectors, of having no sense of religious piety when he does not fast, and of working by the power of Satan when he cures a dumb man. The verses are innervated with the electricity of point-counterpoint, of Jesus' acting and driving home his meaning through his responses to the accusations made against him.

One can feel the massed weight of religious culture, like that of a great cracked wheel, against which Jesus now puts his shoulder; it is the same contest in every incident. Despite Matthew's technique and our familiarity with the verses, we can sense the strain, yes, and the spark that leaps across the space between Jesus and the questioning crowd.

The paralyzed and the dumb, the tax gatherers and the sinners seem incidental in some way to the central struggle between Jesus and the tradition now mounted against him. For this is the contest that Matthew would have us understand, these moments, awesome as the opening of graves, when the Lord, in the plainest of places, joins himself to our history.

Verses 1–8

Then he reentered the boat, made the crossing, and came back to his own town. There the people at once brought to him a paralyzed man lying on a mat. When Jesus saw their faith he said to the paralytic, "Have courage, son, your sins are forgiven." At that some of the scribes said to themselves, "The man blasphemes." Jesus was aware of what they were thinking and said: "Why do you harbor evil thoughts? Which is less trouble to say, 'Your sins are forgiven' or 'Stand up and walk'? To help you realize that the Son of Man has authority on earth to forgive sins"—he then said to the paralyzed man—"Stand up! Roll up your mat, and go home." The man stood up and went toward his home. At the sight, a feeling of awe came over the crowd, and they praised God for giving such authority to men. (NAB)

———◁▷———

Jesus returns, we read, to his own town, to a place where he is less a stranger; yet he is to do unfamiliar things in the compact incidents of these verses, to assault and crack the very foundations of his own culture. It is not just the wonder of the paralytic who rises from his bed before us as he has done over and over again in the readings and preachings of this scene—is there not a field of images, bright as morning clouds, of freeings and healings, of eyes and ears being opened, tongues being loosed, and even the dead shedding their moldering burial cloths, a montage of the miraculous deep in our imaginations?— no, it is something more than the wonder, something larger and more powerful than a kindness to an afflicted stranger. Here, symbolically, is the central message of Jesus because he forges word to action in challenging the ancient belief that sin was the dark seed to which the blight of every illness could surely be traced.

Illness and disfigurement abounded in the ancient world and, as surely as the sun seemed to rise and set over an immovable earth, so the crippled and the deformed, and the wild men shouting in the caves, could only be understood—could only be put into place theologically—if the sores, the dead staring eyes, and the shriveled limbs were the bitterest fruit of the sinful lives of their possessors. Were these people less scientific than we in their search for cause and effect and for some explanatory unity in their world of experience?

Postmodern people have not settled the issue. Are we sick because we sin? Or do we sin because we are sick? Can sin be boiled down to a sliver of psychiatric residue in our souls? We remain unsure of the answers, unsure, most of the time, about how to ask the questions. Sin and sickness, evil and accident are related demons of history. They provide for every hypothesis about the headwaters of our moral existence. Are they filled with light like the dream of an innocent child, or are they fouled like the water swirling around a big-city pier? Jesus is stirring waters of human meaning already roiled by religious explanation.

Just as modern men and women have faith in science and its current metaphors, so the Jewish people worked at piecing their world together with religious ideas. The rabbis wrote of the need for forgiveness of sin before a cure of illness could be expected. It was a staple of their religious outlook and in it, of course, only God could forgive sins.

So Jesus by this action speaks a new religious language; he acts as only God can by declaring that the paralytic's sins are forgiven, that he can arise and walk. The miracle is sweet and filled with light, but the incident is tense and airless, as though the crowds, the crowds that are now with Jesus all the time, have drawn in tightly around the circle of this encounter. It has the feeling of a new power exploding in a small and contained space—and the particles that rain down on the crowd are the wreckage of the religious tradition Jesus has come to perfect.

The scribes accuse Jesus of blasphemy and Jesus makes his own swift claim—as clear and sharp as the blow of a sword—to divine power. He has the authority to forgive sins and to free people for life again. He is the wonder-worker at the center of the crowds as well as the smasher of tablets, the blasphemer pulling the temple of belief down about him, the man at the center of our gaze telling us that he is, in fact, God.

Verses 9–13

As he moved on, Jesus saw a man named Matthew at his post where taxes were collected. He said to him, "Follow me." Matthew got up and followed him. Now it happened that, while Jesus was at table in Matthew's home, many tax collectors and those known as sinners came to join Jesus and his disciples at dinner. The Pharisees saw this and complained to his disciples, "What reason can the Teacher have for eating with tax collectors and those who disregard the law?" Overhearing the remark, he said: "People who are in good health do not need a doctor; sick people do. Go and learn the meaning of the words, 'It is mercy I desire and not sacrifice.' I have come to call, not the self-righteous, but sinners." (NAB)

This is not a section to hurry over while pursuing deeper revelations in the sayings and movements of Jesus that Matthew has yet to tell us. For here we have the very writer of the Gospel at pains to describe Jesus' invitation to follow him in a line that might be neatly printed at the bottom of his sums for that day, an inspiration to explain why they were interrupted and might never be balanced out again—yes, a moment of tidy notation and inclusion of the self, with the modest third-person perspective of a bookkeeper who cannot now leave himself out and who will not make much of putting himself in.

Much thought, we may safely presume, has gone into arranging the account as we now read it. It is a moment of understatement as well as identification, a revelation bright as the evening star concerning Jesus and his essential teachings about religion. Here is the rich grain of theological truth meant to be plucked and eaten, the grain that has been hidden, even though ripe to its heart with nourishment, by those who would rewrap it in decaying layers of custom and ritual.

For the point is that Jesus comes for sinners, for those with some intimate experiences of good and evil, for those as perenially outcast as tax collectors and for those caught up in squalid choices and failed dreams, for the lame and the halt whose wounds, some given and some received, come at close quarters with life. For Jesus not only talks to these people, he dines with them, aware that his sacramental action of pairing deed and word will bring the condemnation of those leaders who identify the obsessive quest for perfection with the worship of God.

This is a passage to be read and reread and preached on even when everything else is ignored, for every generation works to dim the blinding brightness of its meaning, every generation retouches it because its members cannot quite believe it, or will not meditate deeply on its implications. Religion has been cleaned and pressed regularly in the clanking machines of hypocrisy so that we think it belongs to the proper and the pious, to those who stand at a safe distance from the back streets of existence, clucking their judgments at those who have been soiled by life. Yet Jesus proclaims that he has invited sinners rather than the righteous—and the Greek word *kalein*, as used here, means to invite as one would a guest to dinner.

The banquet is for those who have entered far enough into life to sense the powers that are engaged there every day. Life can be appreciated only by men and women who have made passage at its most dangerous crossings. Virtue is not a prize for the fearful; the kingdom is not a subdivision for the self-righteous nor for those who feel they possess the state secret of their salvation. No, the kingdom is for a larger, homelier, and less self-conscious people who understand that they are sinners because they have experienced the yaw and pitch of moral struggle as well as the complexities in what may appear to be the simplest of lives.

With these persons, alive at least to good and evil, Matthew identifies himself. These are the ones invited by Jesus to closeness with him around the banquet table. It remains a staggering story to the dry-souled puritans of every age who never understood that the men and women who are truly filled with light have gazed deeply into the darkness of their imperfect existence.

Verses 14–15

Later on, John's disciples came to him with the objection, "Why is it that while we and the Pharisees fast, your disciples do not?" Jesus said to them: "How can wedding guests go in mourning so long as the groom is with them? When the day comes that the groom is taken away, then they will fast."

<hr/>

A few lines about a homely incident and yet the passage is as mysterious as any we have yet found. Time comes inside out in its telling and Jesus' final words of prophecy are a promise of dread, as deep and foreboding as the first clouds of winter covering the sun.

The words are spoken calmly, indeed, to a certain extent, they are even reassuring for they place events into perspective, aligning the mission of John with that of Jesus, and providing a meditation, with a Jewish wedding as a central illustration, on the themes of joy and sorrow.

Jesus sees into history more clearly than a poet and it would be strange if his own heart did not pound harder as he reveals an awareness of his own destiny. Perhaps only later on will his hearers fully understand what he describes now; the prophecy is slightly oblique and nestled in the ambivalence of metaphor. It is, in fact, a preparation, a way of getting his followers ready, yes, and us as well, for the seeming collapse of his life's work; it is an anticipation of the deepest and most wrenching mystery of our existence—of separation that is the shadow of death itself.

Jesus' whole life is a challenge of death and a pledge of a new life that will rise in us as sweet and clear as spring water. But our lives are set, like a village that gets the sun only half the day, in a situation that is clearly imperfect in which love and death, sin and goodness, intimacy and separation are linked organically in the same vast, poignant truth.

So joy and sorrow can be seeded into the imagery of a wedding feast in which the flowers of celebration already contain the smell of death. It is a bewildering and spectacular mystery, as unjust as John's imprisonment, but as compelling as Jesus' promises. It is a strange yet familiar land, and the very essence of authentic religion is discovered in entering rather than trying to escape it.

This is no simple paragraph even though it reads as truly as the most ancient map of life. These are, after all, words about our own lives in which happiness is the prize of the knowing rather than the naïve. We cannot look away from the abiding experience of separation, that great crack that runs like a fault through the terrain of existence.

The earth is always splitting at our feet and our wholeness is delivered only through the vision of faith that comprehends our condition and its daily terrors of illness and accidents, of aging and misunderstanding, of time getting away from us even in our most precious and splendid moments. Jesus preaches truths for just such a state because he has truly entered it, breaking the power of life's tragedy forever through accepting all of it—from the smallest to the greatest aspect—and redeeming it in his own death.

Verses 16–17

"No one puts a piece of unshrunken cloth onto an old cloak, because the patch pulls away from the cloak and the tear gets worse. Nor do people put new wine into old wineskins; if they do, the skins burst, the wine runs out, and the skins are lost. No; they put new wine into fresh skins and both are preserved."

Who can resist the passage? It is rich and dark with mystery like anything that has aged well; it possesses, in fact, life's texture, that of old cloth, and the smell of wine, the feel of rough patches fraying and of the look of soaked hides dripping in the sun. The very unevenness of our existence can be touched here in these commonsense, yet poetic, sentences about change and decay and the promise of the things that are still coming to be.

The religious destiny of the world is stated in a homely metaphor rather than in an elegant theological abstraction. Pausing for a moment we get a better sense of Jesus the preacher, for he is a poet of our salvation, the Lord of the universe who perceives our experience not in a manifest of laws nor in a detailed numbering of our sins or virtues but in the language of literary imagination.

Jesus is the direct man who cuts to the bone of the matter, the carpenter with a sense of the strength of wood and the power of troubled weather, the man who talks not in mysteries but in metaphors, not, as some commentators would have us believe, to hide his meaning, but because this is the natural language of revelation, the language always fresh because it builds on the experiences we all recognize.

Opening the pages of the scriptures is not like pulling back the lid on a trunk to fill the attic with the compressed odors that are nothing more than ghosts of buried events; it is rather like a walk in the fresh air, a reunion with family and friends, homecoming rather than exile; it is to be engaged with life rather than memory. Jesus is understood better as the fashioner of metaphor, the lively observer whose conversations and prayers are as filled with music as his eyes with light, the sensitive man who loves and laughs and who also feels the pain of betrayals even as he understands and forgives his betrayers. No, the Jesus we meet here is not the hooded mystic attracting people because of some ambivalent magnetism; indeed, he is quite unlike the spectral Lord of the holy cards.

And what he says speaks to us still, for religious leaders of many faiths have resisted the future in every age of history; they have fashioned awkward patches for garments and wineskins, preferring outdated and literal interpretations, for example, that are the very opposite of the lasting language of metaphor which Jesus regularly employs. A new age has indeed dawned in Jesus and, while many proclaim this in words, they have not really freed themselves from the deadly categories of a static world. They sing alleluia but they do not understand resurrection except as an intellectual notion, the life pressed out of it by excessive theologizing.

Such leaders resist life, as though they were afraid that human beings might live it too deeply and discover that the secrets are simple rather than complex; they are fearful that this might subvert their efforts to control and supervise the very flight of the Spirit. Jesus stands vibrantly present in this paragraph, more alive to us than many contemporary preachers, because he speaks in the language that never grows old of the everlasting freshness of the life he gives us.

Verses 18–34

While he was speaking to them, up came one of the officials, who bowed low in front of him and said, "My daughter has just died, but come and lay your hand on her and her life will be saved." Jesus rose and, with his disciples, followed him.

Then from behind him came a woman, who had suffered from a hemorrhage for twelve years, and she touched the fringe of his cloak, for she said to herself, "If I can only touch his cloak I shall be well again." Jesus turned around and saw her and he said to her, "Courage, my daughter, your faith has restored you to health." And from that moment the woman was well again.

When Jesus reached the official's house and saw the flute players, with the crowd making a commotion he said, "Get out of here; the little girl is not dead, she is asleep." And they laughed at him. But when the people had been turned out he went inside and took the little girl by the hand; and she stood up. And the news spread all around the countryside.

As Jesus went on his way two blind men followed him shouting, "Take pity on us, Son of David." And when Jesus reached the house the blind men came up with him and he said to them, "Do you believe I can do this?" They said, "Sir, we do." Then he touched their eyes saying, "Your faith deserves it, so let this be done for you." And their sight returned. Then Jesus sternly warned them, "Take care that no one learns about this." But when they had gone, they talked about him all over the countryside.

They had only just left when a man was brought to him, a dumb demoniac. And when the devil was cast out, the dumb man spoke and the people were amazed. "Nothing like this has ever been seen in Israel," they said. But the Pharisees said, "It is through the prince of devils that he casts out devils."

───────◆───────

We are caught up here in the art of Matthew—for, with the orderly motives of a bookkeeper who may have given up gathering taxes but who cannot live without his accounts both balanced and neatly entered, the writer has been arranging the paragraphs so that by the time the dumb man speaks we will have witnessed ten healings and not less than that. It is the kind of number that satisfies both the accountant and the poet in Matthew, and if we do not consciously add them up from our stance in time it does not mean that their rhythm has not worked on us: Who knows what subtleties stir the deepest waters of our souls?

Matthew has filled these paragraphs with echoes from the Old Testament, into which he has dug like a preacher reaching into an old bag of sermons for his favorite quotations. There is a purpose here—one that does not strike us, because the scholars tell us in their solemn way that

Matthew actually misunderstood the Old Testament, making prophecies out of statements that were never meant to give previews of the Messiah.

But Matthew has been working carefully to demonstrate that Jesus is the fulfillment of all the signs and visions of the ancient writers, that in Jesus' life one recognizes the promises whose echoes have continued to fall, like tumbling white water, down the ledges of history. Give good marks to the biblical students who plumb the roots of Greek and Aramaic words like dentists determined to get to the jawbone of all our sensibility. But so few scholars understand poetry that one is tempted to side with Matthew, at least to trust his feeling for the mystery of religious writing, and not quickly to think that he was naïve about the presence or absence of literal truth in what he was putting down.

It is worth our meditation: for Matthew's genius, after all, may be that he has lived with his own conflicts, that he is both an accountant and a seer, that he both proves and reveals, that the very tension of these chapters rises from his own soul, giving them life and wonder. We see the man of dreams and the man of numbers forging a new creation to describe the New Creation and leaving us, all these centuries later, caught up in a vast scene, full of order and yet broken free of the constraints of time—a scene that makes us aware of the power and force of Jesus' presence as he confronts the stale religiosity of the age and divides his hearers into those who are healthy, filled now with sight and hearing and life, and those who remain blind and claim that he works in league with evil spirits.

So we cannot break these incidents down into small and distinct wonders, familiar and dear as they may be from a lifetime of hearing or reading them. We must surrender to Matthew's style and to his staging of events, for it is clear that he has more complicated purposes in mind than merely an orderly account of the Lord's life. No, the healings are set out unmistakably in time and yet they are also filled with symbols—death and darkness, blood and blindness, light and sound—that speak to us in their own way. Not the least of their effects is to make us sense that here, in the person of Jesus, something has welled up out of the age of the prophets—that God's ways are being fulfilled in him.

Verses 35–38

Jesus made a tour through all the towns and villages, teaching in their synagogues, proclaiming the Good News of the kingdom and curing all kinds of diseases and sickness.

And when he saw the crowds he felt sorry for them because they were harassed and dejected, like sheep without a shepherd. Then he said to his disciples, "The harvest is rich but the laborers are few, so ask the Lord of the harvest to send laborers to his harvest."

This is a passage of essential tenderness, a moment in the narrative that allows us to see the world as Jesus did. We are so caught up in viewing him from the outside, from the outlines of his journeys and actions, from the comments of scholars or the reverences of preachers, that we may be surprised at the sudden and utterly simple revelation of Jesus' deepest feelings about human beings. If there is gentleness in the imagery of the Old Testament in which Israel is described as a shepherdless flock—and poignancy beyond that in God's assuming the role of the shepherd, the patient searcher and the welcoming master—Jesus whose heart is moved with pity for all of us.

It is strange that this central notion—what, after all, reveals persons more clearly than an account of their genuine feelings?—this idea of Jesus as anything but harsh, and certainly not a man abstracted by heavenly visions, should be made so little of in religious education and commentary. Many grim-sounding theologians and tight-lipped guardians of orthodoxy have projected a fear that we would miss the divinity of Jesus, so that they have moved back, like ancient worshipers shielding their eyes from the holy of holies, from the humanity of the Lord. Their uneasiness betrays a strange hesitancy of belief, that slightest film of uncertainty that coats the voices of those who borrow their words from others and who have never confronted or thought deeply for themselves about their faith.

For why must we preserve Christ's divinity at the price of diminishing his humanity? This attitude has half-blinded us to the lightning at the heart of the gospel story. God so loved us—He could have a feeling for us and for the swaying bridge of our human passage—that he embraced us with a tenderness that lifts us, scarred and full of the sickness after sin, gently to himself. A portion of our sense of loss, of our wandering like the once leaderless Israelites, derives from our being denied a richer understanding of how profoundly human Jesus is. We need not fear for Jesus' claim to be God; that is strong enough to take care of itself if we believe it to be the truth.

We are drawn more out of ourselves by the enormous mystery of God's invading our history, of his setting the pegs of his tent in our time, of his investment in our very flesh and consciousness. Yes, it is a notion as deep and full of light as the galaxies, a truth that disturbs as well as comforts, an idea almost too big for us because it forces us to change our way of looking at ourselves and each other. That was the purpose of Incarnation—to pitch us, reeling, into the mysteries of the life God gave us and then entered himself, to have us embrace our existence, with all that is mean and uneven about it, and yet to see its promise still.

If we take seriously God's becoming a man, then we must take our human relationships more seriously as well, for each one reproduces the chances and hopes of the Incarnation itself, each one asks us to take on the flesh of the human situation more truly and more compassionately. To become human is a dizzying invitation that is at once the most simple and most difficult of all, because it means we can never, in the name of grandiose spirituality, turn our backs on ourselves, each other, or the world that is spread like a dream around us.

CHAPTER 10

Verses 1–5

He summoned his twelve disciples, and gave them authority over unclean spirits with power to cast them out and to cure all kinds of
diseases and sickness.

These are the names of the twelve apostles: first, Simon who is called
Peter, and his brother Andrew; James the son of Zebedee, and his
brother John; Philip and Bartholomew; Thomas, and Matthew the tax
collector; James the son of Alphaeus, and Thaddaeus; Simon the Zealot
and Judas Iscariot, the one who was to betray him. These twelve Jesus
sent out, instructing them as follows:

"Do not turn your steps to pagan territory, and do not enter any
Samaritan town. . . ."

What kind of power is this and what kind of men? For the power
seems awesome and the men seem ordinary. Is it the author's intention
to make it so or is there something beyond his control here, something
in the very shape and sound of the words, and in every translation they
have suffered, that is filled with mystery and peace? The mystery abides
in the talk of unclean spirits and this strange power—do we understand
it yet?—to cast them out of people.

And why would Jesus grant his followers the ability to cure every
kind of sickness? We have heard the answers many times over; they
have been refined by generations of apologists who would have us understand the need to make an impression on the people of the time, on
the need to build belief on wonders and to anchor the early Church in
the wide-eyed attention they would get.

The passage is as charged as a boiling summer cloud, and the lightning might strike anywhere; these are words to make us draw back, for
there is divine power on the land to burn the sinfulness out of men and
to make the wolves howl at night. Draw your cloak a little closer about
you, for if you can be cured then surely you can be infected. Such gifts
reveal terror loose in the world.

But if the gift were not so grand, if it were simpler it would match the peacefulness that lifts off in the names of the apostles themselves. This roll call of old friends is as reassuring as the promise of miracles is unsettling. These are names that are strong the way old trees are, and there is something homely in the ordering of them: some in terms of their relationships, some in terms of their work, and then, of course, Judas, in terms of his deeds.

Could it be that their power, the strength we feel as they move past us even now, lay in their humanness, in the purity of their hearts and the sweetness of their presence? Were they filled with light so that those who met them could suddenly see more deeply into the once dark and fearful parts of their own souls? Was the healing then, as it may be mostly now, not to break the laws of nature but to bring the peace that allows us to discover our wholeness?

These are not small miracles, this light for darkness and this oil for our wounds. Would those who listened to them be more struck by a dazzling wonder, by tricks even of the most heavenly sort, rather than by a deeper penetration of their own personalities? Does not the very idea of evil as an infestation estrange us from recognizing our own capacity for wrongdoing? Would not such exorcisms make us victims of a stinking infection rather than persons in control of our own best and worst possibilities?

The men called by Jesus seem possessors of another kind of power, one that fits well their utter humanity. It is power, all right, but not one related to spells or curses out of a wizard's book. It is the power that comes from the spirit and that flows through them because they have cleansed themselves in the Lord's presence of their last resistance to grace. It is something we can recognize because in them, the dust rising as they tramp away from us, we can see something of ourselves— in Judas who will despair and Peter who will weep—yes, something of the shape we are putting into our own lives every day.

Verses 6–15

". . . go rather to the lost sheep of the House of Israel. And as you go, proclaim that the kingdom of heaven is close at hand. Cure the sick, raise the dead, cleanse the lepers, cast out devils. You received without charge, give without charge. Provide yourselves with no gold or silver, not even with a few coppers for your purses, with no haversack for the journey or spare tunic or footwear or a staff, for the workman deserves his keep.

"Whatever town or village you go into, ask for someone trustworthy and stay with him until you leave. As you enter his house, salute it, and if the house deserves it, let your peace descend upon it; if it does not, let your peace come back to you. And if anyone does not welcome you or listen to what you have to say, as you walk out of the house or town shake the dust from your feet. I tell you solemnly, on the day of Judgment it will not go as hard with the land of Sodom and Gomorrah as with that town."

———⚭———

We sense Matthew, collector once of taxes and now of the sayings of Jesus, arranging a manifesto, a grand statement for all those who count themselves members of the Kingdom here proclaimed in riveting and practical fashion. The verses radiate the excitement of their first utterance and, standing among the ordinary men called to be his closest followers, we are as absorbed and attentive as they are. We know that the expanded flow of this discourse, with its application to the world beyond, is fed by the torrent of these first instructions. Jesus is direct and precise as he sends these men on a missionary expedition to his own people.

Where else, at this moment, are they prepared to go, how far can they travel away from Jesus on this initial probe? One senses the layers of meaning of the Greek word, *paragellein*, used here to describe his commissioning of his friends and followers. It resonates with ambiguity, for Jesus is at once the military leader issuing orders, the friend calling for help, the teacher giving advice, and, yes, the lord of the Kingdom issuing a command. It is as if, at this extraordinary moment, Jesus casts a net of images over them, reassuring them that they will not be far away from him even as he sends them away, their hearts generous but uncertain and much in need of his strength.

What, we ask ourselves again, is the nature of this Kingdom, so long prophesied and so frequently imagined as bristling with soaring towers floating on the banners of victory? It is difficult not to construct it as a place, for the blessed can enjoy pearls and gold as well as anybody else. Yet the wellspring of this Kingdom is clearly not the power of arms or of positive thinking. It is a spiritual Kingdom and stands, therefore, without boundaries. We enter it through relationship to Jesus who here proclaims its presence. We live in it, not through physical presence but through the power of the spirit that is communicated in friendship with Jesus and in our friendship with each other. If we live in this relationship with Jesus, which is immune to the effects of time and distance, others will feel his presence through us. The transfer of power, something we easily identify as, for example, when people stand by us in bad times, is essentially spiritual. Energy moves from their hearts to ours and we are changed—we are stronger, more faithful, more true to our best selves—because of it. The Kingdom of God, we understand in such moments, is indeed in the midst of us.

This passage commits the apostles not to be grand and distant preachers calling for repentance, but to place themselves into close relationship with people, to enter their homes, sense their capacity to accept the Kingdom in their capacity to receive them. Only then can they heal the people's spiritual weaknesses, hack away the chains of their sinful obsessions, call them back to life from the dead void of sin.

This mystery still baffles us, encounter it though we do in our ordinary life activities. Jesus speaks of no power except that which, as mist to rushing river, is inseparable from its setting. As a Kingdom of human relationships, its tests and experiences are described in attitudes of the human heart, in the wondrous acceptances and wrenching rejections that the apostles can expect to find even as Jesus himself has found them. So Jesus' advice is eminently practical; it matches their imminent encounters with human beings rather than angels. Jesus knows the possibilities and the hazards of the community which he proclaims. All these centuries later one feels the sensible, hard-won truth of his counsel. It would be easier were Jesus to proclaim a worldly Kingdom in which his followers are expected to overwhelm their enemies by force. But this Kingdom, based on opening others to the nature of friendship and love, is far more difficult because, by its essential nature, it makes us vulnerable by giving others the awful power to reject and hurt us.

Verses 16–23

"Remember, I am sending you out like sheep among wolves; so be cunning as serpents and yet as harmless as doves.

"Beware of men: they will hand you over to Sanhedrins and scourge you in their synagogues. You will be dragged before governors and kings for my sake, to bear witness before them and the pagans. But when they hand you over, do not worry about how to speak or what to say; what you are to say will be given to you when the time comes; because it is not you who will be speaking; the Spirit of your Father will be speaking in you.

"Brother will betray brother to death, and the father his child; children will rise against their parents and have them put to death. You will be hated by all men on account of my name; but the man who stands firm to the end will be saved. If they persecute you in one town, take refuge in the next; and if they persecute you in that, take refuge in another. I tell you solemnly, you will not have gone the round of the towns of Israel before the Son of Man comes."

We need the scholar to bring his lantern closer, to raise it above this paragraph so that we can better understand how it was fashioned. One feels Matthew's intensity, his sense of purpose late in the first century, as, like a collator with more material than he can use, he assembles this sturdy bridge of Jesus' sayings without worrying about their strict historical context. They are clearly Jesus' words; one cannot mistake their freshness and directness, the confidence of their tone. And yet we are suddenly well beyond the boundaries of Palestine, in places to which the apostles have not yet traveled, much less imagined. We crane our necks in these Gentile palaces of judgment, looking for a familiar face, a signal about how we were delivered to this alien court, challenged to speak for ourselves about the Kingdom we proclaim.

The students of the Gospel tell us that Matthew, more concerned about the reassurance Jesus offers than the precise moment in which he speaks it, wedges these sentences into place, certain that they are not out of place. This is what Jesus said, the aging evangelist says to an assistant, everybody remembers this, it is the promise of his presence—that he will fill us in times of trial—that is important to include here. Here, here is the place for it. There is something powerfully comforting not only in Jesus' words but in Matthew's editorial judgment.

As he approaches this set of phrases Matthew conveys his sense of personal relationship to Jesus. He sees him as clearly as he did half a century before, is moved as deeply as then, and proceeds with the sureness of a man who knows that the truth of life transcends what seem to be its hardest and best-ordered facts. In gathering these injunctions together, Matthew reveals the Jesus he knows, and we can feel the rightness of his move because it serendipitously captures the excitement, the still living character of the man who one day called him away from his counting table. One feels the immediacy of Jesus as a man, for only someone who knew him intimately could have presented him as we find him here.

Verses 24–27

"The disciple is not superior to his teacher, nor the slave to his master. It is enough for the disciple that he should grow to be like his teacher, and the slave like his master. If they have called the master of the house Beelzebul, what will they not say of his household?

"Do not be afraid of them therefore. For everything that is now covered will be uncovered, and everything now hidden will be made clear. What I say to you in the dark, tell in the daylight; what you hear in whispers, proclaim from the housetops."

———❦———

Jesus speaks in the cadences of the rabbi, alluding to proverbs that have sung in the heads of his followers all their lives. There is something lyrical and free, and therefore immensely attractive, in the way he talks to these men as they head off on their first missionary journey. If his Kingdom is one of relationship rather than royalty, Jesus structures their understanding of their special attachment to him. Your lives, Jesus tells them evenly, must be like mine, do not be surprised if the rhythm of my days is repeated in your own. Everything we have shared together—the friendship we have—is what you can now give away to other persons. Jesus reveals the essentially social nature of his teaching; it is to be made as public as possible. Everyone is welcome to enter the Kingdom that I have prepared you to teach openly.

We pause in wonder at the nature of the Kingdom, that dynamic relationship to Jesus to which everyone receives an invitation. Jesus breaks his inner circle open, casts them, in a sense, like rich seed into the thicketed garden of the world. His words are meant to take root everywhere, because the Kingdom is not an elite organization in which everything is determined by rank, but a family in which the most essential things are determined through relationships. Don't hold back, or form privileged groups, but plunge in among people, as I have done, for each of them is invited to learn in broad daylight the great truths I have taught you in the shadowed life that you have had up until now.

Verses 28–33

"Do not be afraid of those who kill the body but cannot kill the soul; fear him rather who can destroy both body and soul in hell. Can you not buy two sparrows for a penny? And yet not one falls to the ground without your Father knowing. Why, every hair on your head has been counted. So there is no need to be afraid; you are worth more than hundreds of sparrows.

"So if anyone declares himself for me in the presence of men, I will declare myself for him in the presence of my Father in heaven. But the one who disowns me in the presence of men, I will disown in the presence of my Father in heaven."

———∞———

Jesus reads the reactions of his apostles. He understands that they may be afraid of the darkness he urges them to dispel with the blaze of his teaching. Jesus speaks confidently, the way a man does about a hazardous journey he has already made many times. He knows what you can lose on such a pilgrimage, what and what not to fear. Jesus' eyes are alight as he looks from one of his friends to the other, offering that which they—and most other people—need almost more than anything else, encouragement for their lives. The real killers, Jesus says, are those who destroy hope and rob people of a chance for a productive life.

He smiles, for he is sure of what he promises them, aware as only a son can be of what his father is like. There is the hint of good-natured observation as he speaks of the numbering of the hairs on their heads. Is Peter balding, and is this jest a signal of Jesus' understanding of even this minor human problem as he incorporates it into his reassurance about God's care for them? God knows, Jesus says, whenever the sparrows touch the ground. You, when you feel lonely or forgotten or dis-couraged, should draw on this truth for nourishment.

One cannot look up from these verses without feeling the warmth of Jesus' communication. He leaves the disciples not just feeling better, but in some way changed by what he says: stronger, more keenly aware of their relationship with Jesus, and through him with God. We get a vivid sense of his presence as Jesus draws close to them, calming them here as he will in a later storm, the source of their energy as they proclaim his Kingdom in a doubting and fearful world. This is one of those profoundly emotional moments in which time is suspended by the power of a great achievement or the fidelity of a great cause; one does not want it to end, for the truths we live by lie on its open palm for our contemplation.

Verses 34–42

"Do not suppose that I have come to bring peace to the earth: it is not peace I have come to bring, but a sword. For I have come to set *a man against his father, a daughter against her mother, a daughter-in-law against her mother-in-law. A man's enemies will be those of his own household.*

"Anyone who prefers father or mother to me is not worthy of me. Anyone who prefers son or daughter to me is not worthy of me. Anyone who does not take his cross and follow in my footsteps is not worthy of me. Anyone who finds his life will lose it; anyone who loses his life for my sake will find it.

"Anyone who welcomes you welcomes me; and those who welcome me welcome the one who sent me.

"Anyone who welcomes a prophet because he is a prophet will have a prophet's reward; and anyone who welcomes a holy man because he is a holy man will have a holy man's reward.

"If anyone gives so much as a cup of cold water to one of these little ones because he is a disciple, then I tell you solemnly, he will most certainly not lose his reward."

The Day of the Lord is indeed here, Jesus says, drawing, as he has in his injunctions not to be afraid, on the scriptural language that is sunk deep in the consciousness of his hearers. If they share friendship with Jesus, if, indeed, his Kingdom is one of loving relationships, then they should not be surprised at the disruption that its proclamation will cause. Jesus has a poet's sensitivity to the world and to its gathering defensiveness against a message whose utterly simple notions about the way people should love and trust each other are bound to upset the bureaucracies to which culture is anchored. Jesus raises a vision of a universe disturbed at the notion of everyone's being equal in God's sight. He feels, as poets always do ahead of others, the forces coming together on the long plain of the future. He knows that a challenge to the world's idea of kingdoms and power will draw down fierce persecution for him and his followers. Jesus looks into the eyes of the men around him. Do they really grasp the essential point? Do they understand this deepest truth about life in his Kingdom?

We may ask whether we understand and assent to it yet ourselves. For Jesus speaks here of that surrender of self, that death to one's own seeking, that allows a person to pass through suffering to resurrection. There is no phrase easier to quote and more difficult to live by. Jesus is looking into our eyes, repeating again what comes with citizenship in his Kingdom: the challenge of carrying a cross and suffering a death. This is not an invitation to masochists or religious fanatics but the statement of a simple truth to ordinary men and women.

Separation and dying, as good people learn, are essential to healthy friendship and lasting love. The Kingdom is, therefore, made up of men and women who understand this, whose generous intuitions are validated by Jesus' teaching. He does not bring pain into human life but he recognizes it, sets the seal of his own life and death on it, makes its endurance for the sake of others the sacramental experience that enlarges life and delivers peace and blessedness. That is why, in the closing sentences, Jesus underscores the unity of our lives with his in every action in which we give up something of our own—die a death—in order to offer a gift of love.

We can only be silent as Matthew draws this section of his writings to a close. He has massed together sayings of Jesus that prompt us to turn inward, in an examination of ourselves and our values that nobody else can do for us. Here, spoken urgently to us by Jesus himself, are the words of life and eternal life.

CHAPTER 11

Verses 1–6

When Jesus had finished instructing his twelve disciples he moved on from there to teach and preach in their towns.

Now John in his prison had heard what Christ was doing and he sent his disciples to ask him, "Are you the one who is to come, or have we got to wait for someone else?" Jesus answered, "Go back and tell John what you hear and see; the blind see again, and the lame walk, lepers are cleansed, and the deaf hear, and the dead are raised to life and the Good News is proclaimed to the poor; and happy is the man who does not lose faith in me."

——————⟨∞⟩——————

In this choking prison cell, the desert shimmering beyond its rude window, we hear John's dry voice ask one of the great questions of history. Is Jesus the "One" or not? We hear hope dying in the tone of the question, hope barely propped up by the weary determination of the next phrase.

It is a familiar experience for every man or woman who has taken Jesus seriously. What of this preacher from whom we have expected so much? What reference, we wonder in the imprisonment of discouragement, does this Jesus have to our lives and problems? Does he embody the great promise of deliverance from woe that sings like wind through the ancient trees of the Old Testament? Do we, hard-pressed by events, wonder whether religious history is a pipe dream, and whether a Messiah to make sense of it all is merely a projection of all our painful longing?

John spoke up for the truth, but falsehood prevailed in the smirks of the regal and the powerful while he went down into dusty exile. In greater and lesser ways every person who chooses the truth encounters the same fate. The world—blind, smooth, overwhelming—rolls over good people, celebrating itself and its lesser gods of celebrity, influence, and wealth, all the time. Money does talk, for example, very softly but very convincingly even to those who seem the most principled among us. Life's ironic depths energize faith but also test it cruelly. Believing in the real world is not the same as the sweet contemplation of Divine truth; it offers little rest and, often enough, no opportunity for recollection. Believing is done against the odds, in the face of events and forces that say that it cannot be done; it demands a reinvestment of the self when the latter seems all but used up. Can we go on believing in you, John asks, as worn out as any man has ever been by the challenge of faith.

Jesus' answer matches John's question, for it is a catalog of his activity, an inventory of his preaching whose energy, sparking beneath layers of time and translation, electrifies us still. He does not speak of great wonders, of victories over the smugly powerful, of the establishment of an earthly kingdom rich in armies and princes. Jesus defines his work as service to the weak and the needy in a voice so ringing with confidence that we feel its deep spiritual pull. We are not asked to rally like soldiers but to live like believers. Jesus turns us back to everyday, to the plain, hard struggles of existence in which bad things happen to good people and, harder at times to bear, good things happen to bad people. Jesus sends John's questioners back with the evidence of their own senses, the proof of spiritual power at work among the suffering. The greatest sign, however, is that the good news is at last being preached to the poor. You are blessed, Jesus tells them and us, if you understand this, if you are not stunned by something so simple, not put off by truths so profound, not puzzled because you longed for something very different.

Verses 7–15

As the messengers were leaving, Jesus began to talk to the people about John: "What did you go out into the wilderness to see? A reed swaying in the breeze? No? Then what did you go out to see? A man wearing fine clothes? Oh no, those who wear fine clothes are to be found in palaces. Then what did you go out for? To see a prophet? Yes, I tell you, and much more than a prophet: he is the one of whom scripture says:

> Look, I am going to send my messenger before you;
> he will prepare your way before you.

"I tell you solemnly, of all the children born of women, a greater than John the Baptist has never been seen; yet the least in the kingdom of heaven is greater than he is. Since John the Baptist came, up to this present time, the kingdom of heaven has been subjected to violence and the violent are taking it by storm. Because it was toward John that all the prophecies of the prophets and of the Law were leading; and he, if you will believe me, is the Elijah who was to return. If anyone has ears to hear, let him listen!"

These paragraphs are dense as collapsed stars are, rich with the secrets of time and the universe, defying our understanding of them, inviting us to inspect them again and again. Jesus fills the air with metaphor as he recapitulates Jewish belief, proclaims again that the waiting is at an end, that the Kingdom is not entered easily, as a great city by tourists curious about living there, but with difficulty by people desperate to fight their way inside. Are there sentences more puzzling than these, phrases that leave us more uncertain about their meaning and their relevance to ourselves?

John is, of course, familiar. A rough figure, the essential prophet of our common religious imagination, the prophet unafraid of proclaiming the advent of the Kingdom. Such uncertainties crowd around all beginnings; each one, in some way, carries a seed of this Kingdom's beginning. When, we ask, did we fall in love, and when did we finally feel grown up? When did we stumble on the doorstep of wisdom, and when, indeed, does life begin, or, for that matter, come to an end? Life is as thick with mysteries as that of the initiation of Jesus' Kingdom, each of them a reflection of the transitional moments in which we have a chance to grasp the meaning of our lives.

How characteristic of the nature of faith that John should proclaim what he will not live to see, that his belief stretches beyond himself. Every act of faith reaches toward events whose very beginning depends on the strength of its pledge; it is not for us to see its outcome, only for us to make the promise, for us to take the risks that lead to something greater beyond our own time and place. John is not only the example of the gaunt but majestic prophet, but also of the simple believer always working for something or someone beyond the shadow of his own life.

The Kingdom of which Jesus speaks is not at all what some churches have turned out to be, affluent, privileged, serene in the ways of their societies. Jesus' startling vision conjures up a noisy place, a vast, milling gathering into which there is no mannered way of entry. You must want to be there and you may have to fight your way in, struggling to keep your balance, aware of the crowds pressing on every side, aware also of the rightness of all the expended effort, of how such a charged environment matches the longing and needs of human beings. It is a place in which persons recognize who they are, feel at home, share their strength, gaze together into the open jaws of time and fate, a place only for those desperate for life and courageous enough to live it fully. These are the ones who take the Kingdom for their own, not by blind, violent force, but through the spiritual power of their ordinary lives.

Verses 16–19

"What description can I find for this generation? It is like children shouting to each other as they sit in the market place:

> 'We played the pipes for you,
> and you wouldn't dance;
> we sang dirges,
> and you wouldn't be mourners.'

"For John came, neither eating nor drinking, and they say, 'He is possessed.' The Son of Man came, eating and drinking, and they say, 'Look, a glutton and a drunkard, a friend of tax collectors and sinners.' Yet wisdom has been proved right by her actions."

Jesus seems as exasperated as any one of us in this brief section, and closer to us in the human condition because of it, somebody like us rather than somebody very distant and different. Here he speaks in a manner familiar to every parent or teacher, to anyone, indeed, who has ever struggled to remain an adult in dealing with people who exult in the primitive rewards of remaining children. It is easier to be angry with such persons than it is to see deeply into their self-centeredness, the childish ways they clutch, as they did the go-to-bed dolls of their earliest years. There is some comfort in realizing that Jesus reacted with the same impatience that we find rising in ourselves.

We would fail to be adults if we did not recognize these inner reactions, or if we denied them, or willed them into oblivion. Jesus reads the information in his own reactions and uses it in a powerfully poetic way to characterize the resistant immaturity of those to whom he and John have spoken. If I sing of the joys of life, he says, you fail to join yourself to its rhythm. And if John has been a harsh prophet you have refused to cry out for your failures. You have had the texture of life spelled out, and so self-absorbed are you that you miss it altogether. John proclaimed the deaths that are in life and I have sung of the life flourishing out of death itself, and you have ignored us both. You find ways to write us off, to count John a madman and me a glutton. You prefer your childish games to the words that deliver meaning to your lives.

Jesus addresses people who, like so many millions in every age, die before they ever learn to live. They constitute a bewildering mystery in themselves, for they look like adults and seem to involve themselves in the activities of adults. And yet they never seem to get beneath the surface of their lives and they die in a thousand meaningless and unnecessary ways, they die finally of their own childishness, and nobody seems able to save them or even to know how to mourn them properly. These people, living on borrowed emotions, stumbling through the corridors of time like shipboard drunks, are a far greater mystery than the unbaptized children who crowded the territory called Limbo. Perhaps they are a reminder that we are still very close to the beginning of history, that we have only begun to understand the maimed in spirit for whom blessings seem scant, if they exist at all. It remains a nagging and perplexing mystery, some spin-off from the gorged heart of evil, that so many should never taste life deeply enough to be either saints or sinners.

Verses 20–24

Then he began to reproach the towns in which most of his miracles had been worked, because they refused to repent.

"Alas for you, Chorazin! Alas for you, Bethsaida! For if the miracles done in you had been done in Tyre and Sidon, they would have repented long ago in sackcloth and ashes. And still, I tell you that it will not go as hard on Judgment day with Tyre and Sidon as with you. And as for you, Capernaum, did you want to be exalted as high as heaven? *You shall be thrown down to hell.* For if the miracles done in you had been done in Sodom, it would have been standing yet. And still, I tell you that it will not go as hard with the land of Sodom on Judgment day as with you."

--------∞--------

These ten verses constitute a triptych of the Gospel itself, miniatures side by side with cross-sectional views of Jesus' life, a montage of rueful moral judgment, theological revelation, and pastoral understanding. Grouped tightly together, fine as inscriptions on a medallion, these lines could be carried like the most precious keepsake for, at a glance, they resonate with the meaning and presence of Jesus himself.

Here, of course, the hand of the Gospel writer can be felt, for these are the product of an artist's selection, a coda, in a way, for the larger symmetry of the Gospel. This is a poet's montage of verses because of what is left out; we feel Jesus' great sorrow as we might a once powerful kingdom abandoned, in which the dust of chariots settled on merchants and lovers in lanes and courtyards alive with the cries of traders, the noises of life, confident and prospering, everywhere. And here, in these lines of Matthew, we sense only the void of Chorazin and Bethsaida, their living energy suddenly hushed, their sins and failures uncertain and mysterious.

What did happen in Chorazin—an hour, the scripture scholars tell us, north of Capernaum—or in Bethsaida, a fishing village on the West Bank, or in Capernaum itself, that Jesus should pass such a sorrowing judgment, grounded more in pity than in wrath, on them? The interpreters say that these people were indifferent to the preaching of Jesus, that they ignored him as they pursued their varied ambitions.

A modern reader can believe it, for calculated indifference rings with the harsh sound of the modern world, of slave masters and overseers coldly uncaring about the human longings and family ties and chances for life itself of their charges. The contemporary world has grown sick on such scenes, on guards numb to concentration camp prisoners in their hungry agonies, on governments with policies of extinction for troublesome colonies, on the hollow eyes everywhere that are never lighted by sympathy for others.

Still, the passage generates dread and uneasiness, catches the reader up in the mystery of what really took place in those cities, quiet now for hundreds of years, and in its implications for our own lives if, no longer able to feel for the plight of others despite the words of Jesus, we place ourselves so pitiably beyond forgiveness. Modern persons, of course, have a thousand ways of acquitting themselves from the charge of indifference. The world has constructed ways in which we can salve our consciences by signing petitions, or feel morally justified by joining an organization proud of its righteous aims, or comfort ourselves with the illusion of active concern by abstract or philosophical sympathy, by holding close to ourselves the "right" opinions on everything. Perhaps these attitudes are the great sins so mysteriously veiled in this passage, evasions of genuine concern that were ways of life in these all but forgotten villages on which Jesus looked with such sadness so long ago.

Verses 25–27

At that time Jesus exclaimed, "I bless you, Father, Lord of heaven and of earth, for hiding these things from the learned and the clever and revealing them to mere children. Yes, Father, for that is what it pleased you to do. Everything has been entrusted to me by my Father; and no one knows the Son except the Father, just as no one knows the Father except the Son and those to whom the Son chooses to reveal him."

Verses 28–30

"Come to me, all you who labor and are overburdened, and I will give you rest. Shoulder my yoke and learn from me, for I am gentle and humble in heart, *and you will find rest for your souls.* Yes, my yoke is easy and my burden light."

The next passages are also part of this sheer thrust of wall that we must climb at the end of this chapter. Jesus addresses us directly, commanding our attention as he looks into our eyes and makes this claim, at once plain and extraordinary, this revelation of the core significance of the mystery of his taking on our flesh. If we want to know something of God, Jesus says, then look at me. This staggering and implacable assertion about himself remains that central notion with which we must come to grips. This is not a complicated symbol of divinity, not a mystery double-wrapped and coded against those who might understand it. There is nothing, Jesus says, more obvious than what I am telling you. You may approach it with the complicated thinking of adulthood, but it comes down to that utterly simple kind of human transaction which a child unerringly comprehends.

Children grasp almost purely the intentions of others in their regard; they startle us by the direct manner in which they understand our anger, our cajolery, our efforts to mislead them. They also apprehend the simplicity of love that has no ulterior motive toward them; they sense the nature of the relationship we offer to them and no amount of coaxing or reasoning can overcome the intuition of their hearts. That is how we enter relationship with Jesus, as a child does, without craftiness or measures of self-interest, relying on our truest selves as we accept relationship, not with a wild-eyed Messiah, but with the profoundly human Jesus. Our response to this revelation, in which we find the Father, is not through some effort to rid ourselves of our humanity but through our acceptance of it. What is human about us allows us to meet God in what is human about Jesus.

These final words, placed here as carefully by the writer as the keystone by the mason, are among the most understanding uttered by Jesus. If he comes close to tears about the judgment the indifferent towns have called down upon themselves, then welcomes us with a warm and revealing embrace, he speaks here as a brother, as no stranger to us and our lives. Everyone understands burdens. Their feel on our shoulders is a constant of life; we shrug off one and find that we must strap on another, at least as heavy as the one we have just shed. Even Easy Street, human beings learn, is endless, its houses unnumbered, its cobbles treacherous underfoot. Jesus, with a sure feel for the texture of human days, reveals his understanding in a metaphor filled with the creak and sweat of ancient times. If it speaks less directly to contemporary people, it retains force, if only because we can see in it a reflection of Jesus's own sensibility, and thereby catch a glimpse of the agrarian world that filled his eyes. His metaphors are, even at this distance, the surest key to Jesus's way of seeing things, a subtle continuation of his revelation of himself and his Father. A person, in a real sense, is what he or she sees; their visions are mystical not because they see another world but because they can see this one, they are spiritual not because they focus on the skies but because of the richness of their compassion and of their comprehension of even the homeliest of human details. So here stands Jesus, aware of the lowing beasts and their burdens, seeing in them the struggle of every striving life, speaking not of their elimination but of how, following his teaching, we discover the goodness of the fit between us and the weights and sacks of our pilgrimage.

CHAPTER 12
Verses 1–8

At that time Jesus took a walk one sabbath day through the cornfields. His disciples were hungry and began to pick ears of corn and eat them. The Pharisees noticed it and said to him, "Look, your disciples are doing something that is forbidden on the sabbath." But he said to them, "Have you not read what David did when he and his followers were hungry—how he went into the house of God and how they ate the loaves of offering which neither he nor his followers were allowed to eat, but which were for the priests alone? Or again, have you not read in the Law that on the sabbath day the Temple priests break the sabbath without being blamed for it? Now here, I tell you, is something greater than the Temple. And if you had understood the meaning of the words: *What I want is mercy, not sacrifice,* you would not have condemned the blameless. For the Son of Man is master of the sabbath."

———————∞———————

As in one moment we sense that the season has turned, that the child has become an adult, or that we ourselves have stepped irrevocably over some threshold in life, so in this chapter we feel the tension of change in the life of Jesus. If we allow these stories—which may have become dry tableaux through familiarity—to emerge freshly, Jesus steps forward and surprises us with his sure sense of himself and his work. Jesus moves decisively, aware, as some brave people are not when they first go against the grain of their culture, that he challenges a religious bureaucracy whose greatest strength is the weakness of its threatened and unforgiving leaders.

Jesus lances the swollen infection of religious practice that has lost its soul and doesn't know it, that, one feels, still does not understand it twenty resistant centuries later. It is not the idea of religious institutions that is in itself bad; the institutionalists who long ago forgot the purpose of the structure and who cling desperately to its dehydrated beams and dusty treasures are the ones who debase things of the spirit.

These are the enemies of Jesus, these peculiar "survivors," as they might now be called, for they always keenly weigh their opportunities, watching with narrowed eyes the slightest quiver of the scales which hold their power, well defended against ideas that are too profoundly human for them to accept as religiously valid, rich in strategies to destroy their authors.

Jesus is a man who understands very well the immense, blind strength and spiritual inertia of those he takes on in these pages. What is here obvious about Jesus has been hidden in a thousand efforts to portray him over the centuries. He is a man in a way that we have forgotten that men can be, truthful, direct, unmanipulative, profoundly understanding of human nature—aware, then, in the finest point of his soul, of how, as in a mountain range, great heights are matched with the deepest of chasms. Jesus understands what fearful men will do in order to save themselves and to preserve what they construe to be their wealth or influence. These men, trailing the robes and ritual insignia of religious faith, distorting its spirit for their own purposes, selling out human beings by trivializing their hunger for life, are the enemy. They still are.

So they are eager to catch Jesus breaking the law, buzzing among themselves, nodding judiciously, their beards wagging in the sunny lane that runs through the stand of grain. We have him and his followers now, we have them at last. They are holding the stripped heads of grain, flopping reeds of indictment and proof, as they lay their accusation of breaking the sabbath against Jesus. This is the moment of revelation, for Jesus meets them head on, without apologies, battering them, in fact, with arguments from their own tradition. He is intense, compelling, his eyes locked on theirs as he steps toward them, speaking of David and his soldiers hungrily eating the twelve loaves of the temple showbread on the sabbath, and of the work that is done in the temple itself on the day on which the law prescribes that there shall be none.

If you understood Hosea, Jesus says evenly, you would not bully these men with your charges. This is the point that has had to be made over and over again ever since. How remarkable, since Jesus himself is so clear. The Lord wants love, not sacrifice; living people always come before dead observance of ritual. The weight that crushes human beings is that placed on them by religious leaders whose need to dominate blinds them to everything else. Thus is religion, which is meant to free men and women, used instead to intimidate and enslave them. Whoever in history has put the law, the regulation, the tradition ahead of the suffering person stands in the same field of grain smugly making the same accusation against the innocent. How else could we have had so many grim judges handing people over to the torturers through the centuries, forcing their hands into the fire, reading them out of the community instead of welcoming them into it. This sin is the devil's own seed, contaminating the wells of human experience from which the waters of lasting life are raised, splashing like crystal, into the sun.

Jesus uses a phrase which, translated, misleads us into thinking that he is asserting his own claims to authority, even over the sabbath day. In the Aramaic, the saving scholars tell us, "son of man" means simply man; it is the phrase the rabbi employs when he begins any tale of instruction: "There was a man . . ." Thundering still, like echoes that have never left the labyrinthine caverns of time, Jesus' words put the situation as clearly as possible: men and women are masters of the sabbath, not the other way around. They come first, their genuine needs identify the religious nature of life. What else is the purpose of worshiping God, if not to ransom the times and places of ordinary lives? The laws, the temples, the cathedrals, every waft of sacrificial incense, each hymn and prayer offering: these are for the service and salvation of struggling human beings. This is the richest kernel of the grain that has been eaten on the sabbath; there is no possible understanding of religion if the regulations of worship are thought to transcend the human hunger for life itself.

Verses 9–14

He moved on from there and went to their synagogue, and a man was there at the time who had a withered hand. They asked him, "Is it against the law to cure a man on the sabbath day?" hoping for something to use against him. But he said to them, "If any one of you here had only one sheep and it fell down a hole on the sabbath day, would he not get hold of it and lift it out? Now a man is far more important than a sheep, so it follows that it is permitted to do good on the sabbath day." Then he said to the man, "Stretch out your hand." He stretched it out and his hand was better, as sound as the other one. At this the Pharisees went out and began to plot against him, discussing how to destroy him.

————————⋖∞⋗————————

This section of the gospel is alive with movement and color and is heavy with a sense of Jesus' presence as a man. He presses for our attention, drawing closer to us so that we can see his flashing eyes, his work-roughened hands, the bristly edging of beard on his neck, the homely inventory of small scars and blemishes that are the seals on a life lived at work and out of doors; we can smell the odors, clean and strong, that are the unmistakable aura of a real presence. One thinks of how grateful his disciples must be that he speaks up for them so decisively, and of how closely they now follow him, banded together in the shadow of his strength, fearful that he might get too far ahead of them, fearful as well, as Jesus heads for the synagogue, about what he will say or do next. They sense that Jesus has drawn a line in the dust that divides the religious world in which they live, that they have crossed it with him, and that they are being watched by those who, angry and determined, remain on its farther side.

Whether it is a function of the accountant Matthew's careful ordering of events or of a historical account of a tumultuous afternoon, the underlying theme of these incidents, linked as beads are on a string, centers on a sense of values about life and worship. Let us put it to him, the Pharisees say, shouldering Jesus' followers out of the way as they cluster around a bewildered man, his hand curled and useless in his lap. He is convenient for them, just what they need as they challenge Jesus once more about the lawfulness of cures on the sabbath. Say it again, they intimate, break the law that we uphold in this holy place so that your blasphemy will be evident to everyone.

Jesus' answer is good Jewish common sense, very human, resonating with an understanding of the way in which people actually behave. They would, of course, care for a sheep trapped in a pit on the sabbath, anyone with a feeling for life would do the same, and that is what I have come to reveal to you, that people come before regulations, that religion is for them, and not they for religion. You don't need a law, or a religious leader's permission, in order to do good on any day. Goodness lives, not in self-conscious gestures made to bring attention to oneself, but in the utterly simple responses, done before they are mangled by rumination, made to people in need. Yes, and I will defy your rigidity, your exaggerated, soul-killing pieties, in this very synagogue.

Jesus speaks swiftly, the man staring up at him hardly grasps what is happening, and yet he can open this hand that has been bent on itself, and yes, he mutters as he raises it, compares it with his other hand, yes, I can use it again. He looks up into a circle of disapproving faces, into the gazes of men who do not rejoice with him in this recovery, at Jesus' bidding, of himself, his work, his very life in these suddenly unbound fingers. Jesus has not only answered the taunting question of the Pharisees but he has dared to heal on the sabbath. What they feel, what, literally, they cannot stand, is the truth of the man and of what he says. Jesus is too much a man for them, as, indeed, genuine men and women always are for those whose souls are salted with fear, who therefore stand to lose everything if they become party to an honest negotiation and are terrified that the truth will devour them.

What the Pharisees do, in Matthew's tightening account, is what their impoverished spiritual descendants have done so heavy-handedly ever since then. They conspire, their inner weakness a source of strength as it binds them in fear and self-interest, to rid themselves of this disturbing source of truth. There is too much light in Jesus: that is the trouble with truthful men and women—the light of their lives is unbearable to those who love the darkness.

Verses 15–21

Jesus knew this and withdrew from the district. Many followed him and he cured them all, but warned them not to make him known. This was to fulfill the prophecy of Isaiah:

> Here is my servant whom I have chosen,
> my beloved, the favorite of my soul.
> I will endow him with my spirit,
> and he will proclaim the true faith to the nations.
> He will not brawl or shout,
> nor will anyone hear his voice in the streets.
> He will not break the crushed reed,
> nor put out the smoldering wick

till he has led the truth to victory:
in his name the nations will put their hope.

———————◦∞◦———————

We feel like the curious in the crowd drawn to the excitement in the synagogue. Has some wonder occurred? Who is it and what are we to make of it? And Jesus is gone, his followers talking excitedly behind him as, at this moment of high triumph—has he not cured the man, has he not confounded the Pharisees?—he withdraws. A baffling maneuver for the twentieth century, whose light glows from neon rather than from anything as simple as truth. Yet Jesus renounces fame and celebrity, perhaps the opportunity of white heat in which he might have fused his own personality with great political power in a country in which messiahs were making claims in every village. But he is gone, for he wants neither the crown of celebrity nor that of rebel leader. We are left, like the healed man in the temple, staring at a suddenly open hand.

Perhaps it was the truth that shattered the lock on those clenched fingers, the power of the truth in Jesus' eyes and his words, something about the way he looked deeply into the startled man that allowed him to see into his own depths at the same moment. When we honestly face ourselves the outcome is freedom, even as it was for the nameless man in the Gospel. What outraged the Pharisees was that Jesus used the truth so directly, that he refused to dilute its power by diverting it through the hundred brittle pipes and circuits of their corrupted ritualistic observance. Let something as penetrating as truth be used on the sabbath and their magic would be destroyed. Give people the idea that religion is fundamentally a function of their inner selves, of their souls and spirits, and what would happen to those who prosper by controlling their religious aspirations from outside?

What cripples us, we might ask, and keeps us from bringing our truth into the world? Most of us, perhaps again like the man startled by Jesus in the synagogue, understand what holds us back even though we do not like to admit it, dislike inspecting it, would rather look in some other direction for an explanation. Others know the truth very well, live it unmistakably, only to discover the same reaction given to Jesus; the fearful and cramped of heart are uneasy, would like to find something against them, plot, in large and small ways, to rid themselves of these bearers of the truth. Truth has been a chronic irritant for those ambitious for the power that depends on successful falsehood.

Jesus understands this as he pulls away, letting people contemplate the meaning of his words and deeds rather than cluster around him. Yes, his sense of truth can awaken them to themselves, can make them whole, but they are to nourish this as an inner event rather than as a public wonder. Matthew counterpoints Jesus' message with his quotation from the prophet Isaiah, showing, as is his style, the fulfillment of the old promise in the new life of Jesus. Matthew does not want us to miss the meaning of what Jesus is saying about religion, for this is central to all that he preaches. This is the truth too blinding for the religious functionaries of that, and any other, day.

The truth of faith is a slender, glowing element that runs through even the seemingly ordinary and undramatic moments of existence. Even at low intensity, it is a steady source of illumination. Such religious truth is powerful even when it seems faint, even when it seems obscured by the larger events of history. So Jesus recognizes its power even when it burns as feebly as a flame on the last notch of wick; he validates the authenticity of truth, plain in its identity as a reed is, even though it be damaged and seemingly useless. Everything, no matter how bloated, distorted, or broken, is redeemed if it cherishes in some deep recess or coil the slightest sliver of truth. Religion has to do with our discovering that thread of truth in the confusing design of our lives. That is what we can depend on and follow. We save ourselves through discovering and embracing the truth. And, even in the seemingly worst or most wasted of lives, it can still be found as a wondrous edging of saving light.

Jesus speaks as one who gives hope and courage because he understands the disappointments and disillusionments that fill every person's life. His recognition of human weariness and woe is a sign, more powerful by far than miracles, of the salvation he proclaims. So he bids us to search out the ebbing sparks of love that can be found even in seemingly burned-out fires, or burned-out people. Faith bids us to raise the flame to life with the breath of our own spirits. That transaction, Jesus suggests, takes place in the secret places of the human heart more often than it does in temples and cathedrals.

Verses 22–28

Then they brought to him a blind and dumb demoniac; and he cured him, so that the dumb man could speak and see. All the people were astounded and said, "Can this be the Son of David?" But when the Pharisees heard this they said, "The man casts out devils only through Beelzebul, the prince of devils."

Knowing what was in their minds he said to them, "Every kingdom divided against itself is heading for ruin; and no town, no household divided against itself can stand. Now if Satan casts out Satan, he is divided against himself; so how can his kingdom stand? And if it is through Beelzebul that I cast out devils, through whom do your own experts cast them out? Let them be your judges, then. But if it is through the Spirit of God that I cast devils out, then know that the kingdom of God has overtaken you."

Verses 29–30

"Or again, how can anyone make his way into a strong man's house and burgle his property unless he has tied up the strong man first? Only then can he burgle his house.

"He who is not with me is against me, and he who does not gather with me scatters."

———————<∞>———————

Pharisees in any age are prodigal in their accusations. It is their gift, their trademark, their most predictable and reliable response. We are not surprised that, seeking out word of Jesus, watching him from a safe distance, they are afraid of this goodness that is so attractive to others. What is Jesus doing as he looks deeply and compassionately into people's eyes, if not allowing them to experience something that is rare and powerful because it is so profoundly human? He transmits, one senses, a richness of understanding rather than a scouring of shame. Because he sees the truth beneath all their failed chances, he reaches their souls directly, thereby enabling them to assay themselves more honestly and, prize of all compassionate belief, to free themselves from their varied spiritual exiles. The freeing action occurs within as Jesus breathes gently on the cold ashes of their past lives until they bud into light, pinpoints at first, then flame full, purifying and illuminating their beings once more.

It is the very opposite of contrived ritual, of amulets and potions and the ritual paraphernalia of long gone centuries in which magic darkly occupied religion's homeland. Jesus must be challenged for daring to cure in this fashion, for being so cunning in his understanding of evil. He must be in league with the devil himself. Jesus' answers not only silence and infuriate his accusers but also underscore the message he has been preaching with such clarity. They have survived the mummy wrappings of translations and retranslations as well as the prejudiced use to which they have been put across the years. They are startling in their directness, surely a further revelation of Jesus' personality, and in their message.

Satan is then crippled already, Jesus says: if his house is divided, if his own legions are pitted against each other, if evil contains within it such mortal contradictions, then it is feasting on itself, it is being devoured by its own steaming acids; and to those who understand the truth, the devil's great tent is a flapping ruin that seems whole only from a distance. Evil has no chance in a kingdom of truth.

And what is the sign of this Kingdom that Jesus proclaims in such a way that people wonder if he is the son of David? It may be connected with but is not essentially comprehended in the conventional measures of religious observance, the size of churches, how many people fill them, the numbers of priests. People can recognize the Kingdom because it takes on the pain of the world, it addresses itself to suffering, to that most volcanic of mysteries, and defeats it. Jesus is indeed proclaiming a revolutionary gospel because it takes us into the world rather than away from it, into that dread trench of human life in which disappointment, hurt, and suffering are piled like the uncomforted dead of a nightmare war. Jesus' kingdom opens its gates to the brokenhearted and afflicted, to those under siege by life, to those who are acquainted with separation and loss, to that extraordinary assemblage of people making their way past our windows at this very moment.

And this is possible, Jesus says in a powerful metaphor, because he has broken into Satan's house, bound him as a burglar might, and, if he is not dead, he is shamed by his weakness—for Satan himself, full of guile, has been taken unaware and has lost stature among his own divisions, even as a great general might after a defeat that reveals his fallibility. The balance of power shifted in the desert when Jesus turned away from the visions of earthly power and the promises of magic, when he rejected the first Faustian pact through which the world would have been delivered to him on the devil's own terms, the same ones offered over and over to each of us ever since. Evil was crippled and shriveled, its hold on the universe broken by this extraordinary encounter, and the power of Jesus made available to us as we make our own internal choices about the shapes of our lives. And Jesus concludes with a sentence that flashes still like a sword blade in the noonday sun, because, in this deepest of all matters, in this struggle to define ourselves spiritually and morally, there is no neutral ground, no place, despite our dreams of it, for bystanders in a battle no less than cosmic in its significance for each one of us.

Verses 31–33

"And so I tell you, every one of men's sins and blasphemies will be forgiven, but blasphemy against the Spirit will not be forgiven. And anyone who says a word against the Son of Man will be forgiven; but let anyone speak against the Holy Spirit and he will not be forgiven either in this world or in the next.

"Make a tree sound and its fruit will be sound; make a tree rotten and its fruit will be rotten. For the tree can be told by its fruit."

Verses 34–37

"Brood of vipers, how can your speech be good when you are evil? For a man's words flow out of what fills his heart. A good man draws good things from his store of goodness; a bad man draws bad things from his store of badness. So I tell you this, that for every unfounded word men utter they will answer on Judgment day, since it is by your words you will be acquitted, and by your words condemned."

Verses 38–42

Then some of the scribes and Pharisees spoke up. "Master," they said, "we should like to see a sign from you." He replied, "It is an evil and unfaithful generation that asks for a sign! The only sign it will be given is the sign of the prophet Jonah. For as Jonah *was in the belly of the sea monster for three days and three nights,* so will the Son of Man be in the heart of the earth for three days and three nights. On Judgment day the men of Nineveh will stand up with this generation and condemn it, because when Jonah preached they repented; and there is something greater than Jonah here. On Judgment day the Queen of the South will rise up with this generation and condemn it, because she came from the ends of the earth to hear the wisdom of Solomon; and there is something greater than Solomon here."

Verses 43–45

"When an unclean spirit goes out of a man it wanders through waterless country looking for a place to rest, and cannot find one. Then it says, 'I will return to the home I came from.' But on arrival, finding it unoccupied, swept and tidied, it then goes off and collects seven other spirits more evil than itself, and they go in and set up house there, so that the man ends up by being worse than he was before. That is what will happen to this evil generation."

Verses 46–50

He was still speaking to the crowds when his mother and his brothers appeared; they were standing outside and were anxious to have a word with him. But to the man who told him this Jesus replied, "Who is my mother? Who are my brothers?" And stretching out his hand toward his disciples he said, "Here are my mother and my brothers. Anyone who does the will of my Father in heaven, he is my brother and sister and mother."

The atmosphere remains electric as Jesus continues, in this extraordinary grouping of stories, to confront the pseudoreligion of every age, speaking with a profound sense of the inner meaning of the noble ideas destined for corruption by the manipulators of religion. His language is blunt yet poetic, its power doubled by the compelling commonsense character of his spirituality. These phrases slash across time itself, defy the deadening effects of translation, ring true for anyone who will listen.

This, of course, is a recurring preoccupation of Jesus, and here, speaking of the Hebrew notion of the Spirit, he tears open the truth, as a man might a sack of the richest grain, to let it spill out at our feet. People place themselves beyond forgiveness when they so ignore the moral character of people and events that they can no longer judge the good from the bad, when they choke on their own foul indifference. We are not speaking of small stakes or inconsequential events here. Jesus speaks of men and women who have estranged themselves from the truth, forgotten the power and significance of language, exiled themselves in a landscape in which nothing really makes any difference anymore. That is the sin against the Spirit, the sin against life itself.

The possibility of salvation depends on retaining our feeling for life, for the simple meaning of truth and falsity, good and bad, for these constitute the necessary basis for any awareness of the sources and possibility of evil in human affairs. One feels a tingle in reading these paragraphs because they are so timeless, so right, so essential to an understanding of the life of the Spirit. In a way, Jesus is saying that everything makes a difference, that there is no neutral exchange between people in life, that we either give life or take it away from people through our contacts with them, and that a reluctance or a failure to appreciate this heart of all moral truth reveals the dull, lustreless face of evil. So there it is, *that* is what it looks like, as familiar as the flatness of a lie, the death in a false pledge of love, the heavy gloss on the unexamined life.

A theme sprawls like broken-backed lightning through these phrases that tumble from Jesus' mouth like truth that can be held off no longer. Face the simple facts of life and death; you can identify yourself in your deeds and words. It is as astoundingly simple and demanding as that. You stand incarnate in the words that make you flesh; listen and overhear yourself, catch the spiritual timbre of your existence.

Words are filled with power. An age may demonstrate its loss of a sense of sin when persons give their word casually, when lies are as dear as truth if they accomplish a man's ends, when the infinite slicings of blinded law first abuse, then transform, and finally kill the truth. When words lose their power, when they no longer reflect even the ambition for truth, the sense of sin is destroyed, and the vital tree of life—

perhaps that one in Paradise, the taste of its fruit bitter on the lying tongue—is withered permanently.

The dreariest reflection of the loss of the power of words is found in the unguarded—unproductive, the scholars tell us—words that are borrowed from other sources and used as if the speakers had fought through to their meaning on their own. The Christian tradition of spirituality is gutted of strength every time it is translated into the terminology of the latest fad in psychology or personal development. The latter make room for corrupt spirits in the vacant dwellings of shallow spiritual mouthings, in the slogans, phrases, and even political opinions that have no power because they do not come from their speakers' souls. The last state of such persons is, indeed, worse than the first. The touching part of this is their failure to recognize their desperate situation, their inability to locate themselves any longer on the continuum of truth. Everything is relative for the person who has lost a sense of direction.

Who can be surprised that, if we easily surrender our sense of truth and life, if we drain the power from our words, we can no longer call anything or anybody by a rightful name—not sin, justice, or even ourselves? Just such people hunger for a sign, as they did from Jesus, and graft a wonder in as well, for such sensations are easy to read and make religion less demanding on the inner person. Right this way, ladies and gentlemen, to the magical faith that takes the effort out of belief.

This chapter comes to a climax as a symphony does, as Matthew draws together the strains of early passages and themes, and their summation in Jesus' renewal of his most basic claim. For *he* is the sign, greater than Jonah, wiser than Solomon, but those who have lost touch with the power to discern truth, or those infatuated with magic, will never be able to recognize or feel the power of his name. That is the sin that cannot be forgiven and that bewilders people as they argue about their relationship with Jesus. It is not, for those who understand how the Spirit binds people into profound relationships with each other, a question of literal relationships, of blood claims and inheritance rights on legal documents, but of the transcendent power of truth itself, boldly and honestly sought, that makes us brothers and sisters and true followers of Jesus.

CHAPTER 13

Verses 1–9

That same day, Jesus left the house and sat by the lakeside, but such crowds gathered around him that he got into a boat and sat there. The people all stood on the beach, and he told them many things in parables.

He said, "Imagine a sower going out to sow. As he sowed, some seeds fell on the edge of the path, and the birds came and ate them up. Others fell on patches of rock where they found little soil and sprang up straight away, because there was no depth of earth; but as soon as the sun came up they were scorched and, not having any roots, they withered away. Others fell among thorns, and the thorns grew up and choked them. Others fell on rich soil and produced their crop, some a hundredfold, some sixty, some thirty. Listen, anyone who has ears!"

Verses 10–17

Then the disciples went up to him and asked, "Why do you talk to them in parables?" "Because," he replied, "the mysteries of the kingdom of heaven are revealed to you, but they are not revealed to them. For anyone who has will be given more, and he will have more than enough; but from anyone who has not, even what he has will be taken away. The reason I talk to them in parables is that they look without seeing and listen without hearing or understanding. So in their case this prophecy of Isaiah is being fulfilled:

You will listen and listen again, but not understand,
see and see again, but not perceive.
For the heart of this nation has grown coarse,
their ears are dull of hearing, and they have shut their eyes,
for fear they should see with their eyes,
hear with their ears,
understand with their heart,

and be converted
and be healed by me.

"But happy are your eyes because they see, your ears because they hear! I tell you solemnly, many prophets and holy men longed to see what you see, and never saw it; to hear what you hear, and never heard it."

———◦∞◦———

Jesus steps out of the shadows of the synagogues and into the daylight, indeed, onto that most public of places, the seashore, that membrane through which the elements of life mingle and lose themselves in each other. Here as they do nowhere else earth, air, and water fuse in the fire of the sun. The seashore is a natural and comfortable place for human beings. People feel the mixture of their origins on these washed sands that are as mysterious as time and rich in their intimate knowledge of nature's power. Nor is there a setting as vulnerable as a seashore or one on which a person stands freer of every human structure and institution. The sense of mystery is, then, not small at the edge of water, for who can say that its essence is either sand or sea? Jesus places himself in the open here to teach in a way that fits the setting's openness and wonder.

One feels the rock of the boat as Jesus steps into it, the murmur of the crowd gathering itself together, its energy, like that of a sea dweller, compressed and languidly sprawling at the same time. The sea glistens behind Jesus. Beyond the spread of the sand stretch the fields in which farmers are hard at work in the silence on the other side of the wind. Groups of fishermen and others toil in clusters up and down the shoreline, also beyond the carry of Jesus' words. It is a setting both homely and majestic.

This is also a moment of further revelation both about Jesus and about the nature of his message and of religious experience. For just as the line of the tide challenges description as either belonging wholly to the earth or to the sea, religious faith cannot be defined in exact categories. Human beings believe not merely in their souls but in that extraordinary, elusive unity of personality. The meaning of religion is not easily exhausted, it remains always just beyond logical analysis, beyond any numbering or rational definition. As such it matches the mysterious depths of men and women themselves and can only be spoken of in the special language that is closer to poetry than to anything else.

Jesus addresses those who can hear his voice, including his closest friends and followers as well as the strangers drawn to these people now clustered around this boat dragged half out of the water. He is the prophet, the man who attracts and puzzles his listeners at the same time, speaking in parables. *Parable* comes from a word that means to put *side by side* and, as a supreme vehicle of spiritual understanding, describes one thing in terms of yet another. Yes, we say, we have heard this all our lives, and we have listened to the parables read out on Sundays and explained and preached year in and year out. These staples of our cultural religious experience are worn now as smooth as the oldest stones in the structure of our religious imagination. We need to step closer to the boat in this open place that smells of both the land and the sea to hear them again, to catch their freshness, their mystery, and their power.

Sown through these pages, somewhat like the varied seed in one of the most memorable of the parables, are the notions, the backing and filling of Matthew the collector of taxes, the lover of measurement whose apparent difficulty with metaphor makes him seem less distant, a man puzzled by his materials and unsure of exactly how to put order into them. One senses this strongly in his anecdotes of explanation, in the efforts, claimed by some scripture scholars to have been added by a different and later author, to make sense out of the parables that, of their essence, reject easy analysis. One finds passages jarring in their flat literalness, in their lack of faith in the poetic form of Jesus' teaching. The disciples' own demand for an explanation suggests that they may have been the first generation of obsessive believers, haunted by a need to get everything just right and made anxious by loose ends. Religious truth should be absolute in its expression, a fixed standard above the legions, instead of a great banner, never quite fully seen, billowing in the wind so that one side is now revealed and then another.

They need time to become accustomed to this form of discourse that differs so greatly from the everyday exchanges of fishermen and farmers. So, perhaps, do we, for the familiarity of these stories works against our ability to descend into history, to feel the sand underfoot, shielding our eyes from the silver glare of the sea, and to hear Jesus speaking as if for the first time not obscurely, as some suppose, but to reveal the folds of ambivalence in which religious truth is always swaddled. Indeed, let everyone hear what he hears!

These parables also constitute a powerful form of revelation about Jesus himself. It is not the quotations from the Old Testament which, in Matthew's usual manner, underscore comparisons with the ancient prophets. Jesus' identity as a prophet does not depend on proof texts. There is something deeper here, the sense within Jesus himself that he fills the same role as every prophet whose words are as familiar to him as the distant line of hills. Jesus understands, not without discomfort, that he lives the life of the prophet from the inside, that he follows and fulfills the great line of Jewish religious teachers because he shares their spiritual intuitions and loneliness at seeing so clearly those truths to which others, including his family and friends, remain blind. A lack of vision is not a punishment flung down like sores on Job by a dissatisfied and impatient God. We cloud our eyes from within, from a failure to gaze into the mystery as Jesus bids us.

Verses 18–23

"You, therefore, are to hear the parable of the sower. When anyone hears the word of the kingdom without understanding, the evil one comes and carries off what was sown in his heart: this is the man who received the seed on the edge of the path. The one who received it on patches of rock is the man who hears the word and welcomes it at once with joy. But he has no root in him, he does not last; let some trial come, or some persecution on account of the word, and he falls away at once. The one who received the seed in thorns is the man who hears the word, but the worries of this world and the lure of riches choke the word and so he produces nothing. And the one who received the seed in rich soil is the man who hears the word and understands it; he is the one who yields a harvest and produces now a hundredfold, now sixty, now thirty."

Verses 31–33

He put another parable before them, "The kingdom of heaven is like a mustard seed which a man took and sowed in his field. It is the smallest of all the seeds, but when it has grown it is the biggest shrub of all and becomes a tree so that the birds of the air come and shelter in its branches."

He told them another parable, "The kingdom of heaven is like the yeast a woman took and mixed in with three measures of flour till it was leavened all through."

Verses 36–43

Then, leaving the crowds, he went to the house; and his disciples came to him and said, "Explain the parable about the darnel in the field to us." He said in reply, "The sower of the good seed is the Son of Man. The field is the world; the good seed is the subjects of the kingdom; the darnel, the subjects of the evil one; the enemy who sowed them, the devil; the harvest is the end of the world; the reapers are the angels. Well then, just as the darnel is gathered up and burned in the fire, so it will be at the end of time. The Son of Man will send his angels and they will gather out of his kingdom all things that provoke offenses and all who do evil, and throw them into the blazing furnace, where there will be weeping and grinding of teeth. Then the virtuous will shine like the sun in the kingdom of their Father. Listen, anyone who has ears!"

Verses 44–46

"The kingdom of heaven is like treasure hidden in a field which someone has found; he hides it again, goes off happy, sells everything he owns and buys the field.

"Again, the kingdom of heaven is like a merchant looking for fine pearls; when he finds one of great value he goes and sells everything he owns and buys it."

Verses 47–50

"Again, the kingdom of heaven is like a dragnet cast into the sea that brings in a haul of all kinds. When it is full, the fishermen haul it ashore; then, sitting down, they collect the good ones in a basket and throw away those that are no use. This is how it will be at the end of time: the angels will appear and separate the wicked from the just to throw them into the blazing furnace where there will be weeping and grinding of teeth."

"Have you understood all this?" They said, "Yes." And he said to them, "Well then, every scribe who becomes a disciple of the kingdom of heaven is like a householder who brings out from his storeroom things both new and old."

———————⤫———————

There is the excitement generated by a great teacher in the way in which Jesus uses now this image and now that in an effort to express the truth that consumes him. Consider it this way, he says, and then look at it in this fashion. Something as staggeringly rich as God's Kingdom cannot be summed up in one illustration. The Kingdom is a treasure hidden in a field, but it is also a pearl valuable beyond any sacrifice to achieve. And believers are like the leaven sprinkled in the dough, gently causing the whole mass to expand, and again, God's reign resembles the nets that sing out of the hands of the fishermen to land on the water and descend mysteriously and silently into the depths, closing themselves on every kind of fish.

And do you understand what I am talking about, Jesus asks, as great teachers do as they search the faces of their pupils for signs of at least a glimmer of comprehension. The answer is *yes,* rising across the years like a sigh from plain people dazzled and overwhelmed by what they have heard. They cannot understand everything, but they grasp enough, they have been caught by the tension that springs from the ambivalent heart of every parable. They *have* glimpsed something of the Kingdom. And they are rich, Jesus says, looking around at the nodding heads, for they understand how truth that is ancient is always new, how the treasure-house of God's wisdom is ever renewing and inexhaustible. Yes, you have seen something of the true nature of the Kingdom, he seems to say as he slips out of the boat. But he moves away under the burden that all prophets have carried for a while through history, that of being ahead of their time, of realizing that even the most enthusiastic, those crowding close to him now, have only seen, as through a barely opened door, the slimmest fraction of truth.

When Jesus had finished these parables he left the district; and, coming to his home town, he taught the people in their synagogue in such a way that they were astonished and said, "Where did the man get this wisdom and these miraculous powers? This is the carpenter's son, surely? Is not his mother the woman called Mary, and his brothers James and Joseph and Simon and Jude? His sisters, too, are they not all here with us? So where did the man get it all?" And they would not accept him. But Jesus said to them, "A prophet is only despised in his own country and in his own house," and he did not work many miracles there because of their lack of faith.

———————❦———————

Jesus returns quickly to his own town to enter the synagogue once again, to taste the bittersweet waters of the human reaction to prophecy. He cannot do otherwise, as every person who follows an inner prompting sooner or later discovers. Prophets believe in a complex manner not only in their vision of truth but in their own ability to see and to describe it. The prophet receives a certain validation in the reaction of the people of his generation. Anyone who follows the truth, even in a very small way in life, finds the kind of reception that Jesus now encounters. The secular sin against the spirit lies in being right, in seeing something clearly before others do. That is the unforgivable sin of prophets who cannot disown their vision but who may never be thanked in their lifetimes for having tried to share it. That is why so many artists—writers, poets, painters—often receive recognition only after they are dead. They are, as Jesus is said to be here, "too much" for their own time.

A more poignant sentence may exist about Jesus but it would be difficult to find. "They found him altogether too much for them" (NAB). Jesus inhabited the role of prophecy, felt its inner pull and the tension that this generated between him and his world. He seems, at the end of this extraordinary chapter, to stand by himself, all alone, left to search anew for the strength to believe in himself in the midst of those dead to belief in him. It is the loneliness, not of a man out of touch with his world but of a man so deeply in touch that the world had to look away from him. It is one of the starkest images of the entire gospel, a parable in itself, for here, in this shadowed void of his homeland, we get another view of the Kingdom and of the kind of experience that will come inevitably to those who enter it.

CHAPTER 14

Verses 1–12

At that time Herod the tetrarch heard about the reputation of Jesus, and said to his court, "This is John the Baptist himself; he has risen from the dead, and that is why miraculous powers are at work in him."

Now it was Herod who had arrested John, chained him up and put him in prison because of Herodias, his brother Philip's wife. For John had told him, "It is against the Law for you to have her." He had wanted to kill him but was afraid of the people, who regarded John as a prophet. Then, during the celebrations for Herod's birthday, the daughter of Herodias danced before the company, and so delighted Herod that he promised on oath to give her anything she asked. Prompted by her mother she said, "Give me John the Baptist's head, here, on a dish." The king was distressed but, thinking of the oaths he had sworn and of his guests, he ordered it to be given her, and sent and had John beheaded in the prison. The head was brought in on a dish and given to the girl who took it to her mother. John's disciples came and took the body and buried it; then they went off to tell Jesus.

We pass into this section of Matthew's narrative as pilgrims would a vast and sacred valley in which everything is familiar and yet strange at the same time. The mountains huddle about us, white-haired elders filled with harsh wisdom; the plain, aching with heat, stretches before us, a barrier filled with lessons that can only be learned by making passage across it. Even the most resolute pilgrim might hesitate, as Peter does halfway across the verses, for here we find no oasis but a spiritual point of no return. Better to stop at the edge of this section, for, once plunged into the story, there is no turning or looking back. Matthew fits the pieces that suit his purpose tightly together so that the reader senses urgency, destiny unfolding, a claim on the heart as well as the head. Make the pilgrimage again and again and it gains rather than loses power.

That is why we return to these stories whose tension possesses us even though we know their endings. Matthew sweeps a small, sure accountant's gesture toward these carefully filled columns that reveal his intentions as both collector and arranger of the scenes of the life of Jesus. He extends the bold theme of the prophet as standing just before us outlined against the wavy heat. The crowds have pulled back, some because they reject him and others because they do not understand him. The compelling image is that of Jesus on the edge of a mission that, in the tradition of the prophets, he must begin on his own.

His is the feeling known by all men and women as they glimpse the thing they are meant to do in life, the mixture of anxiety and faith that laps like wavelets in the souls of those who understand—often against the odds and all advice—that they have a destiny which they must fulfill. What Jesus here experiences on the scale of a prophet, we all face sooner or later in lesser ways when we understand and strive to fulfill our truest possibilities.

We can appreciate the finest edge of Jesus' emotions, for now his mission, his identity, the unfurling scroll of his days are all clear to him. The path Jesus walks as he broadens his preaching, transfers the power of religious leadership from the Jewish elders to his followers, and approaches the death out of which the life of his church will flower is the road on which believers find themselves every day.

We share the prophets' calling, and understand the pull they feel in their souls whenever they perceive, usually ahead of others, an important truth about our times. In that moment we are confronted with the choice that faced the prophets. It comes down to our attitude toward the truth about persons and events. For if the teachings of Jesus cast a special light on truth, then we must not look away from it, or allow others to distort or misrepresent it. Being followers of the Jesus we can now see clearly in Matthew's story requires us to commit ourselves to the truth in a special way. Most of us are not prophets in capital letters, yet we share their calling to proclaim the truth for transcendent rather than political or highly personal reasons.

Never have we seen an age calibrating the truth with such cunning and for so many diverse ideological reasons. "There is some truth in it," might be the best summary for the phenomenon called "news," its second cousin, "opinion," and those other hybrids—information, hunch, and guess—that clog the world's efforts to understand itself.

The truth in small matters becomes more urgent when the truth of larger matters is so difficult to achieve. Perhaps truth survives in a universe in which it is always at risk because it is infused successfully with the energy of the numberless small truths grasped and lived by ordinary people every day. Perhaps they constitute an invisible yet saving archipelago, the remnant separate yet strong as skeletal bones that hold the organism of truth together.

These ordinary persons are prophets when they recognize the truth about themselves, build it into their relationships and into their work. It is not a cosmic fancy to suggest that truth is nourished by truths plainly and bravely revealed, among other places, in marriages, families, schoolrooms, and workplaces every day. Anonymous believers are the leaven in the dough, the saving remnant who bind the universe together with their truthfulness. We may lack enough faith in the power of truth. Perhaps that is the point of the story of Peter, Everyman in his human enthusiasms and fumblings, as he sinks in the waters across which Jesus calls him. The truth makes us free because it is dependable, it is the rock on which Peter can set the Church, and, although it may be obscured by the rubble of history, it cannot be split apart. Truth nags at the inheritors of the prophetic vocation, not to rend their clothes or spread ashes on themselves, but to live on that crooked way made straight, as John the Baptizer proclaimed: truth itself.

It is interesting to note that in the dramatic story of the death of John, the sensuousness is vital but incidental. Deceived by sexual obsession, Herod delivers the head of the desert preacher to the daughter of Herodias. The air still breathes erotic enticement, that most ancient and misleading of perfumes, in a transaction in which cost and value are permanently confused with each other. Still, this scene, focus of a hundred dismal cinematic evocations of the scriptures, is only the setting for the larger meaning of the passage. The prophet has seen and named the truth of the tetrarch's relationship with his brother's wife. That vision and proclamation of truth—so obvious yet so easily compromised—leads to John's downfall, even as truths too deep for the world will bring about Jesus' rejection as well. The central power of seeing the truth defines seers, those who see clearly and seem to foretell the future because they perceive the truth of the present so accurately.

Verses 13–21

When Jesus received this news he withdrew by boat to a lonely place where they could be by themselves. But the people heard of this and, leaving the towns, went after him on foot. So as he stepped ashore he saw a large crowd; and he took pity on them and healed their sick.

When evening came, the disciples went to him and said, "This is a lonely place, and the time has slipped by; so send the people away, and they can go to the villages to buy themselves some food." Jesus replied, "There is no need for them to go: give them something to eat yourselves." But they answered, "All we have with us is five loaves and two fish." "Bring them here to me," he said. He gave orders that the people were to sit down on the grass; then he took the five loaves and the two fish, raised his eyes to heaven and said the blessing. And breaking the loaves he handed them to his disciples who gave them to the crowds. They all ate as much as they wanted, and they collected the scraps remaining, twelve baskets full. Those who ate numbered about five thousand men, to say nothing of women and children.

Verses 22–23

Directly after this he made the disciples get into the boat and go on ahead to the other side while he would send the crowds away. After sending the crowds away he went up into the hills by himself to pray.

Verses 24–27

When evening came, he was there alone, while the boat, by now far out on the lake, was battling with a heavy sea, for there was a head wind. In the fourth watch of the night he went toward them, walking on the lake, and when the disciples saw him walking on the lake they were terrified. "It is a ghost," they said, and cried out in fear. But at once Jesus called out to them, saying, "Courage! It is I! Do not be afraid."

Verses 28–30

It was Peter who answered. "Lord," he said, "if it is you, tell me to come to you across the water." "Come," said Jesus. Then Peter got out of the boat and started walking toward Jesus across the water, but as soon as he felt the force of the wind, he took fright and began to sink. "Lord! Save me!" he cried.

Verses 31–33

Jesus put out his hand at once and held him. "Man of little faith," he said, "why did you doubt?" And as they got into the boat the wind dropped. The men in the boat bowed down before him and said, "Truly, you are the Son of God."

Verses 34–36

Having made the crossing, they came to land at Gennesaret. When the local people recognized him they spread the news through the whole neighborhood and took all that were sick to him, begging him just to let them touch the fringe of his cloak. And all those who touched it were completely cured.

Matthew's purpose in this section of the gospel is to place the origin of the Church into the context of prophecy, to relate its beginning to the ending of Jesus' life, now made inevitable by his swiftly moving public teaching of truths that are too much for his time. Here too we find the first of Jesus' followers, as human, it would seem, as we ourselves, as uncertain of their direction, as uneasy in taking their faltering steps in faith as we often recognize ourselves to be. We encounter here the chronic hesitancy that makes these apostles brothers to us in the human situation, missing the point, holding back until overwhelmed by the works and wonders of Jesus.

Yes, yes, Peter cries, you are one from God, sent by him to reveal the truth; but we know, as we know ourselves, that this certainty, even in Peter, will be shaken, that the moments of high conviction and religious fervor can wear off in the long, undramatic routine of life. Perhaps religious fervor is too much for average believers. And perhaps it should be, because the Christian life would hardly ring true if it were essentially linked to high spirits, to doubt-proof faith, to prayers always answered promptly and unambiguously. Anybody who has lived very long appreciates that Christianity is lived more in the valley than on the heights and that even its wonders, like a child's first telling of responsible moral truth—Yes, I did it—do not break but do fulfill the natural order of things.

So what prompts modern persons to believe and to commit their lives to the truth? Do we need walking on water, the multiplication of loaves and fish? And, in a question we avoid asking ourselves too loudly, what are we to make of these "miracles" of Jesus? What is the truth about them anyway? If these are literal miracles, exceptions made to the natural way of things, do they contain any greater power of truth than the sayings of Jesus or the shape of his life? Is the revelation in the wonder or in the man who took on our all too human life so fully? These are not small questions and, feeling the spray of the storm and hearing the sounds of the hungry crowd shifting uneasily on the hillside, we must search out our own convictions as we forge, if we have the courage, our answers to them.

Many explanations have been offered that explain these "miracles" as less exceptions made to nature than manifestations of the extraordinary human presence of Jesus himself. Whatever the character of the wonder, it is Jesus who stands in front of us, a man disarming us by his transparent honesty, by a vigor of character and a sympathy of insight, that arrests our attention completely. *Disarming* is the remarkable word that we use to describe those persons who give us a sense that we do not need to be defensive with them. Pope John XXIII, for example, spoke to the world in a way that overcame centuries of hatred and prejudice, that made people, even of diametrically opposed beliefs, feel safe with him. The miracle was the presence of such a pope and one could say that he generated greater confidence in people, as Jesus did with Peter, that he broke through their selfishness, as Jesus did with those hoarding their food on that grassy hillside, where people exulted in discovering that they lost nothing, that there was actually food left over when they shared what they had with each other.

The greatest wonder worked by Jesus flows from the "compassion" he experienced for the crowd. His feeling for the men and women is not rooted in some unrealistic idealization of their potential. His is not the vision of the "noble savage" or of pure hearts sullied by the rude world. The compassion of Jesus is built on a clear vision of the truth about us, an acceptance of us as sinners, as an imperfect people caught up in a struggle in which we sometimes, with the best of intentions, sell out ourselves or others. He transforms those with whom he speaks not because he is a wrathful prophet who wants to scare them to death but because he is so well acquainted with human nature that he can speak to them with understanding richer than that of Solomon. Jesus looks us in the eyes, sees our failings, reads the intentions of our hearts, and extends his hand to us. That is the critical exchange in these dramatic scenes. Jesus sees our weakness and, even factoring that in to his measure of our truth, loves us and brings out our strength. The miracle lies in our relationship with Jesus, through which the defenses we erect against our own truth fall away. Is this miracle enough for anybody? Or do we need something added, something ultimately distracting from what Jesus does for human beings, for the hesitant Peter, for the self-centered crowd on the hillside, for you and me, in other words, all the time?

CHAPTER 15

Verses 1–9

Pharisees and scribes from Jerusalem then came to Jesus and said, "Why do your disciples break away from the tradition of the elders? They do not wash their hands when they eat food." "And why do you," he answered, "break away from the commandment of God for the sake of your tradition? For God said: *Do your duty to your father and mother* and: *Anyone who curses father or mother must be put to death.* But you say, 'If anyone says to his father or mother: Anything I have that I might have used to help you is dedicated to God,' he is rid of his duty to father or mother. In this way you have made God's word null and void by means of your tradition. Hypocrites! It was you Isaiah meant when he so rightly prophesied:

> This people honors me only with lip service,
> while their hearts are far from me.
> The worship they offer me is worthless;
> the doctrines they teach are only human regulations."

Verses 10–20

He called the people to him and said, "Listen, and understand. What goes into the mouth does not make a man unclean; it is what comes out of the mouth that makes him unclean."

Then the disciples came to him and said, "Do you know that the Pharisees were shocked when they heard what you said?" He replied, "Any plant my heavenly Father has not planted will be pulled up by the roots. Leave them alone. They are blind men leading blind men; and if one blind man leads another, both will fall into a pit."

At this, Peter said to him, "Explain the parable for us." Jesus replied, "Do even you not yet understand? Can you not see that whatever goes into the mouth passes through the stomach and is discharged into the sewer? But the things that come out of the mouth come from the heart, and it is these that make a man unclean. For from the heart come evil intentions: murder, adultery, fornication, theft, perjury, slander. These are the things that make a man unclean. But to eat with unwashed hands does not make a man unclean."

———————◇———————

One can see them, their brows knit fine with the lines of puzzlement. Who, after all, had ever heard of such a thing? They look, indeed, familiar, for they step forward in every generation, their facial expressions like those of puzzled bankers convinced of the relationship between righteousness and prosperity. There is a melancholy similarity between certain businessmen and some religious leaders—their faces, well supported by finely clothed bodies, intimating, in the veined structure of the cheeks and the brook-clear eyes, every blessing for their exact observances in both commerce and faith. They are always genuinely puzzled, ready to make a long journey, as these scribes and Pharisees do, to settle for themselves issues for which, in God's well-ordered world, there must be explanations that fit the religious convictions by which they live.

These visitors to Jesus represent an idea of faith that is, in fact, totally opposed to the one which he preaches and lives. Jesus understands this, senses, as well, that religious prophets in every generation will face the same problem that he confronts right now. These men are friendly, they do not wish Jesus harm, but they do not for a moment question the religion, sewn together and carried in their souls as neatly as well-measured sacks of grain and barley. They are, they feel, successful in their practice of faith for they have mastered the intricacies of belief according to exterior rules and regulations. How is it that the followers of Jesus, who must know the prescriptions of the book of Leviticus about what is clean and what is not, do not ritually wash themselves before they take a meal? A small matter, their hesitant voices suggest, like those of bankers noting a modest arrearage in somebody's account. An oversight, perhaps, but puzzling nonetheless in the companions of a man claiming to teach religion. There is every mood of polite and discreet inquiry, no hint that the questioners have anything but complete confidence in their position.

Jesus glances at them with that same penetrating understanding that allows him to forgive earthy sinners, who are, after all, human to the core and, therefore, both understandable and lovable. But there is nothing but coldness behind the filigreed veils of hypocrisy with which these leaders adorn what they identify as religion. Standing before Jesus with the smug patience of those who know how to keep religion in its place—and how to use it to keep others in their place—these questioners do not have it in their hearts, as Jesus does in his, to forgive sinners. They have mastered religion, they know just how to manipulate it in order to control their world. God, they are sure, is pleased with them. God, in the dream of generations of opposing generals, is on their side.

This meeting, seemingly so calm and mannered, is the setting for the most revolutionary of Jesus' teachings, for he will build his Church on an idea of religion that is both simpler and more demanding, more fitting for human beings than that so comfortably and confidently practiced by his visitors. Two incompatible visions of God's expectations from human beings clash here. And, although Jesus speaks as forcibly on this subject as on any other, externalized religion has been a chronic, sometime low-grade, at other times raging infection of the human religious spirit.

We can see the travelers cringe and exchange incredulous glances at Jesus' forthright condemnation of the hook on which they have spitted money and religion together. Nothing disturbs the hypocritical believer more than a bull's-eye on their most obvious and crude maneuvers, those through which they safeguard their fortunes and please God at the same time. What is this man saying, they ask, deeply offended that their custom of swearing an oath to isolate their fortune from any parental claim should be indicted. If Jesus is unambiguous in ridiculing the contradiction of genuine religious sentiment that defines such hypocritical procedures, he is no less explicit in the words he addresses to the assembling crowd. It is not what you eat but what you say that signals your purity in God's sight.

This reverberates like the first cannonade of a long war. It puzzles his followers, who press Jesus at having so upset the Pharisees by his statements. We sense in this confused scene the nervous disciples, unsure of what he means, anxious to keep peace, clustered about him, an extension of the fate of a prophet. Readers who have ever stood up for the truth only to find previously enthusiastic friends holding back, perhaps even remonstrating with them about their boldness, may enjoy a bittersweet smile as they read these verses. For this happens every day, and contemporary prophets, even in what seem to be small matters of truth, often find themselves standing alone.

Equally striking is the clarity of Jesus' reproach to those who imagine that extrinsic religious gestures and rituals can somehow trap God into favoring them. The amazing part is not what Jesus says—it is common sense, after all—but that, to this day, even among his followers, one can detect a swell of nostalgia for extrinsic religious structures. The last years of the twentieth century echo with the mournful laments of many Catholics for the days when religion was straightforward and simple. There are those who would reinstate the cold demands of rule-ridden perfectionism because that approach appeared to offer more control, to reassure believers that they were marching in step on the road to salvation.

Internalized faith is the only kind of religion that can please God—the belief, for which no road maps exist, that wells up like waters inside us. This is the only pure faith, the belief that cleanses us thoroughly because it rises from the deep springs of our own motivations, our truest selves in God's eyes. The scandal lies in the fact that some church leaders, much like the scribes and Pharisees, attempt in every age to concretize the essentials of faith. Simple, honest people know better; Jesus speaks here to reassure them about their convictions rather than to reeducate the hypocrites, who suffer, history tells us, from a terminal illness of the spirit.

Verses 21–28

Jesus left that place and withdrew to the region of Tyre and Sidon. Then out came a Canaanite woman from that district and started shouting, "Sir, Son of David, take pity on me. My daughter is tormented by a devil." But he answered her not a word. And his disciples went and pleaded with him. "Give her what she wants," they said, "because she is shouting after us." He said in reply, "I was sent only to the lost sheep of the House of Israel." But the woman had come up and was kneeling at his feet. "Lord," she said, "help me." He replied, "It is not fair to take the children's food and throw it to the house dogs." She retorted, "Ah yes, sir; but even house dogs can eat the scraps that fall from their master's table." Then Jesus answered her,

"Woman, you have great faith. Let your wish be granted." And from that moment her daughter was well again.

We know what the commentators tell us about this episode in Jesus' life, but it is the exchange with the Canaanite woman at the center of it that compels our attention, comforting us with its profoundly human flavor. Yes, we understand what the scholars who have patiently retraced Jesus' steps tell us. This is his only journey outside Jewish boundaries, a roundabout pilgrimage about which we know little, a period of withdrawal, we are told, as Jesus, sensing a turning point in his mission, prepares his followers for the approaching apocalyptic events of his life, the shape of which he cannot see clearly, and the nature of which is beyond their imagining.

We appreciate the hint of a mission to a larger world than Judea. We have, despite the intervening centuries, gotten to know Matthew by now. He is not subtle in using symbols; the design of his Gospel resembles a garden laid off in neat quadrants in which we are hardly surprised by his plantings. That is why this exchange between Jesus and the woman seeking comfort for her child is so remarkable. It is as different in tone as the territory is for Jesus. And yet it is profoundly human, a vignette seasoned with irony, presenting an exchange between man and woman that could take place this very afternoon in any city in the world.

This woman does not lack wit any more than she lacks persistence. There is something abiding in her confident approach to the young rabbi whose manner so impresses her. She will not be put off but steps forward, and the tension of the risk she takes rises off the page to this very day. She seeks a blessing not for herself but for her child. In a way, she is making a claim for the kind of intrinsic response from Jesus that he has characterized as essentially religious. Yes, yes, she responds to Jesus' restrictive definition of his task, but spiritual concern cannot be limited only to the Jews. You must help, I will not take no for an answer.

Jesus seems to enjoy her, to be as refreshed by her open manner as he is enraged at the elaborately masked deception of the scribes and Pharisees. Here, at last, is a person of transparent honesty. She and Jesus see into each other's eyes, they know where they stand, they can afford to be playful in their exchange of sayings. She possesses that spark of life, innocence of purpose, and guilelessness of self-presentation that are totally lacking in the calculated maneuvers of the religious leaders suspicious of Jesus. This ordinary woman charms him by her directness, by her unschooled sense that a point need not be conceded too quickly, even to a prophet. As the sea breeze smacks of salt, so this incident sings with the power of healthy sexuality. For here, eyeing each other good-humoredly, stand a true man and a true woman enjoying a playful contest, earthy in its realism, tense with every possibility of misunderstanding, rich in benevolent ironies. They are having a good time on a serious subject, sparring about the table scraps that puppies are allowed to enjoy, and Jesus is won over by her.

She has great faith, Jesus tells her, perhaps smiling as he reassures her about her daughter. She is a healthy person, unselfconscious about her wholeness. Her desire for the health of her daughter cannot fail. Its foundation is her own brimming goodness, her largeness of spirit, the generosity with which she gives herself, like a blessing, away to others. Jesus cannot but join his own spirit of compassion to hers. That energy, released by their unguarded and unselfish exchange, guarantees the well-being of her daughter. The lasting message of these verses comes from the beguiling tone of the relationship between Jesus and the woman. Anybody close to it will feel better, and be better, for exposure to it.

Verses 29–31

Jesus went on from there and reached the shores of the Sea of Galilee, and he went up into the hills. He sat there, and large crowds came to him bringing the lame, the crippled, the blind, the dumb and many others; these they put down at his feet, and he cured them. The crowds were astonished to see the dumb speaking, the cripples whole again, the lame walking and the blind with their sight, and they praised the God of Israel.

Verses 32–39

But Jesus called his disciples to him and said, "I feel sorry for all these people; they have been with me for three days now and have nothing to eat. I do not want to send them off hungry, they might collapse on the way." The disciples said to him, "Where could we get enough bread in this deserted place to feed such a crowd?" Jesus said to them, "How many loaves have you?" "Seven," they said, "and a few small fish." Then he instructed the crowd to sit down on the ground, and he took the seven loaves and the fish, and he gave thanks and broke them and handed them to the disciples who gave them to the crowds. They all ate as much as they wanted, and they collected what was left of the scraps, seven baskets full. Now four thousand men had eaten, to say nothing of women and children. And when he had sent the crowds away he got into the boat and went to the district of Magadan.

The chapter closes on the tide of compassion and human understanding—Jesus' appreciation of human beings who, whatever their faults, strive to close their hands on their lives. He sees beyond their affected poses, their minor vanities and sins, to what lies, like gold in the covering sands, within their hearts. The human warmth of these incidents overwhelms their details as the richness of the first full spring day does the scattered reminders of a long winter. This is what Jesus is like; he moves among the ordinary people with a sure understanding of what they are like and of what they need in the way of encouragement and hope to carry on with their efforts to live lovingly. These people need to be fed, indeed, will recognize how much more they are alike than they are different, if they can share a meal together. It is this note—the dominant note of Jesus' relationships with people—that we take away from these verses. We cannot sit down on the ground with these men and women under the shadow of Jesus without feeling closer to them ourselves and without a firmer sense of his sense of values about the nature of religious experience.

CHAPTER 16

Verses 1–4

The Pharisees and Sadducees came, and to test him they asked if he would show them a sign from heaven. He replied, "In the evening you say, 'It will be fine; there is a red sky,' and in the morning, 'Stormy weather today; the sky is red and overcast.' You know how to read the face of the sky, but you cannot read the signs of the times. It is an evil and unfaithful generation that asks for a sign! The only sign it will be given is the sign of Jonah." And leaving them standing there, he went away.

This chapter is like a flexed muscle: an admirably compact symbol of energy expended and energy available, of the mystery of power grown greater through spending itself, of its tension in the face of tasks yet to be done. A reader feels movement, as one does in a modern film filled with quick cuts and sudden transitions, as Jesus stands now on one side of the lake and now on the other—the movement of abrupt departures from homely but familiar places and sudden arrivals in unexpected and majestic settings in which Jesus reveals answers about himself in some of the most solemn of his questions. Jesus wants us to see him more clearly as, in Caearea Philippi, he stands against the background of temples and holy places that constitute a diorama of religious history itself.

The Pharisees and Sadducees—these names, known from our childhood, suggesting nervous men whose faces, shadowed by hoods and cowls, can never be seen quite clearly—press Jesus once again for a sign. These men, the scholars tell us, are not religious or political allies. They huddle together on the rope bridge of their own self-interest which has been set swaying by Jesus' words. Fearing for their own positions, they sour the air with their demands, like those of money-lenders, for collateral, for a sign, hard and firm as a coin, before they give their belief.

Jesus writes a signature note on this chapter with his reply. Just as

Jonah was, in himself and in his preaching to Nineveh, the sign, so he is the sign. There are no wonders beyond those that flow from his feeling for the poor and the afflicted, there is no sign but that which Jesus gives in what he says and does. We can see him, having overturned their question as he will tables in the temple, move away. If they understand anything of the scriptures they will grasp what he has said. Matthew tightens the winch of the narrative, for we see here nothing less than worlds of religious understanding in collision. The Pharisees and Sadducees, still self-righteous and uneasy, watch him go, as do we, perhaps more like them than we care to admit.

We may, indeed, resemble the Pharisees and the Sadducees, if only in our queasy feeling about the way things are going. We seem, as often happens in life, to be caught in a misunderstanding, to stand in the cold void of irreconcilable differences between other people. Surely, we think, something can be done about this, there can be further explanations, some effort to help these leaders understand Jesus better, some strategy that will make him choose a less absolute position. Absolute positions are always discomfiting to lovers of peace and quiet like you and me.

The measure of our uneasiness is a faint reflection of the anger now boiling inside Jesus' taunting opponents. And Jesus' departure is a further sign of his profound reading of their comfortably compromised hearts. Religion cannot be distorted to fit the frame of their perceptions; it is much less complicated and far more sympathetic to the longings of ordinary people ever to please these questioning leaders.

Jesus knows when he has enemies whose ideas of discussion are to persuade him to change, to exchange his vision of the Deity for the small, tinny gods of their devotions. They will not change—and can only harden their hearts against Jesus—because his ideas threaten not their piety but their use of religion as a source of power and prosperity. And the whole point of Jesus' teaching is to smash such false and niggling gods, to restore religion to the heart of the human family once and for all.

Jesus' attitude suggests that we should examine the great clefts and fissures, the broken places of history; they buckle, in almost every instance, on the jagged fault line of the nature of religious belief and motivation. What wars have been waged in the name of orthodoxy!

How much blood is spilled to this day to justify the kinds of washings and rituals which Jesus condemns! Still, the illusion that God can be coaxed into benevolence through such strenuous tricks persists. The distortion of religion in the name of religion: this is the unforgivable sin, the truest sacrilege. Religion itself must be ransomed perennially not through crusades but through its free and fullhearted practice.

Verses 5–12

The disciples, having crossed to the other shore, had forgotten to take any food. Jesus said to them, "Keep your eyes open, and be on your guard against the yeast of the Pharisees and Sadducees." And they said to themselves, "It is because we have not brought any bread." Jesus knew it, and he said, "Men of little faith, why are you talking among yourselves about having no bread? Do you not yet understand? Do you not remember the five loaves for the five thousand and the number of baskets you collected? Or the seven loaves for the four thousand and the number of baskets you collected? How could you fail to understand that I was not talking about bread? What I said was: Beware of the yeast of the Pharisees and Sadducees." Then they understood that he was telling them to be on their guard, not against the yeast for making bread, but against the teaching of the Pharisees and Sadducees.

------------∞------------

The confusion must be like that of a tour group just arriving at a crowded airport. Everybody is accounted for but somebody has forgotten the food. Accusations clash like dull swords as the disciples mill about, unsure of what to do, looking half-sheepishly to Jesus.

One senses that deep understanding of their woe, as well as of their foreshortened vision, in Jesus' next words with them. Will they never understand the larger sense of things? Are they so focused on the literal aspect of events that they cannot grasp his metaphoric way of speaking? It isn't bread that is the concern of Jesus, not that kind of yeast. He speaks of yeast, the word used metaphorically at the time to mean evil influence. He isn't talking about loaves of bread, or the dangers on this side of the lake of using unclean Gentile ingredients to produce some. Jesus appreciates the concern of his followers, but they still do not understand the way he speaks of things, they still do not grasp the point about the yeast of the Pharisees as their pervasive and selfish attitudes that corrupt the whole idea of faith. Is there weariness in his voice as he reminds these followers that they need not worry about food? That has been the central theme of his preaching, the point of contention between him and the various religious leaders, the conflict that is giving an ominous shape to this quickly moving stage of his life.

Oh, that's what you mean! How frequently, having nodded or distracted ourselves during decisive moments in our own lives and times, have we suddenly grasped the fundamentals of some teaching of Jesus that we have heard all our lives but never quite understood before? We can hardly condemn the apostles for human reactions that we have experienced so deeply ourselves. False ideas of religion rise in every age like stars that seem within our grasp. And even when we know better we sometimes reach for them. The stars may hold a secret design of our lives; or some special prayer of devotion will bring us the answer to our problems. We still rub the good-luck charms smooth in our quest for the magic of external religion. An old temptation this, to incorporate superstition into our faith as easily as yeast is worked into dough.

It strikes us now that Jesus attaches so much significance to our understanding of the intrinsic nature of authentic religion. He denounces its opposite as the seedbed for other sins, emphasizing the dangers of superficial faith far more than individual transgressions. Without a mature faith our sense of life—and our sense of sin—are corrupted. We can travel no further with Jesus, nor can we answer the penetrating question he is about to propose, unless we are sure of the healthy character of real faith.

Verses 13–16

When Jesus came to the region of Caesarea Philippi he put this question to his disciples, "Who do people say the Son of Man is?" And they said, "Some say he is John the Baptist, some Elijah, and others Jeremiah or one of the prophets." "But you," he said, "who do you say I am?" Then Simon Peter spoke up, "You are the Christ," he said, "the Son of the living God."

Verses 17–19

Jesus replied, "Simon son of Jonah, you are a happy man! Because it was not flesh and blood that revealed this to you but my Father in heaven. So I now say to you: You are Peter and on this rock I will build my Church. And the gates of the underworld can never hold out against it. I will give you the keys of the kingdom of heaven: whatever you bind on earth shall be considered bound in heaven; whatever you loose on earth shall be considered loosed in heaven."

Verse 20

Then he gave the disciples strict orders not to tell anyone that he was the Christ.

Verses 21–23

From that time Jesus began to make it clear to his disciples that he was destined to go to Jerusalem and suffer grievously at the hands of the elders and chief priests and scribes, to be put to death and to be raised up on the third day. Then, taking him aside, Peter started to remonstrate with him. "Heaven preserve you, Lord"; he said, "this must not happen to you." But he turned and said to Peter, "Get behind me, Satan! You are an obstacle in my path, because the way you think is not God's way but man's."

⁂

Twenty-five miles northeast of the sea of Galilee stands Caesarea Philippi, no accidental setting for the intensely dramatic dialogue of these verses. This destination was not reached easily, and along the way one can hear Jesus' all too human band of followers trying to grasp the things that he has been teaching them for months. The reader feels breathless, as if he had been hurrying along next to them, catching bits of conversation, sensing that they are being drawn toward irresistible convictions. Their tone has changed, they speak more thoughtfully, as simple men do as they come to understand great truths. Jesus has drawn a line, as he often does in the dust to illustrate a point, between the prevailing orthodox view of religious practice, with its endless and exhausting externals, and his own notion of faith that belongs to regions of the heart which are boundless and beyond measure.

Excitement has replaced uncertainty and confusion for the apostles; for Jesus, walking there beside them, the bar of harsh sunlight in his hair—this man, breathing and speaking and calling them friends; this man, real as the distant mountains—is the long dream of Israel come true. They are the first called of the Kingdom that is about to be established, that great revelation of power envisioned by the prophets, the fulfillment of God's great promises to his bride of a nation. They see now who Jesus is but they do not understand fully the nature of his Kingdom which, like the religious domain of the heart, transcends measurement, knows neither south nor north, and consists in spiritual strength rather than earthly power.

Here in this city, with a name that is an echo of Rome, stands a bold temple erected by Herod the Great in a land bristling with the shrines and memories of the Syrian and the Greek deities. The city was formerly named for Pan, and the mountain holds the very cave from which the Jordan rose to wash down through Jewish religious history. The smell of old fires, of offerings to a hundred gods, hangs in the air; the marble temple blinds the viewer's eye with its noonday glare of Roman achievement and power. The history of men's hopes is recapitulated here. It is the right setting for the awesome question that Jesus asks with surprising ease of his followers. It is time for these men to consolidate their growing convictions, time for them to say out loud, for their own sake, what they think of him. It cannot be put off any longer, because men do not really know what they believe until they express it in words; they discover their deepest convictions as they utter them.

Peter is no shadow in the Gospel. We recognize him immediately, for he is always in the center of things, his heart leading him to the most generous commitments and the greatest human blunders. We can still feel the largeness of his spirit, the amiable, childlike quality of his enthusiasm, the roughness of his unselfconscious embrace as he turns and welcomes us into the gathering. How can you not like Peter, this eldest brother in our family of faith, this man without pretense who, in this extraordinary passage, speaks for us all, his willingness running ahead of his understanding as he professes faith in Jesus as the Messiah, the anointed one, the Son of God for whom we have all been waiting?

The familiar exchange still compels our attention, for we witness something that, like Peter, we do not fully understand either. We work out our understanding as we live our lives, as we gradually construct an understanding of the kind of kingdom that Jesus bids us to enter. If his religion has no place for superstition and magic, his Kingdom has no place for merely earthly understandings of triumph and influence. This is a powerful moment not only because of its ecclesiological significance, but because it is not ended until Jesus has explained, with a clarity that has never been surpassed, what we can expect in life. Following him is not following a book of directions, it consists in living a life marked by the same rhythms that can be found in his own.

The majesty of conferring the keys of leadership on this wonderful rock of a man, Peter, conveys that rare sensation of time's circle being broken open and of God's breath on the back of our necks for an instant. A blink, and we are rooted again in time, as, indeed, we are with Peter's characteristically human protest about Jesus' future suffering. He still does not understand fully as he throws his arm around this man he understands to be the Messiah. But Peter must get behind Jesus if he is to follow him truly.

The sublime moments of these verses are counterpointed by Jesus' simple, incisive description of what human life is like for those who follow him. Religion, he underscores again, is not just in practices; it rises, as mist above the fields, from everyday life. There is no magic, no incantation, no sacrifice of the still warm hearts of birds and beasts that establishes relations with the divinity. That is the very opposite of taking on life as it is, of fulfilling the imperatives of love, of embracing the paradox that otherwise engulfs us: that we save our lives when we are generous enough to give them away, and that we throw them away when we attempt to save them. Death cannot contain Jesus, the gates of hell cannot hold him in, and death does not defeat those who come to know it in its thousand intimations in the sacrifices made out of love for others.

The final section of this chapter is not only a charter for a Church, it is the great seal on the essentially tragic understanding of human life that is essential to any religious vision. If there are no tricks, there are no shortcuts, and the natural medium of religious expression, the culture in which it thrives, is ordinary, everyday existence. That is made up of friendship and work, of living for more than our own gratification, of giving our lives for others and discovering it again in the very process. Nothing worthwhile occurs unless we yield up something of ourselves, unless, in other words, we accept the deaths of each purposeful day. But these break open, as time does in the previous verses, to a fuller and richer life.

This is the mystery within mysteries, the heart of the religion Jesus speaks about. What, we must ask, do we think of Jesus and what he says to us? Who, indeed, do we say he is? The old question, repeated by a thousand preachers and retreat masters, remains fresh. It is *the* question. Having followed just beyond the circle of the apostles for so long now, watching and listening as Jesus repeats his essential theme about God's relationship with us as contrasted to the lifeless notions of the prevailing religious leadership, we find that it is a question for our own time. The effort to manipulate religion for public influence of one sort or another makes the reader pause to reflect on how often Jesus, who makes himself so clear, has been so distorted by those who use him for their own purposes. And Jesus makes claims on us that are hardly ambiguous. If in this passage he becomes more conscious of his divine nature, his question demands that we do the same through our answer.

Verses 24–28

Then Jesus said to his disciples, "If anyone wants to be a follower of mine, let him renounce himself and take up his cross and follow me. For anyone who wants to save his life will lose it; but anyone who loses his life for my sake will find it. What, then, will a man gain if he wins the whole world and ruins his life? Or what has a man to offer in exchange for his life?"

"For the Son of Man is going to come in the glory of his Father with his angels, and, when he does, he will reward each one according to his behavior. I tell you solemnly, there are some of these standing here who will not taste death before they see the Son of Man coming with his kingdom."

Bring the light closer, we bid the scholar, for these lines are a source of puzzlement, a contradiction to every idea of a kingdom of love and relationship. What are we to make of Jesus as he utters these words? The scholars nod, bend over the page, turn back with an invitation to let time and place drop away from us, to travel to the Palestine of Jesus and to sense the religious imagination of the people to whom he speaks.

The Jewish people conceived of a great crack in their history, on one side of which was the present while the great, coming age of God rose up on the other. The fissure was what they understood as the Day of the Lord, that time spoken of over and over again in the Old Testament books which they knew so well. They were crammed with imagery of terrible upset, of families divided against each other, of brothers handing brothers over to judgment.

We can understand Jesus better—and appreciate his poetic genius more—if we comprehend the way in which he called up these vivid and terrifying scenes. His hearers cannot look away, for it is obvious that he understands the minds of his Jewish listeners. If this, he says, if the way you imagine the Day of the Lord to be, then understand that your waiting is over. That moment which you envision as one of upheaval has arrived, for the Kingdom no longer dwells in expectation. It is, through my presence, already among you, reworking your relationships, ushering in a Day of the Lord that is powerful but very different from the one you expect.

So too, Jesus says, in an enigmatic phrase, some of you won't return from preaching the arrival of this Kingdom before the Son of Man comes. We scratch our heads from our far-removed viewpoint. What has Matthew inserted here? How are we to understand these notions, scattered elsewhere as well, that a Second Coming was imminent, and that this notion dominated the minds of the earliest believers? We turn again to the students, those patient searchers, who tell us that, once again, Jesus speaks forcefully, not of the end of the world, but of the nature of the Kingdom that is the center of his ministry.

The Kingdom is here, the Kingdom is already throwing itself open for those who wish to enter. Before you get back, this community of people will, in the spiritual power of loving and trusting relationships, have established itself. It won't be as you have imagined it but, because you initiate this chain of relationships to me through your preaching, the Kingdom will be a reality before you return to tell me of your travels. It will rise wherever you have been in my name. Jesus is not evoking some dramatic scene in which the curtain trembles uneasily above the stage of history. This is not apocalypse and judgment on a grand scale that Jesus foresees. No, it is a subtler, more ordinary face for a Kingdom that comes to life in the wake of proclamation. What you have all waited for is here. Perhaps Jesus speaks dramatically because even now it is difficult for us to recognize that the Kingdom exists in the invisible web of our relationships of love and friendship. Perhaps we need the lightning to flash so that we can see what is around us already.

CHAPTER 17

Verses 1–8

Six days later, Jesus took with him Peter and James and his brother John and led them up a high mountain where they could be alone. There in their presence he was transfigured: his face shone like the sun and his clothes became as white as the light. Suddenly Moses and Elijah appeared to them; they were talking with him. Then Peter spoke to Jesus. "Lord," he said, "it is wonderful for us to be here; if you wish, I will make three tents here, one for you, one for Moses and one for Elijah." He was still speaking when suddenly a bright cloud covered them with shadow, and from the cloud there came a voice which said, "This is my Son, the Beloved; he enjoys my favor. Listen to him." When they heard this, the disciples fell on their faces, overcome with fear. But Jesus came up and touched them. "Stand up," he said, "do not be afraid." And when they raised their eyes they saw no one but only Jesus.

Verses 9–13

As they came down from the mountain Jesus gave them this order. "Tell no one about the vision until the Son of Man has risen from the dead." And the disciples put this question to him, "Why do the scribes say then that Elijah has to come first?" "True," he replied, "Elijah is to come to see that everything is once more as it should be; however, I tell you that Elijah has come already and they did not recognize him but treated him as they pleased; and the Son of Man will suffer similarly at their hands." The disciples understood then that he had been speaking of John the Baptist.

———————◆◇◆———————

This story, again as familiar as any we know, underscores our need to come to terms with Jesus. We may be fascinated by this passage, a sunlit rose window resplendent with glorious images from Jewish history as well as from Jesus' own life. For if we enter the clouds that rise above the momentous events of the Old Testament we feel God's nearness to his people and to the great figures, Moses and Elijah, who encountered him on other mountain tops. Moses comes down from Sinai with the tablets of God's commands, and on Horeb Elijah, in one of the sweetest of all biblical stories, finds God not in thunder but in the still, small voice. Our religious imagination seems flooded by these larger-than-life figures, these mysterious men who, after their tumultuous lives, seem to slip away from our sight—Moses to the quietest grave, Elijah as if into the heavens. Is it not for Elijah that a place is set at the Passover service to this day?

This section rumbles like a summer sky with every intimation of power and grandeur. If the lightning-split clouds remind us of the vastness and unity of nature, this scene binds together the memories and longings of a believing people, speaking to our conscious and our unconscious, to the deepest rings of our common experience. We hear the echoes of the prophets as well as of the baptism of Jesus. It is as if a great tapestry of Salvation History is flung out before us to identify Jesus for himself and for us. If we do not understand the nature of the manifestation, we feel its intensity as it confirms Jesus in his role, as if his prayer on this slope had been so great that it had bled this vivid understanding of his role out of those who beheld it. God speaks in the wispy cloud, the colors brighten as a full grasp of Jesus' biblical lineage, of his Divinity, comes to those closest to him. It is powerful and human, not only because of Peter's characteristic exuberance in his delight in the moment and his resolve to do something practical about it, but in the way in which this billowing royal tent is pegged over the mysterious chasm that runs beneath Jewish history and all genuine religious experience.

The scholars remind us that, in Luke's version of this same scene, Moses and Elijah speak to Jesus "of his departure." The word used electrifies us: *exodus*—this word used of the departure of the Jewish people out of Egypt into the trackless desert on whose far edge lay the Promised Land; *exodus*—a word which summons up the abiding mystery that flows from the lives of Moses and Elijah through that of Jesus to our own—this word means a going out into the unknown with trust in God. *This* is the way for all believers, not to build tents in the shimmering atmosphere of glory but always to give that up, to accept the mystery of separation to fulfill our mission. At the heart of this glorifying experience we find this fissure through which Jesus must pass in order to carry out his role as successor to Moses and Elijah.

Separation is the enormous mystery that is the condition of our religious pilgrimage. It is the lining of the vital experiences through which we ourselves experience a kind of transfiguration. There is no great love, for example, that does not accept separation as one of its essential elements. Lovers cannot merge their identities for good; they come up against the strangeness of their separateness even in their richest moments of union. They find that parting—sharing in some fashion in this Exodus experience—is necessary if they are to share their love with others, if they are to raise children, entertain friends, do any of the hundreds of things that impose separation on people who love each other. That is what we recognize here. The theophany, mighty as it is, draws us inevitably to the reality of the Exodus in our lives. We are linked, if we follow Jesus, not only to the effulgent mystery of his glorification, but to the homely reality of giving up the self, of departing from what we know in order to possess it more truly.

This is a mystery blinding in its intensity. We still do not like to look at the separations and deaths to ourselves that are inevitable in lives fully and lovingly lived. Better, with Peter in his boisterous enthusiasm, to stay at this high point of affirmation than to follow with Jesus as he accepts his own departure to Jerusalem and the final acts of his mission. The passage, ringing with glory, turns our gaze down the slopes toward the often shadowed valley in which most people lead their lives. There we find the setting for the kind of religious experience of which Jesus has been speaking. It has little to do with the minute observation of detailed rules. It concerns rather those things which cannot be measured at all: loving someone throughout a lifetime, making sacrifices in our lives for the benefit of those who follow after us, raising a child, keeping our word, forgiving each other for our failures, standing together in the bad weather of life. Our Exodus leads us not through strange and exotic places but through the very middle of our quite ordinary lives.

Verses 14–20

As they were rejoining the crowd a man came up to him and went down on his knees before him. "Lord," he said, "take pity on my son:

he is a lunatic and in a wretched state; he is always falling into the fire or into the water. I took him to your disciples and they were unable to cure him." "Faithless and perverse generation!" Jesus said in reply. "How much longer must I be with you? How much longer must I put up with you? Bring him here to me." And when Jesus rebuked it the devil came out of the boy who was cured from that moment.

Then the disciples came privately to Jesus. "Why were we unable to cast it out?" they asked. He answered, "Because you have little faith. I tell you solemnly, if your faith were the size of a mustard seed you could say to this mountain, 'Move from here to there,' and it would move; nothing would be impossible for you."

A small leave-taking before the great one whose long shadow now falls permanently across Matthew's pages. The departure from the slopes of the mountain, the return to the pressing needs of the people: our own lives are recapitulated in this narrowest of spaces between the verses. Even for Jesus these sacramental high points come infrequently. He lives in the pull and drag of the crowds, with the honed sensitivity to human suffering that only a man as comfortable with metaphor as he is could understand. Jesus came for these people who grope, as most people do, for the right direction in life, for blessings for their families, for the return of health for their children. He returns to them all the time after his retreats for prayer and reflection. And here, perhaps, we find a key to help understand why he can bring peace to the epileptic child and his followers cannot.

Jesus is besieged with people, like the Canaanite woman and this man, who do not ask for something for themselves but for others— often, as here, for their children. If the Canaanite woman is a pest to his closest followers, she is a delightful and loving woman who is completely unselfconscious in her pleading for her daughter. So the man so touchingly concerned about his boy approaches Jesus without a thought for himself. This anonymous man and woman might be patrons of all intercessors, of all those who forget themselves as they seek good for others. Trust is here the ripest of fruits split open for us. A mystery still, but we can see it more clearly as we watch Jesus in his responses to this man and woman. Each is caught in that special pain that only parents with afflicted children can know. Their hearts are wrenched out of place because of their love for their sick offspring. This suffering is a function of the experience of hurt, a searing reality for all those who make themselves vulnerable through giving their hearts to others. There is exquisite pain for those in our universe of trust who are lost or hurt in some way. That is what this man and woman feel. It is what motivates them, fittingly or not, to present themselves to Jesus, to entrust themselves and their children to him. They sense something about him that allows them to approach him confidently. They know that he will understand.

What Jesus transmits is that quality of interest and compassion that rises from the poetic edge of his soul. Where the apostles lack faith—and why they cannot heal—is in their human sensitivity to the suffering of others. Peter is a great bear of energy but he is consumed with himself. So are the other apostles, who find this loving woman a nuisance who must be gotten rid of. They cannot see as deeply as Jesus, they fail to perceive the human stories beneath the beseeching faces all around them. Their lack of faith is not so much a defect of belief in God as a failure to believe deeply enough in his creatures. Freed of the burden of poetic sensitivity, they are compromised in their ability to enter into the mystery of trust with other persons. Healing follows not from magic or tricks but from the human price paid for giving heartfelt concern to others. We have all known people who, without seeming to do anything special, make us feel better by their presence. They heal us of anxiety, strengthen us, cure us as surely as the distressed are cured in the Gospel. They do look into our lives with a feeling for our troubles; they understand, and we feel they believe in us, that they are trustworthy. The ability to appreciate the common pains of the world is what enables Jesus to heal them.

Verse 21

(As for this kind [of devil], it is cast out only by prayer and fasting.)

Verses 22–23

One day when they were together in Galilee, Jesus said to them, "The Son of Man is going to be handed over into the power of men; they will

put him to death, and on the third day he will be raised to life again."
And a great sadness came over them.

These episodes are footnotes about the nature of existence. Even the
closest follower of Jesus cannot heal people until he can peer without
flinching into their well-deep hearts. Wherever Jesus looks he sees the
private troubles of other people and their struggles, sometimes hero-
ically brave, to deal with them. The apostles, puzzled still by metaphors, have not yet developed the compassionate vision that will inevitably be their greatest strength. They are, then, overwhelmed with
grief, at the sure vision Jesus has of the rejection and suffering that rise
up before him. He knows what is in the hearts of good people and in
the hardened hearts of those who count him a threat to their corrupt
view of religion. All human sufferings finally flow together in the com-
pletion of Jesus' work. The apostles only feel on their hearts the impact, like that of a battering great log on a door, of the immensity of
their loss.

Verses 24–27

When they reached Capernaum, the collectors of the half shekel came
to Peter and said, "Does your master not pay the half shekel?" "Oh
yes," he replied, and went into the house. But before he could speak,
Jesus said, "Simon, what is your opinion? From whom do the kings of
the earth take toll or tribute? From their sons or from foreigners?" And
when he replied, "From foreigners," Jesus said, "Well then, the sons
are exempt. However, so as not to offend these people, go to the lake
and cast a hook; take the first fish that bites, open its mouth and there
you will find a shekel; take it and give it to them for me and for you."

Jesus is self-possessed in this encounter with Peter, and the reader is
struck by the change in their relationship, for they seem closer, easier
in their ways with each other. Jesus continues, Matthew tells us, "without giving him time to speak." He knew his man well. Yet there is a
mood of intimacy here, a singling out of Peter as the agent of this
episode in which the temple tax is paid in order not to upset those who

would misunderstand it if they claimed an exemption. One might elaborate theories of relationship to civic and ecclesiastical authority, but at the risk of missing the charm of the scene. Is there a hint of playfulness here, as Jesus urges Peter to go back to his fishing in order to make enough money to pay the tax? There is every suggestion of the poet speaking as Jesus, in the picturesque fashion of the age, speaks of his apostle's hard work in a way that lightens it, makes it seem wonderful because money comes out of the very hook marks in the fish he catches. Those who wish it to be a miracle, to see Peter, streaming water, prying open a fish's mouth and extracting a shining coin, will miss the human alternatives of this exchange. It is no accident that Jesus indicates that what Peter earns will pay the tax for just the two of them. Peter, impulsive, generous, and masculine, stands closest to Jesus in carrying out his mission.

CHAPTER 18

Verses 1–4

At this time the disciples came to Jesus and said, "Who is the greatest in the kingdom of heaven?" So he called a little child to him and set the child in front of them. Then he said, "I tell you solemnly, unless you change and become like little children you will never enter the kingdom of heaven. And so, the one who makes himself as little as this little child is the greatest in the kingdom of heaven."

Verses 5–7

"Anyone who welcomes a little child like this in my name welcomes me. But anyone who is an obstacle to bring down one of these little ones who have faith in me would be better drowned in the depths of the sea with a great millstone around his neck. Alas for the world that there should be such obstacles! Obstacles indeed there must be, but alas for the man who provides them!"

Verses 8–9

"If your hand or your foot should cause you to sin, cut it off and throw it away: it is better for you to enter into life crippled or lame, than to have two hands or two feet and be thrown into eternal fire. And if your eye should cause you to sin, tear it out and throw it away: it is better for you to enter into life with one eye, than to have two eyes and be thrown into the hell of fire."

———⚭———

Jesus is not preaching a way of life that is as cumbersome and awkward as that of a beast with an ill-tied burden. Faith is not a balancing act with rule-filled baggage; it expresses itself, and finds its truest test, in the way we live with each other. That is what is on his mind as he responds to the all too human questions of his disciples about rankings in God's Kingdom. Who, indeed, will be first? It is the question of many a preening ascetic caught up in the subtle, long-undiagnosed but always fatal narcissism of spiritual perfectionism. Setting out to look like a saint from the outside is not far different than setting out to have that twentieth-century attribute of success, the "right look."

Jesus cuts to the heart of the matter. He takes a child on his knee as he speaks. Still, twenty centuries later there are those who cannot hear what he so clearly says. He is not emphasizing an artful striving for lowliness, or that adults should surrender independent responsibilities; no, he emphasizes the quality that comes close to defining the essence of a child. A child, above all, is unselfconscious, incapable of artifice, and capable, then, of grasping the attitudes and motivations of others with a clarity that is astounding.

The Kingdom belongs to the people who aren't trying to look good or impress anybody, including themselves. The reason is simple and remains their essential goodness, holiness, call it whatever you like. God smiles on those people who are not aware of themselves and are not full of plots about how to seize the world's attention. The first citizens of the Kingdom Jesus preaches are the lovers who give themselves without studied awareness to their spouses, children, students, and friends.

These wonderful people reveal God freshly in every generous and unplanned impulse of their hearts. They have a special sensitivity to others, knowing as surely as a mother does with her children when to give and when to withhold, when to open them to life and when to let them be children for a little while longer. Such loving people, not thinking about how their actions will be interpreted or whether they will get good marks or gold stars for their behavior, are the ones who save the world.

Such persons are the only known antidote to sin, to that initiation into worldliness that is taken by many as success. These loving people generate in others the very values which they live every day. They are childlike in their ability to read the motivations and manipulative attentions of those who live by a less generous code. Their clear view of good and evil is never obstructed by barriers constructed inside themselves. Others will not stumble in their way through life because of them. The world of sin is a universe of false ideals, of power and influence sought for their own sake, of winning at all costs, at any price in failure of honor and decency.

Better, indeed, to be thrown into the fiery refuse dump that stood in the valley of Hinnom where children were once sacrificed to Moloch. Those who initiate the young or the inexperienced into a world of deceiving values are unproductive, they add nothing to the lives of those around them. They are, as trash is, worthless, fit only for throwing away. Here we confront the profound existential demand at the root of Jesus' teachings.

Either we give life to others in our relationships with them, or we drain them of it. Life can be taken out of others in rivulets and drops, in the small daily failures of inattention, that bitterest fruit of self-absorption, as surely as by the terrible strokes to their hearts. Sin sprouts, as mold in the right medium, whenever the effect of our relationships with them is to diminish rather than to enlarge them. There is no neutral corner in our human encounters, no antiseptic arena in which "nobody else is hurt," or "nobody else knows about it." We either make people a little better, or we leave them a little worse. We define our belief and moral posture every day. The Kingdom belongs to those, as artless as children, who love others simply and directly, without thinking about anything but them.

Verses 10–14

"See that you never despise any of these little ones, for I tell you that their angels in heaven are continually in the presence of my Father in heaven.

"Tell me. Suppose a man has a hundred sheep and one of them strays; will he not leave the ninety-nine on the hillside and go in search of the stray? I tell you solemnly, if he finds it, it gives him more joy than do the ninety-nine that did not stray at all. Similarly, it is never the will of your Father in heaven that one of these little ones should be lost."

————⦿————

Jesus stretches a hand toward the hills, for his question introduces images that are as familiar as the glare of the Mideastern sun. It is also a parable that has lived on in the imagination of the race because of its gentleness and its pledge of concern for all the missing. History is filled with missing persons, those who never had a chance to live their lives

173

and those whose families and nations have been torn out of their native soil, of men and women who have missed their chance for love, of human beings lost in the deepest crevices of the centuries, of the millions gone with nobody to miss or mourn them. The story registers deeply within this loss-plagued civilization because of its promise that God sees into our souls, sad as children's weeping about desperate cruelties of life.

The plateau, the scholars tell us, on which the sheep grazed in this territory of Jesus was a narrow shelf, broken and ridged with gullies, and the villagers often sent their herds together, tended by a band of shepherds who were expected to seek out stray animals, to return their bones and skins to their community if they were found dead, to account for every animal. One shepherd could pursue the missing sheep because the others were well tended by his companions. And the people rejoiced when, long after the main body of the herds had descended, the one who had sought out the lost sheep was suddenly outlined, the small animal slung on his shoulders, against the fading light.

It is a tale that gives off emanations of a childhood home safe from the world and its problems, of a family circled by a fire or at a meal, experiencing the deepest peace of their lives in and through their relationships with each other. This powerfully evocative parable is about God's family and his care for each of its members. It is not a tale of royalty, of God as a king waiting for the praise of the ranks of his fearful court and servants, but of God searching in the dark and in the farthest places, as a good shepherd or a good father would, for a missing member of the family. At its best the Church remembers that the essential metaphor of Jesus' religious teachings is the family, and that it is meant to offer shelter against the multiplied loneliness of the contemporary world.

Verses 15–18

"If your brother does something wrong, go and have it out with him alone, between your two selves. If he listens to you, you have won back your brother. If he does not listen, take one or two others along with you: *the evidence of two or three witnesses is required to sustain any charge.* But if he refuses to listen to these, report it to the community;

and if he refuses to listen to the community, treat him like a pagan or a tax collector.

"I tell you solemnly, whatever you bind on earth shall be considered bound in heaven; whatever you loose on earth shall be considered loosed in heaven.

The words in these paragraphs have grown harsh over the years. They seem to underscore exclusion, as if Jesus, like a canny politician, had suddenly modified his stand on a controversial issue. How, one wonders, did this happen? Has this chapter, with its references to a church, been used by the Church to strengthen its human institutional aspects at the expense of a certain generosity of spirit? A slight change of emphasis here, a shift of wording there, and the passage comes to justify excommunication after phrases that have emphasized the efforts a person must go to in seeking reconciliation with others.

Some scholars suggest that a gradual adaptation of Jesus' words has taken place over the years, that Jesus emphasizes the importance of nourishing relationships because they are the setting for the ordinary mysteries of love and trust. It does not make sense to read of searches in the night for lost sheep on one page and a more militant, if not downright angry, attitude toward the erring on the next. How can treating them like tax collectors and Gentiles be thought of as an exclusionary punishment when Jesus counted these as his own friends, when, indeed, he called Matthew away from his accounts to be one of his closest followers?

Jesus is really telling his hearers to reach out, as he did, to these recalcitrant persons, to make room for them as he did for the cultural outcasts in his own life. The believer always makes the effort to keep people in relationship and never to exile them from his heart. The energy of these sayings has been misappropriated for institutional ends and we have been made poorer for it. Readers must reclaim Jesus' meanings as the ones that resonate best in their own loving hearts, in their commonsense feeling about life, in what they have learned about the human heart and its problems at close range. They know that, when all is said and done, only love and forgiveness count, and that Jesus could have urged no less in these lines.

175

Verses 19–20

"I tell you solemnly once again, if two of you on earth agree to ask anything at all, it will be granted to you by my Father in heaven. For where two or three meet in my name, I shall be there with them."

Verses 21–35

Then Peter went up to him and said, "Lord, how often must I forgive my brother if he wrongs me? As often as seven times?" Jesus answered, "Not seven, I tell you, but seventy-seven times.

"And so the kingdom of heaven may be compared to a king who decided to settle his accounts with his servants. When the reckoning began, they brought him a man who owed ten thousand talents; but he had no means of paying, so his master gave orders that he should be sold, together with his wife and children and all his possessions, to meet the debt. At this, the servant threw himself down at his master's feet. 'Give me time,' he said, 'and I will pay the whole sum.' And the servant's master felt so sorry for him that he let him go and canceled the debt. Now as this servant went out, he happened to meet a fellow servant who owed him one hundred denarii; and he seized him by the throat and began to throttle him. 'Pay what you owe me,' he said. His fellow servant fell at his feet and implored him, saying, 'Give me time and I will pay you.' But the other would not agree; on the contrary, he had him thrown into prison till he should pay the debt. His fellow servants were deeply distressed when they saw what had happened, and they went to their master and reported the whole affair to him. Then the master sent for him. 'You wicked servant,' he said, 'I canceled all that debt of yours when you appealed to me. Were you not bound, then, to have pity on your fellow servant just as I had pity on you?' And in his anger the master handed him over to the torturers till he should pay all his debt. And that is how my heavenly Father will deal with you unless you each forgive your brother from your heart."

———⤜∞⤛———

These last sections underscore the sweet spirit of this chapter. Those who have corrupted religion into harsh judgment, into a strange fellowship ready to pass sentences from which there is no appeal, cannot have pondered these verses. There is no limit to forgiveness, Jesus tells us, as Matthew, the obsessive, relishes the perfect number seven multiplied by itself and by ten to emphasize that there is no quota on forgiveness.

Each saying develops another aspect of Jesus' teaching on this subject. Jesus cannot tell us often enough, or in ways sufficiently different, that loving others is the fundamental religious experience of living, that redemption is tied up with the mystery of forgiveness because in the tragic grandeur of existence people are always hurting each other, that there is no survival, there is no salvation outside our relationships. The Church, if anything, must profoundly understand and champion this truth against all those who distort religion into a merciless and cold imperative. Faith is for the beleaguered in need of friendship, not for the proud and powerful. The Church is meant to be like a family, perhaps as defined by Robert Frost: "the place where, when you have to go there, they have to let you in." Everything else is a misunderstanding, no matter with what righteousness it may be proclaimed.

How many times, Jesus seems to ask, must I tell you these things? Seventy times seven? What perverse chancre eats at the heart of religious bureaucracy that it so regularly forgets that religion concerns itself with trust and hope and love, the common mystical experiences which, in their ability to give and enlarge life, surpass all the miracles that have turned the moon to blood or cleft pathways in the sea? "Where two or three are gathered," Jesus tells us—wherever, in other words, men and women are in genuine relationships with each other— they meet in my name and spirit, and I am with them.

Jesus defines a startling faith, one that incarnates itself through the way in which we make ourselves present to each other. There is no faith, no mystery, and no revelation of God in relationships of manipulation and deception, in relationships of untruth and seduction. And Jesus is not there either. He is present only as we are present, unselfconscious as children, living from principles deep within us, from hearts tender as those of shepherds, as ready to forgive as we want to be forgiven, encountering the mysteries of religion in the common experiences that bind us together in a way that laws never can.

CHAPTER 19

Verses 1–9

Jesus had now finished what he wanted to say, and he left Galilee and came into the part of Judaea which is on the far side of the Jordan. Large crowds followed him and he healed them there.

Some Pharisees approached him, and to test him they said, "Is it against the Law for a man to divorce his wife on any pretext whatever?" He answered, "Have you not read that the creator from the beginning *made them male and female* and that he said: *This is why a man must leave father and mother, and cling to his wife, and the two become one body?* They are no longer two, therefore, but one body. So then, what God has united, man must not divide."

They said to him, "Then why did Moses command that a writ of dismissal should be given in cases of divorce?" "It was because you were so unteachable," he said, "that Moses allowed you to divorce your wives, but it was not like this from the beginning. Now I say this to you: the man who divorces his wife—I am not speaking of fornication—and marries another, is guilty of adultery."

Jesus moving again, the crowd forming and reforming itself as easily as a microscopic organism around him, people looking up from their chores at the noise and excitement. Is a prophet passing by? Yes, and more than a prophet, comes the reply, for people are changed by being in his presence, they are better for being with him, for hearing him, and feeling his healing touch. We are not surprised to see a group of Pharisees hurrying, like men entitled to push others aside, toward Jesus. Now, *now* in front of the crowd they can force Jesus into a compromising position on a question that is as delicate now as it was at the time. What, they ask, their elaborate piety covering their smug certainty that they have him on the spot, does Jesus teach about divorce?

The calmness of Jesus' self-possession—that quality that stills the anxieties in those before him, who are healed by the strength of his presence—endures, as light traveling endlessly from a star to earth, through the piled-up centuries to arrest our attention now. Jesus understands this effort to manipulate him and does not hesitate. He looks directly into the faces of his questioners as he speaks, then sweeps the expectant faces of the crowd. The crowd is silent and still, calmed as the sea was by his words.

Jesus speaks of the ideal of marriage, calling up the imagery of the biblical Paradise and God's purposes in offering a life to be shared on every level by husband and wife. Jesus speaks of the depth of friendship in marriage, of the way man and woman find what they can discover in no other way when they give themselves into each other's care without reserve or condition. It remains the ideal to touch the larger crowd grouped around the gospel at the present time. As Jesus looks at the men and women clustered beyond the inquiring Pharisees, he sees into the lonely chambers of their hearts, he senses longings, very much like our own, for the love that gives light to the universe.

Love is the great mystery, root and stem of any experience that can be called religious. We find everything in each other by letting go of everything for each other, we enter life by way of love that asks us to accept a thousand deaths for its sake; we find ourselves, in the essential dynamic of Christ's teaching, when we lose ourselves. If we are to resemble the little children in their lack of self-consciousness, it is only so that we can bear our undefended, unpuffed-up selves as gifts to each other. The whole mystery of our dying and rising, of surrender and triumph is forever balanced in the everyday mystery of being true friends.

Genuine marriage is a revelation of friendship, a manifestation of God, a source, true as any cited in dusty theological manuals, of our comprehension of the largest of truths about ourselves and our world. In the friendship of marriage—for this is what Jesus describes rather than a purely technical union—we get a glimpse, a cosmic hint about God's innermost nature, of his intentions, as our perennial suitor, in our regard. How else could we ever imagine a God who wants to share his life with us if we did not feel that same impulse toward another person? Marriage is, then, not a legal brief in a dried-out binding but a beacon flashing a signal about God's personality across the universe.

Jesus cannot speak of this holy of holies except as an ideal that necessarily transcends human limitations and failings. This great flare burns with a Divine fire and no man can quench it. How else can Jesus speak to us of this relationship, this way of living a whole life together, this prism for God's power and glory, except as an unbroken whole? He knows the exceptions that his contentious inquisitors will mention. Moses' exceptions, he says quickly, were made in view of the people's resistance to God's teaching, an exception that reveals the face of man rather than the face of God. No, Jesus says once more, searching the expectant faces, you cannot sully marriage by using this ideal to justify those incestuous unions—lewd conduct or *porneia*—that do not represent marriage at all.

This section, like the finest evening of a changing season, cannot be dealt with hurriedly. The reader must enter its mood, let it settle in the soul, savor its depths repeatedly before the richness of its proclamation about human relationships comes through. Jesus, in all his teaching, has pointed toward love as a gift within us that, at the price of great sacrifice and greater joy, we must share with others in order to enter into the mystery of redemption. He understands human shortcomings, failures of every kind, but these do not lessen the ideal or our need to strive toward it. God is found in the very effort to live the mystery of marriage.

Verses 10–12

The disciples said to him, "If that is how things are between husband and wife, it is not advisable to marry." But he replied, "It is not everyone who can accept what I have said, but only those to whom it is granted. There are eunuchs born that way from their mother's womb, there are eunuchs made so by men and there are eunuchs who have made themselves that way for the sake of the kingdom of heaven. Let anyone accept this who can."

———————∞———————

Well, then, the disciples say, crowding around him afterward, if this is so, then a man might better avoid marriage, for then he would not be so bound. Men say the same thing today, offering countless reasons to avoid marriage, to describe it as just a piece of paper, or an unnecessary formality. There is more than a tinge of chauvinism in these remarks, a hint of something near to changeless in the male psyche in its vigilance for means of escape, for life and love on terms comforting to immature men.

Jesus flavors his idealism with an answer that displays an understanding and acceptance of the facts about human nature. He knows what the world is like, is acquainted with the infirmities and hesitancies of human beings. The reply holds up to this very day. Not everybody can live this way, and it is a grace from God that enables some people to do so. Jesus may, in his poet's soul, be speaking of what he has felt in the crowd of people who have been following and listening to him so intently. He brims over with his awareness of the shortcomings and honest difficulties of the men and women all around him.

That is the wellspring of his compassion for them; he knows what their lives are like, appreciates that, in an aspect of the mystery that blinds the onlooker like the sun glaring on the shields of the enemy, some people are more favored than others, that some are lucky and some seem cursed, that love, powerful even in slivers, may not be within everyone's reach. Jesus seems to speak out of a comprehension of the sadness of the history that stretches before him, of the years, fields beyond fields running but never reaching the horizon, filled with illness and early death, of cruelties and misunderstandings, of the thousand circumstances that will make it difficult for so many people ever to grasp the ideal of marriage.

It may remain a dream for many, yes, he understands that, in the variety of graces, some people may freely forsake a life of intimate friendship with one person in order to give themselves in the service of friendship in the Kingdom with many. There are all kinds of possibilities, Jesus says, and men and women must be free to choose the way on which they can move best. What is remarkable about this passage is that, far from being harsh and stern, as it is often interpreted, it is gentle, compassionate, rich in wisdom about the struggles of people to do the best they can. Yes, we might say, that is a teaching about freedom that anybody who has lived very long, or gazed into the hearts of ordinary people, can accept because it is in itself so accepting of them.

Verses 13–15

People brought little children to him, for him to lay his hands on them and say a prayer. The disciples turned them away, but Jesus said, "Let the little children alone, and do not stop them coming to me; for it is to such as these that the kingdom of heaven belongs." Then he laid his hands on them and went on his way.

Verses 16–22

And there was a man who came to him and asked, "Master, what good deed must I do to possess eternal life?" Jesus said to him, "Why do you ask me about what is good? There is one alone who is good. But if you wish to enter into life, keep the commandments." He said, "Which?" "These": Jesus replied, *"You must not kill. You must not commit adultery. You must not steal. You must not bring false witness. Honor your father and mother,* and: *you must love your neighbor as yourself."* The young man said to him, "I have kept all these. What more do I need to do?" Jesus said, "If you wish to be perfect, go and sell what you own and give the money to the poor, and you will have treasure in heaven; then come, follow me." But when the young man heard these words he went away sad, for he was a man of great wealth.

Verses 23–26

Then Jesus said to his disciples, "I tell you solemnly, it will be hard for a rich man to enter the kingdom of heaven. Yes, I tell you again, it is easier for a camel to pass through the eye of a needle than for a rich man to enter the kingdom of heaven." When the disciples heard this they were astonished. "Who can be saved, then?" they said. Jesus gazed at them. "For men," he told them, "this is impossible; for God everything is possible."

Verses 27–30

Then Peter spoke. "What about us?" he said to him. "We have left everything and followed you. What are we to have, then?" Jesus said to him, "I tell you solemnly, when all is made new and the Son of Man sits on his throne of glory, you will yourselves sit on twelve thrones to judge the twelve tribes of Israel. And everyone who has left houses, brothers, sisters, father, mother, children or land for the sake of my name will be repaid a hundred times over, and also inherit eternal life.

"Many who are first will be last, and the last, first."

———◇———

This chapter is a family album for the reader. Everyone is familiar, we have met the children, the young man, the ponderous rich, and the bewildered, all too human disciples many times before. The stories offer us variations on themes that are intensely familiar to us; they are concerned with the nature of religion and the kingdom or way of life to which we are invited, and with the character and quality of our relationships with each other. These are bound up with each other, inseparable as breath and life. They are stories that indict calculation and selfishness and every notion that a code or formula exists that, like a properly rubbed lamp, will produce a powerful jinni who will lead us safely to a place of reward. The illustrations offer telling details about the impacted attitudes that make it difficult for some people to follow the way that Jesus is going. Is there a suggestion that such dullness of spirit on the part of his closest followers and others has begun to take its toll of Jesus? Is his compassionate understanding tested by the self-interest he finds all around him?

His followers want to protect him from the children but, as he has said before, only those as open and undefended as these children may enter the Kingdom. The Kingdom. What does he mean? Is it heaven, the reward for virtue, a place beyond the clouds in which all our human needs will be met superabundantly? Or is Jesus here, and in later verses, describing something that cannot be satisfactorily defined in geographical terms? And is the Kingdom something of the future in which we reserve places by being faithful to the rules and regulations of humanly organized religion? Or is it of another order of experience altogether? Does it resemble something like friendship or love, a state of the heart accessible only to those whose spirits are as generous and loving as that of God himself? Is the Kingdom a mode of relationship with Jesus that is essentially spiritual, to which one makes entrance only by the inner route of opening our hearts to him through the way in which we love and serve the family of men and women all around us? These verses overflow with such hints. The Kingdom is not something we break into through our claims to have performed righteous deeds; it is entered when we break out of preoccupation with ourselves, and our wealth, and our possessions.

These incidents bear the same weight of meaning even as they repeat similar phrases—the Kingdom, eternal life, entering into life. These refer to qualities of life that are beyond the grasp of the first-century narcissists whom we encounter in these paragraphs. The young man, like many persons in our own time, is, despite his comfortable life, unhappy but unsure how to do anything about it. *Do* is the operative word of his self-infatuated question. For there is nothing we can *do*, unmotivated by a loving heart, that can make purchase of the Kingdom for us. He turns away finally, back to the cramped world of his possessions.

It is no different for those who, as if they had stepped out of twentieth-century newspapers, identify worldly wealth with spiritual success. The air becomes close in this section, as if so hungrily breathed by the wealthy that it has lost its freshness. We must move away, seek an uncontaminated space far from those who confuse wealth with God's blessing on their lives. Jesus means what he says here: it is difficult to enter a kingdom of relationships by way of calculations, by the standards of the bottom line. Yet this has been a recurrent dream, especially in America, where preachers, distant cousins to those who questioned Jesus, identify worldly success as God's blessing on the righteous. It is difficult but not impossible, Jesus says, for it is a kingdom of grace freely given by God.

Even the disciples want to know what they are going to get out of following Jesus. They have not yet understood the Kingdom or its demands for entering into relationship by following him. He is headed for suffering and death, for the pain of sacrifice that leads to resurrection, to the "fullness of life" of which Jesus speaks to the rich young man, and which, lamentably, is still often translated as "perfection."

The startling message of these pages is about the nature of the Kingdom. It is not far off, nor is its entrance governed by rules and regulations. We are in the Kingdom when we open ourselves as guilelessly as children to relationships with Jesus. The heart, offered in service to others, is the medium of this relationship. We are already in the Kingdom if we understand that religion and love are matters of the inner person rather than of the external keeping of rules of behavior. Eternal life does not refer to unending life in the sense that we have often heard it explained and, indeed, commonly use ourselves. It refers, first and foremost, to "what befits God" (Greek *alionios*), that is, to God's character, to his loving, generative, and giving essence. We enter the Kingdom when our hearts, breaking free of the bonds of selfishness, reflect that same self-giving in our lives with other people.

There are no tricks, no manipulations of extrinsic religion that can buy a person the experience of relationship to God that is the essential characteristic of the fullness of life of which Jesus speaks repeatedly. Look back at the little children, climbing unselfconsciously on Jesus' knee. Of such is the spiritual kingdom we enter when we love others without thinking about ourselves. It is *the* message of all these verses, *the* message of all Jesus' preaching.

CHAPTER 20

Verses 1–16

"Now the kingdom of heaven is like a landowner going out at daybreak to hire workers for his vineyard. He made an agreement with the workers for one denarius a day, and sent them to his vineyard. Going out at about the third hour he saw others standing idle in the market place and said to them, 'You go to my vineyard too and I will give you a fair wage.' So they went. At about the sixth hour and again at about the ninth hour, he went out and did the same. Then at about the eleventh hour he went out and found more men standing around, and he said to them, 'Why have you been standing here idle all day?' 'Because no one has hired us,' they answered. He said to them, 'You go into my vineyard too.' In the evening, the owner of the vineyard said to his bailiff, 'Call the workers and pay them their wages, starting with the last arrivals and ending with the first.' So those who were hired at about the eleventh hour came forward and received one denarius each. When the first came, they expected to get more, but they too received one denarius each. They took it, but grumbled at the landowner. 'The men who came last,' they said, 'have done only one hour, and you have treated them the same as us, though we have done a heavy day's work in all the heat.' He answered one of them and said, 'My friend, I am not being unjust to you; did we not agree on one denarius? Take your earnings and go. I choose to pay the last comer as much as I pay you. Have I no right to do what I like with my own? Why be envious because I am generous?' Thus the last will be first, and the first, last."

———∞———

Jesus' reply to Peter bridges the division of these chapters. Jesus looks into Peter's puzzled face. Although Jesus has spoken often about the mystery of the reversal of relationships in the Kingdom, of the emptiness of worldly power and the fullness of loving service, his closest follower still imagines that an earthly triumph lies, like a splendid city rising suddenly out of the desert, at the end of their journey together. A man wants to be up front so that onlookers will see how favored he is, how easily he gets the attention of the master. Jesus smiles at his eager friend. At least there is no dissimulation in Peter; he bursts out with his feelings, his plans, his expectations, a little boy of a big man still. This unretouched humanity is lovable. Listen, Jesus says, let me tell you about this again. Peter's face grows solemn, his brow creases, for he knows that the truth is embedded in Jesus' stories as freshness is in the sea breeze or autumn in the long days of harvest.

We listen attentively with the apostle, as Jesus calls forth a gallery of actors who have performed this scene for us times beyond counting. They seem like relatives in the photographs, flat and darkened as long stretched hides, faces in which we see our own features fixed with eternal expressions in gatherings long concluded when we were born. The only way we know these forebears is in these small timeless panels of a lawn party, a wedding, an everyday scene with a lost world in the background. We search their faces to understand them better, indeed to understand ourselves, for we are still writing the story of which they are a part.

So here the estate owner, the workmen, the vineyard rustling in the early fall sun. This is the only time we see them, they move in our imagination like the generations before us, the whole living spread of their existences stretched out, like a once lithe animal preserved leaping in an ancient ice floe. We strain to hear more of what they say or do, but this is the only record we have; it is vivid, as a picture of the past is, because we recognize the depth of its still puzzling truth. The story is told to us as much as it is to Peter because it proclaims again the nature of the God whose Kingdom Jesus preaches. We knit our brows with Peter because Jesus speaks of the wholeheartedness which, even in an instant, makes us equals in the Kingdom. Love that gives itself can be fully present and powerful in that very moment of its expression; it doesn't depend on duration, but on depth; it is, in fact, a mystery outside of time and its ordinary calculation, beyond numbering, and no mathematical model of it can ever be constructed. The Kingdom exists in relationships of love, not in the rank orderings of power, not in the childish insistence on a kind of measured justice that means nothing in God's eyes.

Still, in looking up from the page just as in looking up from the photograph album, we feel that we have had an experience that cannot be measured. We have broken free of time and sensed something of the

measureless realm of the spirit; we sense that real love does not have
dimensions, beginning or end, that it is part of a mystery that is beyond
the calipers of justice or human estimation, that it is the essence of
God's own life and of Jesus' own kingdom.

Verses 17–19

Jesus was going up to Jerusalem, and on the way he took the Twelve to
one side and said to them, "Now we are going up to Jerusalem, and the
Son of Man is about to be handed over to the chief priests and scribes.
They will condemn him to death and will hand him over to the pagans
to be mocked and scourged and crucified; and on the third day he will
rise again."

Matthew, collector of the sayings of Jesus about a sphere that is
without horizons and whose magnetic north lies in the energy of love,
will nonetheless put them carefully in order. He is like the obsessive
keeper of the picture album, cutting and fitting the events and themes
of the family's saga so that they appear rational and linear. But, just as
the photographs cannot contain the elusive dynamism of the people
whose images they bear, so neither can Matthew's well-ordered and
logical arrangement of Jesus' life. Still, it has the advantages of the
family album because it allows us to view the past, and, through meditation, through loosening our own insistent rationalism, to feel the heat
and light of other times, to see Jesus, with followers as human and
time-bound as we ourselves, inviting us outside of temporal values.
Matthew's method also permits us to see Jesus in the context of Jewish
history as a successor of the suffering servant, as the man in one way as
fixed in his period as we are in our own, the inheritor of its customs, the
speaker of its language, the man familiar with the rhythms of its mystical symbols. In this prediction of his suffering we hear Jesus underscoring the character of his Kingdom as for the third time he raises a vision
of the suffering that lies before him.

Matthew inserts this in a chapter in which Jesus is pressed not only
by the realization stirring within him of the betrayals of trust that lie
before him, but also by the fact that his followers still have not grasped
the nature of his preaching or of the spiritual rather than earthly power

to which they must surrender themselves. Matthew's careful cutting and pasting of this passage reminds us that Jesus is fulfilling prophecy even as he proclaims his Kingdom. We sense urgency, a last chance to get the point as we hurry to join the still confused disciples on the road to Jerusalem.

Verses 20–28

Then the mother of Zebedee's sons came with her sons to make a request of him, and bowed low; and he said to her, "What is it you want?" She said to him, "Promise that these two sons of mine may sit one at your right hand and the other at your left in your kingdom." "You do not know what you are asking," Jesus answered. "Can you drink the cup that I am going to drink?" They replied, "We can." "Very well," he said, "you shall drink my cup, but as for seats at my right hand and my left, these are not mine to grant; they belong to those to whom they have been allotted by my Father."

When the other ten heard this they were indignant with the two brothers. But Jesus called them to him and said, "You know that among the pagans the rulers lord it over them, and their great men make their authority felt. This is not to happen among you. No; anyone who wants to be great among you must be your servant, and anyone who wants to be first among you must be your slave, just as the Son of Man came not to be served but to serve, and to give his life as a ransom for many."

Verses 29–34

As they left Jericho a large crowd followed him. Now there were two blind men sitting at the side of the road. When they heard that it was Jesus who was passing by, they shouted, "Lord! Have pity on us, Son of David." And the crowd scolded them and told them to keep quiet, but they only shouted more loudly, "Lord! Have pity on us, Son of David." Jesus stopped, called them over and said, "What do you want me to do for you?" They said to him, "Lord, let us have our sight back." Jesus felt pity for them and touched their eyes, and immediately their sight returned and they followed him.

But here the family is at it again, and so too, in as human a touch as we will find, is the chauvinistic editing of Matthew. Once a tax collector always a tax collector. The scholars tell us that, based on the oldest Gospel, Mark, it is clear that Matthew offers a cover-up for the reputations of James and John. They are the ones still numb to spiritual things as they press their case for favored positions in the Kingdom. Matthew, assembling his material when these men had become highly revered in the young Church, spares them this evidence of their ambition by blaming it on their mother. Matthew is not the last highly placed church elder to deal so insensitively with women or to be so defensive about his brother church officials. If Matthew's retouching is regrettably human, so too is the picture beneath the scraped-away paint. The men vie for the first places and Jesus, still patient with his followers, explains the nature of the Kingdom to them—and to us— once again.

We think again for ourselves about Jesus' message, for it is easily forgotten or corrupted, and we, much like James and John, are still prey to the ravaging tempters of fame and position. We are often as blind as the men in the following passage, but we do not have their understanding of their condition. We do not know how obstructed our vision is if we still aspire to power and celebrity and do not care what means we use to achieve them. What does it require of us to become servants in the sense in which Jesus speaks of himself in these words? How can we join in ransoming the world by serving it?

I recall listening to Cesar Chavez, the farm organizer, speak of his own decision to accept a life in which he would work for a great cause at five dollars a week. He talked about the "first fear" that men must face. They worry that others may be able to take their possessions away from them, that they may lose everything if they give themselves to this seemingly powerless kind of servanthood. This is the great fear that makes people hesitate, that turns them back to goals of power and money instead of the good purposes of working for the good of others. Once a man gets past that first fear, Chavez said, then he can move ahead because he no longer worries about losing everything and he discovers the power that comes to those who can no longer be bought off by money or the promise of influence.

The first fear still grips most of our hearts because, although we are inspired by Jesus' revolutionary proclamation about the nature of relationships in the Kingdom, we hesitate. We hesitate even to ask, as the men in the next verses insistently do, to be cured of our blindness.

But we have heard Jesus say this in many ways now: his Kingdom is not a hierarchy of power, but a community of people who love and give themselves for the good of others. It is a Kingdom that reveals itself not in armies arrayed for battle or in great treasuries filled with gold, but in the character of the human relationships of its members. The Kingdom is roughly equivalent, as we have learned, to a way of life, to what Jesus means when he speaks of eternal life. We pierce the shell of time when we respond in trust and love to others; we find ourselves living beyond its crimping grasp and we are no longer affected by the terrors that it holds for those who place power above love. The Kingdom exists wherever people love; they are living an eternal life, God's own life, already. But nobody loves, and nobody understands this, if they have not faced and passed beyond that first fear that they might lose everything in the process.

CHAPTER 21

Verses 1–11

When they were near Jerusalem and had come in sight of Bethphage on the Mount of Olives, Jesus sent two disciples, saying to them, "Go to the village facing you, and you will immediately find a tethered donkey and a colt with her. Untie them and bring them to me. If anyone says anything to you, you are to say, 'The Master needs them and will send them back directly.' " This took place to fulfill the prophecy:

> Say to the daughter of Zion:
> Look, your king comes to you;
> he is humble, he rides on a donkey
> and on a colt, the foal of a beast of burden.

So the disciples went out and did as Jesus had told them. They brought the donkey and the colt, then they laid their cloaks on their backs and he sat on them. Great crowds of people spread their cloaks on the road, while others were cutting branches from the trees and spreading them in his path. The crowds who went in front of him and those who followed were all shouting:

> "Hosanna *to the Son of David!*
> Blessings on him who comes in the name of the Lord!
> Hosanna *in the highest heavens!*"

And when he entered Jerusalem, the whole city was in turmoil. "Who is this?" people asked, and the crowds answered, "This is the prophet Jesus from Nazareth in Galilee."

———⋘———

Jerusalem holds us in the grip of its shifting crowds, forcing us to move with them, stumbling, holding on, the white buildings rising and falling around us, carrying us through the drifting smoke and noise as easily as a tide. The air is rich with the smells of earth, animals, roasting meat, and alive with the splintered cries of birds and beasts, of men and women calling through the spring light to each other. People spill through its gates like grain out of a slashed open sack, more than two million of them, entering the Holy City for Passover.

Jesus heads into this river of energy, knowing that it will carry him to the end of his pilgrimage, understanding that the slaying of the lambs, as surely as the cries of the prophets, are signs of whose meaning he will make purchase with his life. Jesus heads into Jerusalem quite aware of the moment, and well prepared for it through the arrangements he has already made for the donkey that is tethered near its colt. The master needs them. One can hear the phrase being passed from friend to friend. These are words men and women have ached to hear not only as a signal to set the animal free but also to kindle the fuse coiled throughout the nearby villages. Jesus will enter Jerusalem, matching the glory of the feast as lightning does the majesty of the sky. Jesus, the prophet of their expectation and the lamb of their deliverance, with a sense that the shouts of acclamation at the beginning of the week will turn to derision by its end.

We have stood here, trying to hold our place in the surging throng, ever since we were children, waiting for Jesus, waiting, indeed, for the drama of the coming days to work itself out. It is difficult to see Jesus clearly as he rides through the tunnel of branches, for the people shoulder us as rudely as Mideastern crowds do to this day. Still, for all the shouts, for all the excitement of the people as they ask their awaited king for mercy, it seems like a tableau, an event remembered or carefully reenacted for us. Even as the news of Jesus' arrival eddies swiftly around us, turning the teeming city's atmosphere electric, it is difficult to keep him in view as a living person, or to enter his consciousness of this moment, as filled with dread as with joy, as he presents himself as the Messiah. Yet this is an essentially dynamic experience; Jesus enters Jerusalem forever on his way to celebrate the everlasting Eucharist.

The moment demands that we steady ourselves and allow the event, like the curling wave of the city's excitement, to wash over us. Jesus cuts through time to present himself to each of us as our savior, as the person who is the focus of all of history. We find him in the tumult of the street, in the disordered celebration of an improvised royal welcome, we find him not with the kings or the religious leaders but in the middle of sinners like ourselves. Perhaps we have become so accustomed to the set-piece scene of Palm Sunday that we have lost sight of one of its most important aspects. Jesus proclaims himself a king of ordinary people, a messiah for sinners in the noisy streets of a great city. The week will recapitulate what we have already learned as we have moved with Jesus and his disciples throughout the country. He is the unexpected expected one who identifies the essentials of religious experience—the fundamentals of God's relationship to his people—in far simpler fashion than the theologians of his day. The mystery is one of human hearts rather than finely inscribed rules. He lays claim to his titles in the heart of everyday existence, in the maw of heartbreak and meanness, of broken dreams and promises, proclaiming that it is to bring healing and comfort to suffering persons, rather than new heavenly guarantees to the righteous, that he has come. This week is for them—and so, astoundingly enough, it remains at this moment as we watch Jesus jouncing on the back of the simplest of animals, through the pattern of the stirring branches, into our own star-crossed lives.

Verses 12–14

Jesus then went into the Temple and drove out all those who were selling and buying there; he upset the tables of the money changers and the chairs of those who were selling pigeons. "According to scripture," he said, *"my house will be called a house of prayer;* but you are turning it into a *robber's den."* There were also blind and lame people who came to him in the Temple, and he cured them.

Verses 15–17

At the sight of the wonderful things he did and of the children shouting, "Hosanna to the Son of David" in the Temple, the chief priests and the scribes were indignant. "Do you hear what they are saying?" they said to him. "Yes," Jesus answered, "have you never read this:

> By the mouths of children, babes in arms,
> you have made sure of praise"?

With that he left them and went out of the city to Bethany where he spent the night.

———❦———

Jesus, intent on coupling the makeshift acclamation of his messiahship with a practical symbol of his teaching, strides into the courts of the temple, raising the memory of Judas Maccabeus who cleansed the house of God after its profanation by Antiochus Epiphanes two centuries earlier. The Court of the Gentiles is a circus of noise, an intersection of commerce in sacrificial doves and money changing so that people could make their offerings with acceptable coins. The noise and the cries, the sound of the cooing birds, the flutter of their wings, the clink of money, and the coarse haggling across the tables of exchange: the scene has been acted out all across religious history and we are all too familiar with it. We have seen it in the preachers hawking indulgences in St. Peter's Square, in the carnivals of religious gimmicks set like the tents of gypsies outside shrines, we have seen it in the morning's mail of cures promised for donations, and we have shrunk back from it in the moulted shell of commerce left in the wake of papal visits.

Jesus overturns the stalls and tables of the sellers and money changers to underscore the message that has been central in his dialogue with the scribes and Pharisees. Their argument has been about the nature of religious belief and practice. Jesus has insisted on its being a matter of the converted heart even if that beats in the chest of a person struggling with sin; the religious leaders of the day locate it in the external behavior of people, even if their hearts are far from set on the ways of God. The overturned tables symbolize the overturned hypocrisy of those who cannot understand and do not accept the internal faith that Jesus preaches. The drama of this incident should not blind us to its simple and yet majestic meaning.

That significance is, in fact, underscored for us by the fact that those who know the burdens of life, the blind and the lame, remain with him. They understand what he has been talking about; he is the messiah of their expectation, and what he says and does possesses the power to strengthen and cure them. We must remain behind in this hall that still reverberates with the noise of the retreating merchants. The afflicted—and which of us cannot be counted somehow in their number—recognize Jesus as Lord of their burdened hearts. We are healed, as they are, by the way he looks into our lives, and the shouts of joyful children, fresh as spring rain, cleanse us. We are not surprised at the outrage of the chief priests and the scribes. What do they know of simplicity of heart and the pure voices of children? They cannot accept and will not tolerate a Messiah with such a sympathy for the plain wonders of life.

Verses 18–22

As he was returning to the city in the early morning, he felt hungry. Seeing a fig tree by the road, he went up to it and found nothing on it but leaves. And he said to it, "May you never bear fruit again"; and at that instant the fig tree withered. The disciples were amazed when they saw it. "What happened to the tree," they said, "that it withered there and then?" Jesus answered, "I tell you solemnly, if you have faith and do not doubt at all, not only will you do what I have done to the fig tree, but even if you say to this mountain, 'Get up and throw yourself into the sea,' it will be done. And if you have faith, everything you ask for in prayer you will receive."

———————∞———————

There are human aspects to this surprising passage as powerful as archeological discoveries that reveal our oldest ancestors as our brothers and sisters. The discovery that a man previously classed as "primitive" had been laid out on a bier of spring flowers made him seem like a long lost relative, for only human hands intent on tenderness and affection for someone who loved and was loved could have arranged such a burial. The same feeling rose off the recently uncovered footprints, millions of years old, of a family apparently out for a walk together. And here Jesus, in the midst of great and draining events, feels hungry and, in the most natural of ways, walks to the roadside and searches a newly leafing fig tree for the fruit, as sweet and old as biblical dreams of plenty. Such ordinary actions remove the shadows of majesty that sometimes fall across Jesus' face in this worked and reworked narrative.

Still the story is puzzling. Is Jesus' anger a signal of a man so pressured by the quickly moving days collapsing in misunderstanding and rejection that he displaces his frustration on a tree that would not, by its very nature, bear fruit until the fall? The commentators offer a half dozen interpretations, some of them technically complex, some of them astoundingly pious, but hardly any of them dealing with the central emotion of the incident, Jesus' anger. One thinks of Jesus' bearing the burden of every prophet: he feels things more keenly, reading the men and women around him accurately because he so sensitively picks up the finest breath of their attitudes and reactions. He also understands the hostility and fear beneath the pious facades of the religious leaders who question him endlessly, defensively, hypocritically.

Perhaps we are watching Jesus the poet at work, startling his followers, who seem almost impenetrable, searing into their minds this extraordinary image. He senses that the tree is already dying, that it is forever barren, that it is, then, a natural symbol of the infertile religion with which he is in conflict. The fullness of its foliage hides the death that the branches already embrace. Jesus has singled out the unfruitful life, the useless existence numb to love and relationship, as the waste of sin. He has spoken of Gehenna, the smoldering refuse dump: his metaphors have been stark and clear but still not comprehended even by those closest to him.

Very well then, he recapitulates these themes as he addresses this dying tree. Religion that looks good but has no substance is the enemy of both God and men. Religion that emphasizes externals but remains empty inside is a cursed and worthless construct. *That* is what I am talking about, he says to his disciples, remember this tree already bent under the weight of its own death and you will understand what I teach you about God and the Kingdom.

Still, the disciples, like men rubbing sleep from their eyes, focus only on the slowly dying tree. Jesus must draw them to the real source of spiritual power, the faith that flowers from within themselves, the religion whose strength is lasting because it does not depend on the exterior. He is not done with metaphors to dazzle their imagination as he speaks of mountains that can be moved by those whose trust is dug deep in their souls. Jesus emphasizes to them—and to us these long years later—that religion rooted within us is bountiful beyond any dreaming of it, and the source of the love that is the energy of God's Kingdom.

Verses 23–27

He had gone into the Temple and was teaching, when the chief priests and the elders of the people came to him and said, "What authority have you for acting like this? And who gave you this authority?" "And I," replied Jesus, "will ask you a question, only one; if you tell me the answer to it, I will then tell you my authority for acting like this. John's baptism: where did it come from: heaven or man?" And they argued it out this way among themselves, "If we say from heaven, he will retort, 'Then why did you refuse to believe him?'; but if we say from man, we have the people to fear, for they all hold that John was a prophet." So their reply to Jesus was, "We do not know." And he retorted, "Nor will I tell you my authority for acting like this.

Here we see Rabbi Jesus, learned in his tradition and its devices, as deeply and appealingly Jewish as he is anywhere in the Gospel. And here come the eternal bureaucrats of religion, the chief priests and elders making themselves foolish, revealing their own pettiness and shallowness as they test him on the question of his authority. Smug, oily, over-polite, they exchange knowing glances as they put their question to this calm, appraising young man who has challenged their power to manipulate others in the name of religion.

Jesus, in the rabbinic style they recognize only as it falls around them like a fisherman's net, places them in a dilemma. If there is one thing that the religious bureaucrats have disliked down through the ages— think of the inquisitors haughtily regarding Galileo, the bishop judges sniffing righteously at Joan of Arc, the ecclesiastical leaders of every century confidently condemning those who for good reasons have broken bad religious laws—it is the dilemma, fierce as the grip of the devil's own pincer, caused by their own manipulation of truth.

To Jesus' piercing question, which forces them up against their own fears, they give the answer that is always on the lips of the timorous. "We do not know," the classic escape, the hurried withdrawal of those who flee because they have no principles to stand by and no solid truth to stand on. They have already turned their backs, enraged by the embarrassment that close-up contact with truth always causes them. Truth is the burning coal that seals and scars their lips, the great fundament of the universe on which they eternally stumble.

Verses 28–32

"What is your opinion? A man had two sons. He went and said to the first, 'My boy, you go and work in the vineyard today.' He answered, 'I will not go,' but afterward thought better of it and went. The man then went and said the same thing to the second who answered, 'Certainly, sir,' but did not go. Which of the two did the father's will?" "The first," they said. Jesus said to them, "I tell you solemnly, tax collectors and prostitutes are making their way into the kingdom of God before you. For John came to you, a pattern of true righteousness, but you did not believe him, and yet the tax collectors and prostitutes did. Even after seeing that, you refused to think better of it and believe in him.

Matthew places these stories like central stones in the great arch through which passes his vision of what scholars call "salvation history." Matthew's plan is not to erect a portal of remembrance about failed heroic events, but rather a gate through which the living experience of salvation through Jesus still moves. Matthew, we are told, reveals the dynamic nature of salvation history as a continuing process in which Jesus' death and resurrection are the decisive events. So he carefully selects his materials to show the fulfillment of prophecy in the Kingdom that transcends space and time and roots itself in history, triumphing over rejection by God's beloved Israel and breaking into the world beyond it.

Matthew has lived to see Jerusalem overrun by the Romans, knows of the destruction of the Temple, feels that there is now a wholeness to the first part of this story of Jesus. He is anxious for us to see the mystery of salvation thrust into time through the Church whose life flows directly from this last apocalyptic week of Jesus' life. Our guide arranges the text for larger purposes than chronological history: he wants to fuse the themes of Old Testament expectation and New Testament fulfillment, and the Church itself will boldly add a verse early in its history to complete the work of the man we call Matthew, but who, from all accounts, is not only the aged apostle, but a synthetic presence bringing a roundedness to his memories as well as his vision.

These stories of Jesus are well-observed vignettes, tales that ring true because they have the human heart, with its best and worst chances, in focus. Who has not smiled in recognition of these two sons, used as examples of obedience in a hundred barely remembered sermons? But there is something deeper here, the point that Jesus makes over and over again, the interpretation of authentic religious faith that will bring him in a few days to his death. Pseudo-faith boasts of external observance but is internally bankrupt, estranged from the human experiences of love and trust that give it meaning. Genuine faith may not be self-conscious enough to make great promises, but it gives of its inner strength when human need makes demands on it.

Love, Jesus explains in language that makes his followers listen carefully, can live in the heart of those judged by hypocrites to be exiles and sinners. It cannot breathe, however, in the closed-off personalities of those who carry religion like a shield of self-justification and a sword of judgment. Don't you remember, Jesus asks movingly, how the tax collectors and prostitutes trusted John the Baptist while you did not? Don't you understand, he turns to put the question to all of us, don't you understand that the signal of faith is given by people who trust and love each other and in no other way? It remains *the* question about the nature of religious faith in our own day.

Verses 33–46

"Listen to another parable. There was a man, a landowner, who planted a vineyard; he fenced it around, dug a winepress in it and built a tower; then he leased it to tenants and went abroad. When vintage time drew near he sent his servants to the tenants to collect his produce. But the tenants seized his servants, thrashed one, killed another and stoned a third. Next he sent some more servants, this time a larger number, and they dealt with them in the same way. Finally he sent his son to them. 'They will respect my son,' he said. But when the tenants saw the son, they said to each other, 'This is the heir. Come on, let us kill him and take over his inheritance.' So they seized him and threw him out of the vineyard and killed him. Now when the owner of the vineyard comes, what will he do to those tenants?" They answered, "He will bring those wretches to a wretched end and lease the vineyard to other tenants who will deliver the produce to him when the season arrives." Jesus said to them, "Have you never read in the scriptures:

> It was the stone rejected by the builders
> that became the keystone.
> This was the Lord's doing
> and it is wonderful to see?

I tell you, then, that the kingdom of God will be taken from you and given to a people who will produce its fruit."

When they heard his parables, the chief priests and the scribes realized he was speaking about them, but though they would have liked to arrest him they were afraid of the crowds, who looked on him as a prophet.

———⋘———

Listen again, Jesus bids his religious adversaries, and see if you can grasp the meaning of my life and of the fate now taking shape both for me and for those of you who condemn me. We are deep now in the art of Matthew, for his intention is to link Jesus' mission both with the ancient imagery of Isaiah and with the fresh experience of the first-century Church. This crucial confrontation with the chief priests and Pharisees defines positions which are spiritually irreconcilable.

The manipulators of faith may kill the vineyard owner's son but they complete the design of their own fate at the same time. The religious leaders of Israel reject themselves and their birthright as they turn on Jesus; they invite the Lord of the vineyard to destroy them and to give his trust to others. Jesus brandishes the parable like a smoking brand before the angry faces of his opponents. They back away, grumbling, bent on the fulfillment not of God's design for Israel but of their out-of-joint plot against Jesus.

Lacking hearts for love, strangers to courage, they are governed by a feeling for the darkness. They must move cautiously because these people think Jesus is a prophet. The darkness, yes, the darkness is the place for their plotting, the lightless void in which their weightless souls are forever at home.

Matthew and others have, we are instructed, included the quotation from a psalm sung in the early Church in celebration of Jesus' resurrection. But it is Jesus' death, that of the slaughtered son, that gives birth to the Church. This is the awful event that seeds the vineyard, throws it open as God's good Kingdom to Gentiles as well as Jews, this is the living mystery Matthew wants us to recognize as the Church. Majestic, compelling, overwhelming as the final movement of a great symphony is, these passages invite contemplation rather than analysis. We enter the verses, sense the breaking seams of time, lose ourselves in the enormous mystery of history's ransoming and our salvation.

CHAPTER 22

Verses 1–10

Jesus began to speak to them in parables once again, "The kingdom of heaven may be compared to a king who gave a feast for his son's wedding. He sent his servants to call those who had been invited, but they would not come. Next he sent some more servants. 'Tell those who have been invited,' he said, 'that I have my banquet all prepared, my oxen and fattened cattle have been slaughtered, everything is ready. Come to the wedding.' But they were not interested: one went off to his farm, another to his business, and the rest seized his servants, mal-treated them and killed them. The king was furious. He dispatched his troops, destroyed those murderers and burned their town. Then he said to his servants, 'The wedding is ready; but as those who were invited proved to be unworthy, go to the crossroads in the town and invite everyone you can find to the wedding.' So these servants went out on to the roads and collected together everyone they could find, bad and good alike; and the wedding hall was filled with guests.

Verses 11–14

When the king came in to look at the guests he noticed one man who was not wearing a wedding garment, and said to him, 'How did you get in here, my friend, without a wedding garment?' And the man was silent. Then the king said to the attendants, 'Bind him hand and foot and throw him out into the dark, where there will be weeping and grinding of teeth.' For many are called, but few are chosen."

This story, transformed by Matthew from Luke's spare account of a simple meal into an allegorical wedding feast, descends, as if into an archeological dig, into the deepest territory of the soul. It reaches that level of longing beneath everyday experience that we all recognize, to that space through which time seeps steadily and irreversibly away from us, that center of terror-filled intuitions about our mortality. The brightly lighted wedding feast is surrounded by a mood of longing, by a tragic sense of things lost, a mourning for experiences passed by for too little, for times whose clocks cannot be turned back, and for days that can be neither reclaimed nor relived.

One cannot meditate on this parable without coming up against the press of time itself and the mystery of how it holds our promise and our destiny. What we do is, in some sense, permanent; there are consequences to our choices that we cannot ignore, there is a pattern in the design we make for our own existences that ultimately reveals their meaning. We clothe ourselves for life, make ourselves ready for it or let it slip by, certain that we can negotiate a pact, Faustian or otherwise, that will deliver us. This parable makes us think seriously about our spiritual and moral condition. Do we understand the conditions for entering this feast of a Kingdom, or do we exile ourselves in that special selfishness that we call sin?

This story repeats again what we have already heard: that the Kingdom of God is in our midst, that we are invited to enter, and that we need only make ourselves worthy for the occasion. The central feature of this spiritual domain is a relationship with God that is mediated through our relationships with each other. We cannot buy or talk our way in, we can only love ourselves into the company of God and our brothers and sisters. A person enters by letting go of the self rather than clutching tightly to it. We are properly dressed when we achieve the openness of heart that makes us available for friendship. The Kingdom is not an earthly citadel held by the powerful, the "entitled" of every age, no, it is more like a family which only thrives and gives life through the power of love, and is therefore accessible even to the poor and disinherited.

We enter God's Kingdom not through the carrying out of the awkward maneuvers of Pharisaic religion but through presenting ourselves emptied of self-concern, intent on serving others. The irony of membership in this Kingdom is that people may acquire it without even knowing it. Jesus wants them to recognize that through leading loving lives they make themselves recognizable as God's guests. That is why its citizens, brothers and sisters to each other, gather at a festive meal, for it is on such an occasion that we remember and mark the experience of friendship and love. What other meaning do wedding feasts have, except as joyous moments that underscore sacrificial love as the lifeblood of family existence? Whether we enter the feast depends on ourselves and the free choices we make in the time we have with each other.

Verses 15–22

Then the Pharisees went away to work out between them how to trap him in what he said. And they sent their disciples to him, together with the Herodians, to say, "Master, we know that you are an honest man and teach the way of God in an honest way, and that you are not afraid of anyone, because a man's rank means nothing to you. Tell us your opinion, then. Is it permissible to pay taxes to Caesar or not?" But Jesus was aware of their malice and replied, "You hypocrites! Why do you set this trap for me? Let me see the money you pay the tax with." They handed him a denarius, and he said, "Whose head is this? Whose name?" "Caesar's," they replied. He then said to them, "Very well, give back to Caesar what belongs to Caesar—and to God what belongs to God." This reply took them by surprise, and they left him alone and went away.

———∞———

There is an electric silence, broken only by the sounds of these disciples of the Pharisees—the swish of their garments, the clack of their sandals—as they make their way, counting their strength in their numbers, toward Jesus, calm, expectant, on the edge of bemusement at this wedge of self-important questioners. The unusual Greek verb that means *to ensnare a hunted animal* is used to describe the intentions of the Pharisees as they hatch yet another of their plots to make Jesus compromise himself in his speech. One senses that Jesus observes the group from a certain psychological distance. He picks up their motivation, the restlessness of their self-justification, and can stand aside from the hostility that consumes them. They cannot ensnare him because he stands apart from them, avoiding emotional reactions that would deliver a portion of his soul to them.

He feels the bite of their greeting, for "Master" (or "teacher" elsewhere) is the title used by nonbelievers. They have left out nothing in their strategies of baiting him, of annoying him enough so that he might, even for a moment, lose the self-possession through which he maintains his mastery over them. The Pharisees and Sadducees confront Jesus because he commits what for them—and for their successors as intransigent religious leaders down the centuries—remains the unpardonable sin. Jesus tells the truth. That is what makes them defensive, that is why darkness hates the light, and why hypocrites find this such an enormous offense against their perverse spirit.

At some level, hypocrites understand the power of truth. That is why they fear it so and attempt to disguise or to distort it at every turn. The truth holds together like a fist, while the falsehood of their preaching is like a splay-fingered hand. They cannot enter into relationship with Jesus because he is right and they would have to change themselves in order to become part of the Kingdom that he proclaims. Powerful hypocrites will forgive a person anything except being right. That is why the truthful people of history so often find themselves in exactly the place that Jesus now stands, condemned without a trial because they will not compromise themselves, because they will not make a deal at the price of their integrity.

Jesus is ready for this group and throws them off guard by a witty question about their own question. You, he says, are the ones who carry the coin whose use troubles you. Look at its inscription, for you barter in the Roman emperor's name when it is to your advantage. In a sentence he tears away the gauzy hypocrisy in which their question has been presented to him and forces them to take a look at their own double standard. He will not be caught in the clumsy snare which, set for him, has caught them in its unyielding teeth. Jesus can tell the difference between church and state, making a distinction not so much to identify long-term political theology but to identify the chronic character of hypocritical religion. It is, of course, too much truth for them to bear and, enraged, exchanging glares, they move angrily away, feeling the pathetic and dangerous strength that has marked all the weak men in history.

Verses 23–33

That day some Sadducees—who deny that there is a resurrection—approached him and they put this question to him, "Master, Moses said that if a man dies childless, his brother is to marry the widow, his sister-in-law, to raise children for his brother. Now we had a case involving seven brothers; the first married and then died without children, leaving his wife to his brother; the same thing happened with the second and third and so on to the seventh, and then last of all the woman herself died. Now at the resurrection to which of those seven will she be wife, since she had been married to them all?" Jesus answered them, "You are wrong, because you understand neither the scriptures nor the power of God. For at the resurrection men and women do not marry; no, they are like the angels in heaven. And as for the resurrection of the dead, have you never read what God himself said to you: *I am the God of Abraham, the God of Isaac and the God of Jacob?* God is God, not of the dead, but of the living." And his teaching made a deep impression on the people who heard it.

W̲e are as spellbound as the surrounding crowds as Jesus deals with another testing question from the Sadducees and offers us an insight into the mystery on the other side of our frustrations with time and chance, that life with God that is promised to those who make themselves into friends of Jesus. One is struck first, however, with the indefatigability of these questioners. Their smugness refreshed, their confidence in their manipulative religious schemes renewed, they confront Jesus once again. One imagines that teams of questioners are being dispatched by the distracted and fearful religious leaders. Their power is at risk, there must be a way to deal with this troublesome but clever man whom the people revere as a prophet. We shall catch him in his words yet, we will trap him in the maze of laws and distinctions in which we have made truth our captive for years.

The case is put afresh in terms of the levirate marriage, that law which required a man, for the sake of earthly immortality, to raise up offspring for a brother who died childless. Living on, according to this vision, lay in preserving one's name into future earthly generations. Here, the Sadducees say, is a problem for the man they refer to contemptuously as teacher. Their whole purpose is sardonic because they do not believe in resurrection of the body. The Pharisees, on the other hand, imagine an afterlife of dulled literalness in which the dead return to the conditions of this life, favorably revised and greatly improved. So they exaggerate their case, choosing the mystical number seven to footnote its ridiculous character. If men do return to their former lives, what sense can they make of them? How, teacher, would you sort out these seven brothers as husbands to one wife in the time to come?

Jesus makes a deft incision in their sarcasm, exposing the disease of their spirit to the air. He will not be caught up in this posturing. They do not understand at all, he says, sweeping them with his eyes, they do not grasp God's words or God's ways. People who are taken into God's presence do not lose each other, but we cannot understand the nature of their new relationship in this radically transformed state. Our metaphors fail us because our new relationship with God is the fulfillment of what we have experienced in the richest of our relationships on earth.

Jesus refers to angels to indicate a state of presence with God that transcends these petty theological games. Nor, Jesus insists, binding his questioners with his intensity, can we understand God's power except He be a God of the living, a God whose relationships are not with dust or memories, but are always in the present, that sphere which we invade in the heightened moments of true friendship and love. God is not tied down by history, nor by your rules or ideas that are as narrow and cramped as your own souls.

And we, standing near the back of the transfixed crowd, watching the Sadducees squirm under Jesus' words, what can we understand of the life whose eternal mood hangs in the spring air? We cannot understand the great mysteries as conditioned by earth and time, those perennial sources of frustration for longing souls. Some light breaks through in the best moments of this life when we sense the soaring character of the spirit or the time-conquering immediacy of genuine love. But these remain hints and flashes about the life in God toward which we are borne by our relationships with each other. We take a breath and seem to understand something and we let our breath out and the vision is gone. Our very frustration is a signal of the vastness of the reality that seems just beyond us. Jesus' way of speaking to us has touched the eternal part of us. What else could we be but spellbound?

Verses 34–40

But when the Pharisees heard that he had silenced the Sadducees they got together and, to disconcert him, one of them put a question, "Master, which is the greatest commandment of the Law?" Jesus said, *"You must love the Lord your God with all your Heart, with all your soul, and with all your mind.* This is the greatest and the first commandment. The second resembles it: *You must love your neighbor as yourself.* On these two commandments hang the whole Law, and the Prophets also."

Verses 41–46

While the Pharisees were gathered around, Jesus put to them this question, "What is your opinion about the Christ? Whose son is he?" "David's," they told him. "Then how is it," he said, "that David, moved by the Spirit, calls him Lord, where he says:

> The Lord said to my Lord:
> Sit at my right hand
> and I will put your enemies
> under your feet?

"If David can call him Lord, then how can he be his son?" Not one could think of anything to say in reply, and from that day no one dared to ask him any further questions.

———————⚮———————

As the Sadducees retreat, the Pharisees are more determined than ever to catch Jesus in the glistening web of their strategies. They will send a lawyer, a wily expert in the turn of the phrase and the nuance of the divine regulation, to conduct what amounts to a cross-examination of Jesus. The naïveté of his question reveals the impoverished spirits of his companions just as Jesus' majestic answer reveals the harvest-like richness of his soul. A question by a tinny-voiced lawyer prompts a luminous answer about God, human beings, and the Kingdom in which they meet through Jesus.

The answer constitutes a meditation in itself, the only words we need to recall the essence of Jesus' teachings, for he here declares that these commandments to love our God and our neighbor are bound together, fed by the same bloodstream, inseparable even for the fine-edged chisels of the Pharisees, the summation of the whole law and the prophets. This, Jesus declares again, is the essence of religion. It is not found in tortured regulations or magical incantations. God's blessings cannot be bought or bartered for, they cannot be wrestled out of him even by the most strenuous ascetic. Men and women who love generously receive them freely and live, in fact, by their power even if they are not aware of it. The greatest of graces go not to those who strive self-consciously to claim them, but to those who don't have time to think about themselves as they make sacrifices for the sake of their children, their neighbors, and their friends. Jesus' Kingdom, he reiterates, is one of love, and that is its only sign.

The remarkable thing in the history of spirituality is how Jesus' perfectly clear words have so often been ignored or distorted by those who share the dream of the Pharisees of a God whose attention can be commanded by our small tricks, of a Deity beguiled by our obsessive manipulations. Jesus is never more profoundly understanding of human life than in this moment in which he identifies the hidden wealth of simple people in whose generous lives we discover our only trustworthy ideas about God's love for us.

In this exchange and the concluding one, in which he confounds the same contentious Pharisees with his own question about the Messiah, Jesus stands, as he did among the overturned tables in the temple, making his claim and revealing his religious vision of God and men united in a Kingdom of love. He does not propose a revolution against the government, but against the religious leaders who preserve their power by crippling the human spirit. His words are a great hymn in our ears as we turn to the ordinary tasks of our everyday lives, for in these, rather than in deadly rules, lie our only opportunities to express God's love through our own love for each other. It remains the only signal that has ever moved a cold and longing world.

CHAPTER 23
Verses 1–4

Then addressing the people and his disciples Jesus said, "The scribes and the Pharisees occupy the chair of Moses. You must therefore do what they tell you and listen to what they say; but do not be guided by what they do: since they do not practice what they preach. They tie up heavy burdens and lay them on men's shoulders, but will they lift a finger to move them? Not they!

Verses 5–12

Everything they do is done to attract attention, like wearing broader phylacteries and longer tassels, like wanting to take the place of honor at banquets and the front seats in the synagogues, being greeted obsequiously in the market squares and having people call them Rabbi.

"You, however, must not allow yourselves to be called Rabbi, since you have only one Master, and you are all brothers. You must call no one on earth your father, since you have only one Father, and he is in heaven. Nor must you allow yourselves to be called teachers, for you have only one Teacher, the Christ. The greatest among you must be your servant. Anyone who exalts himself will be humbled, and anyone who humbles himself will be exalted.

The hand we call Matthew's assembles here a collection of Jesus' sayings that bridges the confrontations with his religious enemies and the last great discourse of the Gospel. A mosaic of leftover pieces, it is nonetheless powerful in its impact not only for its unambiguous content—the message is not veiled in a parable—but because a passionate Jesus stands before us, a revelation in himself of his deepest teachings and beliefs. His unmistakable anger builds to a climactic mournfulness, sad as a woman's lament for children who would never be born, for the rejecting people of Jerusalem on whom his tenderness will never be spent. The sayings may have been gathered together but they bear the unmistakable human seal of deep feelings called up from the deepest reaches of Jesus' soul.

This is a condemnation of the exaggerations of Pharisaic Judaism, constituted by a relatively small group of "separated ones" who almost two centuries before had given themselves, for the sake of a Jewish faith preserved free from foreign dilution, to lives of vigilant observance of legal and ceremonial Judaism. Their lives were one long rehearsal, a symphony orchestra endlessly tuning up by playing tortured variations of the Law. The thrilling quality of their dedication—zealotry is always impressive—became obscured by the legal corruption of their daily practice. Large numbers of them fell into the only sin which Jesus ever condemns in such unmistakable fashion, that of hypocrisy, that endless doing that is finally an undoing of the whole purpose of religion.

Jesus' deep feelings are apparent as he moves directly to his point. Believers are to follow the Pharisees as long as they remain faithful to the religious vision of Moses. They are not to follow them, however, when, in the classic symptom of virulent hypocrisy, they say one thing and actually do another. Religion dies at the hands of those who think that they can manipulate it like merchants made dusty by their endless weighing and measuring of grain. The spirit is stifled by men who use the authority of religion to control others, sending them sagging under great spools of regulations, watching them stumble and refusing to assist. The Pharisees' power rises from the burdens they heap on the backs of sincere Jews; their gratification comes out of the primitive manipulation of people's fears of displeasing their God.

Religion, Jesus has said repeatedly, cannot be built on such fear, for it gives men and women no insight into the God who offers them life as a place of freedom rather than a prison for their loving spirits. In other places Jesus contrasts love not with hatred but with that fear associated with the impossible task of ever making oneself presentable to a distant and perfectionistic God. One can never be perfect for there will always be a new law, and with it a new interpretation, a fresh hair to be split by the keenest ecclesiastical razor. Such religion is a trackless place, Eden overgrown, in which people experience a lonely spiritual alienation from their best human instincts.

And yet, despite what is the cleanest, clearest condemnation of Pharisaic religion in the Gospel, the perverted spirit of legalism, like the vilest seed of the overgrown Garden, has flourished on the trellis of the centuries. Jesus calls men and women out of the fear that forces them to think that they can save themselves by holding still and not breathing, by looking away from God's great green world and from each other, by finding ever more demanding fasts and vigils to coax approbation from Him. Yet they remain afraid, for their idea of God is very different from that preached by Jesus. Only a terrifying Deity can give rise to hypocrisy, because there is no safe way to worship him. But a loving and understanding God is loved in the same way in which we love each other, humanly, imperfectly, with the generosity of the love making up for our inevitable failures.

Jesus' words are not directed solely to a small band of zealots who corrupt Judaism, but to all religious leaders across the bands of time. Jesus speaks with such deep feeling because he wants his words to echo in all the courts and temples of history. He calls urgently, lovingly, to offer us friendship rather than domination, a Kingdom of relationships rather than regulations, a kind of life in God that matches and does not contradict what is most richly human about us. Jesus preaches a Kingdom that is more a family than a Spartan company of ascetics.

Is the Good News too good for us to bear? Is it possible that religion can be so wondrously simple, and that it grows best where goodhearted people do not worry about rules as they respond in love to others? It is difficult enough to get justice out of a lawbook; is it possible to find love —or hope, or faith—in one? Jesus looks across the vales of the ages, scanning the other vines that leech their substance from the taproot of hypocrisy. Bad religious practice brings out the worst, the least developed sides of men and women. Jesus sees in the Pharisees and in all the generations beyond them the desperate preening of themselves and fawning over others that characterize vain religious leaders. They are always in plentiful supply.

Perhaps Matthew, according to some commentators, is warning against a hierarchical organization in the Church, using his last energy to inveigh against this all too immaturely human development that would corrupt Christ's message and lock his Church in endless ambivalence about its earthly power and its spiritual instincts. Whether that is Matthew's intention or not, it is clear that Jesus speaks about his followers as having equal relationships with each other and that the eternal temptation of hypocrisy can be observed in the striving for first positions, titles, and power. We stand quietly for a few moments. These words are not yet dead even though they have been safely denatured by defenders of an outmoded and dying hierarchical model of Christianity. Perhaps, two thousand years after their utterance, we are beginning to hear them for the first time.

Verses 13–15

"Woe to you scribes and Pharisees, you frauds! You shut the doors of the kingdom of God in men's faces, neither entering yourselves nor admitting those who are trying to enter. Woe to you scribes and Pharisees, you frauds! You travel over sea and land to make a single convert, but once he is converted you make a devil of him twice as wicked as yourselves.

"Woe" carries its deepest meaning in its sound. The Greek word *ouai* signifies wrath mingled with sorrow. That is why these powerful denunciations, arranged according to the mystical number *seven* as if they were counts in an indictment, seem both as fresh and as ominous as fog at sunrise. There is a lingering quality to Jesus' feelings about these falsifiers of religion as if, knowing they, like the poor, would always be with us, he must extend his condemnation to the limits of worldly time.

So Jesus' words speak not just to a sect as dead as the husks that now skitter across the desert places where its monasteries once stood, but to the resistant strain of hypocrisy that even now infects religion. The words are blunt: rules and regulations are a barrier to the Kingdom of relationships that Jesus proclaims. They lead people away from discovering themselves as they discover each other and force them into exhausting and alienating forms of religion. Religion is meant to help us possess fully our humanity, not to feel wretched under its burden.

Even more powerful in view of history's sad clashes of orthodoxies are Jesus' words about making converts to a false vision of religion. Nothing has ever failed for Christianity as much as the Crusades. One grows dizzy counting the battles allegedly fought about the nature of the "true faith." Such motivation lies beneath the terrorism that makes the headlines every day, and the intimidation that is exercised more anonymously but just as righteously to urge ordinary people into practices and sects that claim to have *the* secret combination to God's treasure-house of favor.

Jesus has all these in mind, and, if the wrath of his woe is for hypocrites, the sorrow is for those so manipulated by them that they are denied access to the Kingdom. The greatest modern experience of this condemned hypocrisy is found not only in exotic, Eastern religions, but in any and every Christian sect that claims to have a monopoly on the Spirit. The Kingdom, however, is not entered through some elaborate series of gates, nor through the delirious recitation of supposed prayers in the Spirit, no, it is entered as it always has been, through the experiences, simple and ordinary, of trusting, loving, and serving each other throughout a lifetime. What Jesus teaches is, in a very real sense, too simple and too wonderful for those with a need for magic to comprehend.

Verses 16–22

"Alas for you, blind guides! You who say, 'If a man swears by the Temple, it has no force; but if a man swears by the gold of the Temple, he is bound.' Fools and blind! For which is of greater worth, the gold or the Temple that makes the gold sacred? Or else, 'If a man swears by the altar it has no force; but if a man swears by the offering that is on the altar, he is bound.' You blind men! For which is of greater worth, the offering or the altar that makes the offering sacred? Therefore, when a man swears by the altar he is swearing by that and by everything on it. And when a man swears by the Temple he is swearing by that and by the One who dwells in it. And when a man swears by heaven he is swearing by the throne of God and by the One who is seated there.

———————∞———————

Hypocrite comes, the scholars inform us, from the Greek *hupokrites,* which means *one who answers.* This came to be the word for *actor,* the one who *pretends* to feelings that come from a script rather than from the inner self. We come face to face here with the behavior that merits denunciations whose heat, like that of a city aflame, we can feel at a great distance. There is enough food for a lifetime of meditation in the truth that Jesus forgives everything else easily, that he is comfortable with sinners who remember how to love, but that he cannot and will not have a relationship with pretenders in the Spirit.

To the hypocritical believer we may apply elements of the diagnosis that modern psychiatry gives to a *borderline personality*. It is said, for example, that such persons act *as if* they had what we recognize as normal personalities, that their facade can deceive others, but within they are filled with unmanageable rage which they gratify through manipulating instead of having real relationships with others. They have difficulties with trust so they have enormous problems with living.

The hypocrites censured by Jesus act *as if* they were religious, using a facade to cover their own impoverished inner selves. They manipulate others because they do not know how to trust or truly love them. That is why the Kingdom of Jesus is so threatening to them. They can enter only as themselves and this is a requirement that is beyond them. Their inner rage is channeled into the deceptive abuse of the quality of trust that characterizes genuinely religious people.

So they take oaths but build into them a dozen clauses through which they can escape; they have a new interpretation and an excuse for every evading of every promise made in the name of religion. They want to look good, one of the pervasive temptations of the contemporary world, and not really be good. Appearance will make up for reality, they feel, even in relationships as finally inseparable as those with other persons and with God. They quiver on a borderline that is the no-man's-land of the soul. The hypocrite, the actor speaking someone else's lines in the only truly sacred business we know—loving God in loving each other—places himself outside the Kingdom. These woes, these mixed cries of wrath and sadness, are for the destiny brutally carved out by religious hypocrites for themselves.

Verse 23

Woe to you scribes and Pharisees, you frauds! You pay tithes on mint and herbs and seeds while neglecting the weightier matters of the law, justice and mercy and good faith. It is these you should have practiced, without neglecting the others.

Verses 24–26

"Blind guides! You strain out the gnat and swallow the camel! Woe to you scribes and Pharisees, you frauds! You cleanse the outside of cup and dish, and leave the inside filled with loot and lust! Blind Pharisee! First cleanse the inside of the cup so that its outside may be clean.

———— ∞ ————

This last line is a coda for this section—for, in its imagery and emphasis, it sums up Jesus' central teaching. One senses that Jesus pauses for a moment, his hearers hunched forward in attention, as he offers an ironic sketch of the hypocrite who, precise in what is unimportant and deliberately unknowing about what is, stretches muslin tight over the mouth of the wine jar to prevent a gnat from making his cup unclean. The hearers chuckle, the tension is broken for a moment, as Jesus conjures up the sight of a man who, focusing on an insect, swallows the camel he missed.

This counterpoints the sense of values that lies at the heart of mature belief. Those within the Kingdom are there because they understand what is spiritually and humanly important in life. What Jesus underscores are not weightless observances of regulations but the matters of life that have heft to them: justice, mercy, good faith. These are the ways religion is manifest, through these God's nature is revealed and He is also fittingly worshiped. What we do with each other provides the fundamental definition of our religious sense. These works of the heart cannot be made up for by dull acts of the uninformed will. Blessed are the clean of heart; they see God because, first of all, they see each other.

Verses 27–28

"Alas for you, scribes and Pharisees, you hypocrites! You who are like whitewashed tombs that look handsome on the outside, but inside are full of dead men's bones and every kind of corruption. In the same way you appear to people from the outside like good honest men, but inside you are full of hypocrisy and lawlessness.

Verses 29–32

"Alas for you, scribes and Pharisees, you hypocrites! You who build the sepulchers of the prophets and decorate the tombs of holy men, saying, 'We would never have joined in shedding the blood of the prophets, had we lived in our fathers' day.' So! Your own evidence tells against you! You are the sons of those who murdered the prophets! Very well then, finish off the work that your fathers began.

Verses 33–36

"Serpents, brood of vipers, how can you escape being condemned to hell? This is why, in my turn, I am sending you prophets and wise men and scribes: some you will slaughter and crucify, some you will scourge in your synagogues and hunt from town to town; and so you will draw down on yourselves the blood of every holy man that has been shed on earth, from the blood of Abel the Holy to the blood of Zechariah son of Barachiah whom you murdered between the sanctuary and the altar. I tell you solemnly, all of this will recoil on this generation.

Jesus pauses again as the crowd members, reassured about their own good instincts, relieved by his words of some of the weight that the Pharisees have piled on their backs, exchange glances. They settle down again as Jesus, drawing on sights they have seen on their pilgrimage into Jerusalem for the Passover, arrests their attention again. The roadside is crowded with the tombs of the dead and, according to the kind of law Jesus repudiates, anybody who comes in contact with them automatically becomes unclean and ineligible to participate in the greatest of Jewish religious feasts.

The practice has been to whitewash these tombs to protect passersby from accidental, contaminating contact with them. All along the way, these people have seen these tombs gleaming in the fine spring sunlight. They are the metaphor for the machinations of manipulative religion: for what, even at great effort, is made to look good outside remains a repository for the rot of death within. This is a bold signature on these denunciations of false religious practice, on the killing hypocrisy of the religious leaders of the day.

Jesus returns to the theme of the destiny which the hypocrites are pursuing. They are fulfilling that of their forefathers which is remembered in the slaying of every prophet in the books of scripture. There is nothing new about the motives or action of these deceitful men, these frauds and vipers. They want, as so many in our own time, to look good, not to be good. They desire to manipulate and to kill in the name of faith. Throughout history, they hold up the robes and insignia of their religious authority to justify their condemnation of the truth and their murder of the prophets. Always for a good reason, of course: for the good of the Temple, for the good of the Church. How many good people have been sentenced to one kind of death or another by ecclesiastical leaders as numb in spirit as these!

Matthew's account is flavored bitterly by his own experience of the first-century Church. He has lived long enough to understand that the deadening hypocrisy Jesus condemns is the permanent enemy of the Kingdom. It will live on in judges and inquisitors, in ecclesiastical administrators who prefer appearances to truth, in people who would rather surrender control of their souls to rules than take responsibility for themselves. It is a prospect still filled with woe and we, on our way to the feast of the Spirit contained in every ordinary day, walk by the tombs of death that dazzle but cannot blind us to the vision of the Kingdom, truthful as it is simple, that Jesus proclaims.

Verses 37–39

"Jerusalem, Jerusalem, you that kill the prophets and stone those who are sent to you! How often have I longed to gather your children, as a hen gathers her chicks under her wings, and you refused! So be it! Your house will be left to you desolate, for, I promise, you shall not see me any more until you say:

Blessings on him who comes in the name of the Lord!"

———— ∞ ————

Jesus turns to view the bewildering dream of Jerusalem at Passover, the beloved city, the wife, daughter, and betrayer of Yahweh. This lament, filled with longing and sadness, haunts all of religious history. Matthew, some scholars suppose, arranges these words to express the immediacy of his own early experience of a suffering band of believers, of Jerusalem overrun and its temple destroyed as if in fulfillment of prophecy, in order to prepare for the last discourse of the five that are the pillars of his narrative.

Even so, these words speak to us on their own. Jesus uses a language which every human being understands, that of heartbreak. Everybody has known rejection; all men and women have, at one time or another, felt wounded by somebody they love. There is no experience closer to the bone of our existence than the one not just described but deeply felt here by Jesus. The language of revelation is not in the thrumming prayers of Pharisaic religion, not in the drumbeat of its rituals, nor in the sound of its washings and incantations. Religion expresses itself in the language of the heart. How else could it, since it is rooted in the most common of our human experiences, in those simple interludes in which we believe, hope, and love each other?

Jesus concludes this extraordinary section by whispering of his sorrow at the people who plunge after their destiny by turning away from his offer of love. The faith of his Kingdom is connected with just such experiences, known to everyone and not reserved for high priests or, for that matter, for high moments of ecstatic vision or garbled prayer. Jesus feels for Jerusalem because nobody can deter it from the fate it has blindly chosen by turning aside from what is human for an illusion of faith as thin and superficial as the whitewash on the rot-filled tombs. It is a moment of supreme sadness that is also profoundly religious. It is the kind of moment which, in the effort to love, we come to more often than we like. These are the moments which, accepted and lived through, redeem our hearts and our lives. They are a sign that we have already entered the Kingdom.

CHAPTER 24

Verses 1–6

Jesus left the Temple, and as he was going away his disciples came up to draw his attention to the Temple buildings. He said to them in reply, "You see all these? I tell you solemnly, not a single stone here will be left on another: everything will be destroyed." And when he was sitting on the Mount of Olives the disciples came and asked him privately, "Tell us, when is this going to happen, and what will be the sign of your coming and of the end of the world?"

And Jesus answered them, "Take care that no one deceives you; because many will come using my name and saying, 'I am the Christ,' and they will deceive many. You will hear of wars and rumors of wars; do not be alarmed, for this is something that must happen, but the end will not be yet.

Verses 7–14

For nation will fight against nation, and kingdom against kingdom. There will be famines and earthquakes here and there. All this is only the beginning of the birth pangs.

"Then they will hand you over to be tortured and put to death; and you will be hated by all the nations on account of my name. And then many will fall away; men will betray one another and hate one another. Many false prophets will arise; they will deceive many, and with the increase of lawlessness, love in most men will grow cold; but the man who stands firm to the end will be saved.

"This Good News of the kingdom will be proclaimed to the whole world as a witness to all the nations. And then the end will come.

Verses 15–22

"So when you see *the disastrous abomination*, of which the prophet Daniel spoke, set up in the Holy Place (let the reader understand), then those in Judaea must escape to the mountains; if a man is on the housetop, he must not come down to collect his belongings; if a man is in the fields, he must not turn back to fetch his cloak. Alas for those with child, or with babies at the breast, when those days come! Pray that you will not have to escape in winter or on a sabbath. For then there will be *great distress such as, until now, since* the world began, there never *has been,* nor ever will be again. And if that time had not been shortened, no one would have survived; but shortened that time shall be, for the sake of those who are chosen.

This fifth and last discourse rushes before us like a turbulent, apocalyptic moat which we must cross to enter the Kingdom completed in the death and resurrection of Jesus. The scholars refer to it as the "eschatological" discourse, Jesus' words on "the last things," a treasured theme of theologians and students of scripture. For the ordinary person, buffeted by the contradictions and frenzy of contemporary life, this is no easy subject and, therefore, not an easy crossing to make.

Matthew underscores that just as Jesus entered the temple previously, now he leaves it, speaking no longer to the crowds but only to his disciples. Matthew offers us a symbolic transition to the establishment of a new Church. Jesus, sensitive, observant, steeped in the scripture, keenly aware of the intentions of his enemies, a man acquainted with human selfishness and its inevitable consequences, speaks to his close friends of the unseen future which he can feel coming as a person can sense the approaching locomotive in the slightest quiver and hum of the rails.

Matthew is no stranger to the poetry of apocalypse, to that literary genre which, as in a dream, condenses time and events, fits contradictory notions together, and sets them afloat in a symbol-filled sea. The purpose, as in the dream, is to convey a vision of reality whose truth is embedded not in a literal reading of its startling imagery but in tracking down the chains of association set off by these figurative presentations. This is a region of shadowed and uncertain perspectives which makes little sense to the obsessive, conscious side of ourselves. We must loosen the rigid controlling mechanisms by which we "make sense" of the world every day whether it makes sense or not. Let the symbols speak to our unconscious, which takes their windblown seed like the waiting earth and gives them life.

We are more comfortable if we permit the nonrational side of ourselves do some of the work for us. Readers enter this long stretch of verses as they might an art gallery. They must let the pictures speak to them. Indeed, if they put an earphone on and allow someone else to impose rational meaning on the special art before them, they will only work against their own capacity to absorb, at a level beneath awareness, the lessons that can only be learned by the unconscious. The confusions in verses which seem rationally contradictory may have occurred because Matthew, stirred in his depths by his eyewitness to first-century events, attempted, through the accountant's imperative for order, to make too much sense of them.

This territory is as human as any other in this book, and twentieth-century readers will be at ease if they suspend their critical faculties and do not try to match symbols with specific historical events or ages. The fearful, sure that God waits behind the clouds to set the earth afire, trap themselves in prophecies against which Jesus warns us in this very discourse. Perhaps no style of writing has been so consistently misused by the oversimplifiers of religion than the alogical panoramas of history found in passages such as these. Let the readers wander as they might in the Vatican Museum, that fabled collection that invites them into time itself in order to allow the visions of a thousand artists speak to them about the family they belong to. In the long run, one might ask, what tells us more of last-century London, the novels of Dickens or the census reports of the city, and where is the mood of turn-of-the-century France found, in the paintings of the Impressionists or the tax records of the time? The truth of the startling transformation of history by the life and work of Jesus—how it is the same and yet greatly changed—is the subject of this section.

One is struck by the fact that, although the disciples typically press Jesus for more details, his concern is for those who suffer for their beliefs. He wants to console and encourage them rather than frighten them further. They will not be abandoned, even though the worst temptation of the coming time will be to think that they are. Jesus speaks into the maw of pain confronted not just by early Christians but by every believer across time who attempts to live by principles. We may read here of first-century travail but it symbolizes our own. In the midst of the extraordinary prophecy, Jesus' concern is that we understand that he understands and will always be with us.

Our meditation may well be on whether we expect a wondrous deliverance from the sufferings and deaths of everyday life or whether we can see, as the prophets do, that the canvas of time is of one piece and that our greatest stresses arise, as they do across its surface, from facing our particular challenges bravely. Better still, readers may finish this section and allow their own associations to float gently to the surface of their consciousness: there they can identify for themselves the central challenges to their own faith and courage. It is to these that Jesus speaks so urgently.

Life for believers may not be much different than it is for nonbelievers. Indeed, Jesus suggests that life in the Church may be difficult to distinguish from life in the pagan void. So the inheritance of sin will be reinvested in every age, and within the Church itself the faithful will find failures and betrayals. It will be a heroic enterprise, hardly free from power seekers and their firstfruits of corruption, a life of suffering and grace.

Is Jesus prophesying a vision of a Church whose religious leaders will often be as blind as the Pharisees? Does he offer encouragement because the Church will be saved in every age by the anonymous faithful who believe in him and share his love with others? Jesus speaks here to the common persons, the people going about their everyday business, taking care of their homes and raising their children, the bearers, in the long run, of the world's worst burden of suffering and heartbreak. They will be comforted, for they are the chosen who, against all odds and every discouragement, reveal his teachings in their generous and hopeful lives.

Verses 23–28

"If anyone says to you then, 'Look, here is the Christ' or, 'He is there,' do not believe it; for false Christs and false prophets will arise and produce great signs and portents, enough to deceive even the chosen, if that were possible. There; I have forewarned you.

"If, then, they say to you, 'Look, he is in the desert,' do not go there; 'Look, he is in some hiding place,' do not believe it; because the coming of the Son of Man will be like lightning striking in the east and flashing far into the west. Wherever the corpse is, there will the vultures gather.

Verses 29–31

"Immediately after the distress of those days the sun will be darkened, the moon will lose its brightness, the stars will fall from the sky and the powers of heaven will be shaken. And then the sign of the Son of Man will appear in heaven; then too all the peoples of the earth will beat their breasts; and they will see the Son of Man coming on the clouds of heaven with power and great glory. And he will send his angels with a loud trumpet to gather his chosen from the four winds, from one end of heaven to the other.

Verses 32–35

"Take the fig tree as a parable: as soon as its twigs grow supple and its leaves come out, you know that summer is near. So with you when you see all these things: know that he is near, at the very gates. I tell you solemnly, before this generation has passed away all these things will have taken place. Heaven and earth will pass away, but my words will never pass away.

Verses 36–41

But as for that day and hour, nobody knows it, neither the angels of heaven, nor the Son, no one but the Father only.

"As it was in Noah's day, so will it be when the Son of Man comes. For in those days before the Flood people were eating, drinking, taking wives, taking husbands, right up to the day Noah went into the ark, and they suspected nothing till the Flood came and swept all away. It will be like this when the Son of Man comes. Then of two men in the fields one is taken, one left; of two women at the millstone grinding, one is taken, one left.

Leaders with a good sense of those they truly represent often speak through the screen of the media—above the heads and beyond the comprehension of reporters intently focused on daily wonders, even beyond the keen analytic powers of the shrewdest observers—directly to the hearts of their people. Journalists may misunderstand and so misreport them. Their people get the message clearly. Jesus does something like that in these paragraphs and in the bridge of parables that connects this with the next chapter of Matthew. Standing just beyond the disciples we hear what even they, fixed so on the immediate moment, may not fully comprehend. Jesus is not scattering biblical signs as much as he is speaking to the inner good sense of the ordinary people who understand somehow that their lives are caught up and redeemed in his.

The warnings are about false prophets, about a religion reduced to the size of their wizened hearts, and about the generations of quacks and frauds—the misled and the misleading—who stretch across the horizon of his vision, faithful to their faithlessness, making of religion something that it is not and never was intended to be. The distortions of religion constitute a ravaged apocalypse of religion's true possibilities. Its leaders will always be clever and may even play on the deepest needs of others by seeming to work wonders. But, Jesus says, there are certain rules of thumb by which you will be able to identify and distinguish them from me.

They will chant of wonders and cures, they will lead people on wild and disruptive pilgrimages, disordering rather than settling their lives. And they have a taste for secrecy, as if the truth of faith were meant only for an elite of believers. Anyone who preaches a secret source of salvation stands revealed by that very action. I've told you all this beforehand, Jesus says in almost anguished tones, so that you will not be misled by them. Jesus seems to sigh, as if he could not warn people enough that prophets who are blood brothers to the Pharisees lie in wait in every age with plans for the spiritual lives of others. They commit the unforgivable sin because they intimidate the lonely and hurting and use their manipulated loyalty for their own purposes.

The faith I preach, Jesus says in bold metaphors, is public and unmistakable. Trust your good sense about it, because there will be nothing deceitful or falsely dramatic about it. Its inherent drama arises from the fact that what I teach meets and makes sense out of the pain and suffering of everyday life. The Kingdom I preach, he says urgently, is not an exclusive club, not an arcane society searching in dark places for magic. No, the power of my presence—of my coming in my authority —is irresistible because it will address the unanswered questions of time and will reassure you that God's will is being worked out in it. When I come, your lives rather than the skies will be lighted up and you will feel the rightness of it. In an instant, the crooked ways will be made straight and the rough ways plain, and you will find your faith justified.

The world, Jesus assures us, will have a new consciousness of itself. But this will never be delivered by those who offer escapes from life through their distortion of belief. The greatest enemies of good people will always be those who almost sound religious themselves and who hawk promises, indulgences, or healing as confidence men once sold wondrous cures from the backs of wagons. In these passages Jesus tells us to listen to our own experience because it will be a reliable sounding board about the difference between those who believe and those who only believe, for other reasons, in believing. You will, Jesus promises, be able to tell the difference.

Verses 42–51

"So stay awake, because you do not know the day when your master is coming. You may be quite sure of this that if the householder had known at what time of the night the burglar would come, he would have stayed awake and would not have allowed anyone to break through the wall of his house. Therefore, you too must stand ready because the Son of Man is coming at an hour you do not expect.

"What sort of servant, then, is faithful and wise enough for the master to place him over his household to give them their food at the proper time? Happy that servant if his master's arrival finds him at this employment. I tell you solemnly, he will place him over everything he owns. But as for the dishonest servant who says to himself, 'My master is taking his time,' and sets about beating his fellow servants and eating and drinking with drunkards, his master will come on a day he does not expect and at an hour he does not know. The master will cut him off and send him to the same fate as the hypocrites, where there will be weeping and grinding of teeth."

———————∞———————

We break here into a clearing in which familiar tents stand deeply staked in the ground of our imagination. We have visited these places many times before, we know the characters waiting behind the lowered flaps to enter the cycle of Sunday scripture readings to act out their varied destinies for us. We have often seen the torches of the bridesmaids flickering in the night, just as we have felt the tension radiating out ahead of the imminent return of the master of the wicked servants. We have held our breath while yet another householder demands an accounting of how his servants have managed the weights of silver he has given them to invest.

Still, the mood of vigilance grasps us. We wonder, as we sometimes do about other events whose sad outcomes we know, if time cannot be stopped so that we can shout a warning into the narrative, we wonder if these characters may not on their own change their attitudes and so their fates at the same time. But they remain fixed in their choices, pursuers of designs laid down by themselves years before, eternally wrongheaded and shortsighted about their values. Perhaps we are, in some sense, as fixed as they are about our choices and, if we had as much perspective as we have on these stories, we might shout a warning to ourselves, or spend our energies in more life-giving ways. Are we, as fixed in place as these familiar figures? Have we observed a split between what we say and what we do, or are we too well defended against our rationalizations to see that we may not be as different from the hypocrites as we would like to think?

What mood hangs over this familiar encampment if not that of the immediate nature of our lives? For most of us existence is strung out along a series of anticipated and remembered events like strutted wires running to the horizon. We talk about what we have done, we plan about the future along the pathway marked by graduations, births, anniversaries, and successive tests of achievement. We are forever in the business of recollection and expectation. Life seems to reside in what we have finished or in what we are about to do.

This parable stirs us to sense the immediacy of life, to realize that it does not consist in milestones but in the spaces in between them, in the nameless days of bending to our duty, in the character we reveal when we are off camera. Big events do not commemorate themselves as much as they draw together the meaning that inheres in the long days and weeks of undramatic living through which we share ourselves with others, either enlarging or diminishing their existence. The design of our lives—and the destiny we pursue even when we are not aware of it —is found in how we live in between the encouraging and sacramental commemorations of our days.

We make small but steady investments of our moral and spiritual qualities every day, chiefly in our relationships with others. What, it is sometimes asked, do people do all day? Not very much, is their usual answer. Those with a sense of the immediate quality of truly moral lives understand that, as a matter of fact, people do everything that is of true importance every day. They have a choice between being truthful or not, of loving or withholding themselves, of being faithful or not, of bringing their full selves into the experience of living or of putting that off, or leaving it to another time. These parables cause us to focus on the unfolding wonder of our lives and to realize that, in a real sense, everything is at stake every day. Jesus is not asking us to live holding our breaths for fear of judgment, or in bomb shelters among the canned goods that offer stale hope for survival, but in the midst of our ordinary lives with each other.

"Then the kingdom of heaven will be like this: Ten bridesmaids took their lamps and went to meet the bridegroom. Five of them were foolish and five were sensible: the foolish ones did take their lamps, but they brought no oil, whereas the sensible ones took flasks of oil as well as their lamps. The bridegroom was late, and they all grew drowsy and fell asleep. But at midnight there was a cry, 'The bridegroom is here! Go out and meet him.' At this, all those bridesmaids woke up and trimmed their lamps, and the foolish ones said to the sensible ones, 'Give us some of your oil: our lamps are going out.' But they replied, 'There may not be enough for us and you; you had better go to those who sell it and buy some for yourselves.' They had gone off to buy it when the bridegroom arrived. Those who were ready went in with him to the wedding hall and the door was closed. The other bridesmaids arrived later. 'Lord, Lord,' they said, 'open the door for us.' But he replied, 'I tell you solemnly, I do not know you.' So stay awake, because you do not know either the day or the hour."

———— ✧ ————

We can hear the rustle of clothing, the flap of torch-flame, we sense the last-minute urgency that is of no avail as this tightly constructed drama is played out before us. Perhaps we puzzle at this scene, nestled as deep in another culture as the pearl in the meat of the oyster. Jesus is making the same point in all of these tales: readiness is a long now rather than an improvised then. The way into the wedding feast—and his Kingdom—leads through ordinary life.

We can smell the guttering lamps, hear the bewildered cries of the foolish bridesmaids, and we can feel the impact of the master's words. *I do not know you.* Jesus emphasizes the quality of ongoing relationship that distinguishes the lives of believers. The shepherd, he has told us earlier, knows his own, just as they know him. But here a last-minute relationship cannot be manufactured. Either it has existed in what only seem like the uncharted stretches of life or it does not exist at all. His is a Kingdom of relationships, a place defined by the kind of experiences —believing, hoping, loving—that remain perennially crucial to life.

We must, Jesus insists, burn with our own oil. We cannot borrow it at the last minute from others, because it is generated from within ourselves through the process of trying to live generously, thoughtfully, and reliably with others. The night is quiet again around the wedding feast whose doors are barred. It provides a moment in which to understand that our spiritual energy is replenished only by spending it, and that life cannot be stored up, put off, or waited for, that for persons truly alive Jesus comes every day.

Verses 14–30

"It is like a man on his way abroad who summoned his servants and entrusted his property to them. To one he gave five talents, to another two, to a third one; each in proportion to his ability. Then he set out. The man who had received the five talents promptly went and traded with them and made five more. The man who had received two made two more in the same way. But the man who had received one went off and dug a hole in the ground and hid his master's money. Now a long time after, the master of those servants came back and went through his accounts with them. The man who had received the five talents came forward bringing five more. 'Sir,' he said, 'you entrusted me with five talents; here are five more that I have made.' His master said to him, 'Well done, good and faithful servant; you have shown you can be faithful in small things, I will trust you with greater; come and join in your master's happiness.' Next the man with the two talents came forward. 'Sir,' he said, 'you entrusted me with two talents; here are two more that I have made.' His master said to him, 'Well done, good and faithful servant; you have shown you can be faithful in small things, I will trust you with greater; come and join in your master's happiness.' Last came forward the man who had the one talent. 'Sir,' said he, 'I had heard you were a hard man, reaping where you have not sown and gathering where you have not scattered; so I was afraid, and I went off and hid your talent in the ground. Here it is; it was yours, you have it back.' But his master answered him, 'You wicked and lazy servant! So you knew that I reap where I have not sown and gather where I have not scattered? Well then, you should have deposited my money with the bankers, and on my return I would have recovered my capital with interest. So now, take the talent from him and give it to the man who has the ten talents. For to everyone who has will be given more, and he will have more than enough; but from the man who has not, even what he has will be taken away. As for this good-for-nothing servant, throw him out into the dark, where there will be weeping and grinding of teeth.' "

———◆———

Jesus pauses, as a master teacher might, wondering if, despite all his examples, his hearers have really caught the point. Even his disciples usually ask him an off-the-mark question, an indication that they are so fascinated by the sensational that they do not even look for the treasures buried in the field of everyday life. He takes a breath and leads them inside a thickly peopled story that gives them another view of his Kingdom.

This drama is like an old movie, the kind no longer made and more precious for that. We can watch it again and again. Ironically, one of Jesus' points, one that should be pondered by men and women who cannot bury and let go of the Catholic Church of their childhood, is that nothing remains the same, that we cannot stop time, despite the illusion offered by old movies, that nothing is more important for believers to understand. The essence of the life of grace is that it continually reshapes itself around the imperative of generous love, that men and women who truly love understand that dying to themselves is the price of keeping that love fresh, that love is a verb spoken forever in the present tense. Life in the Kingdom—and, therefore, in the Church that preaches it—is not life in a museum in which the humidity and temperature are held constant in order to hold the decay of the past at bay. Life finds change hard but commits itself to it, reinvesting its resources endlessly, instead of burying them in sterile safety.

This kind of life is further illuminated in the explanation of the servant who has placed his weight of silver in the cold tomb of the earth. Master, he complains, I knew that you were a hard man, and *I was afraid.* Fear, Jesus underlines again, is the enemy of life, for it breeds a deadening caution, a holding back, a stagnant waiting until people can no longer recall what they are waiting or saving themselves for.

Risk is the nerve ending laid open by love. It is fear that kills love, that terror that if we give our heart to others they may wound it terribly. It is the deepest and darkest of human fears and it is not overcome by easy slogans inscribed on banners. Risk is not a theoretical idea but an existential reality in which we feel the hot breath of demons on our necks. But it is the basic element of love, the secret core of fuel for the furnaces of the universe. Believers cannot bury themselves away and hope to be good stewards of their gift of life; they can only risk some loss—surely the countless small deaths of every day—to themselves as the inevitable cost of constantly enlarging it.

Jesus searches the faces of his followers. Do they understand, he wonders, that he is about to live out on a cosmic scale the truth of the parables that he has just told them?

Verses 31–40

"When the Son of Man comes in his glory, escorted by all the angels, then he will take his seat on his throne of glory. All the nations will be assembled before him and he will separate men one from another as the shepherd separates sheep from goats. He will place the sheep on his right hand and the goats on his left. Then the King will say to those on his right hand, 'Come, you whom my Father has blessed, take for your heritage the kingdom prepared for you since the foundation of the world. For I was hungry and you gave me food; I was thirsty and you gave me drink; I was a stranger and you made me welcome; naked and you clothed me, sick and you visited me, in prison and you came to see me.' Then the virtuous will say to him in reply, 'Lord, when did we see you hungry and feed you; or thirsty and give you drink? When did we see you a stranger and make you welcome; naked and clothe you; sick or in prison and go to see you?' And the King will answer, 'I tell you solemnly, in so far as you did this to one of the least of these brothers of mine, you did it to me.' "

Verses 41–46

"Next he will say to those on his left hand, 'Go away from me, with your curse upon you, to the eternal fire prepared for the devil and his angels. For I was hungry and you never gave me food; I was thirsty and you never gave me anything to drink; I was a stranger and you never made me welcome, naked and you never clothed me, sick and in prison and you never visited me.' Then it will be their turn to ask, 'Lord, when did we see you hungry or thirsty, a stranger or naked, sick or in prison, and did not come to your help?' Then he will answer, 'I tell you solemnly, in so far as you neglected to do this to one of the least of these, you neglected to do it to me.' And they will go away to eternal punishment, and the virtuous to eternal life."

Spread before us is a scene that has delighted legions of preachers and retreat masters. They have conjured it up as skillfully as a Hollywood producer in order to terrify the good people spread in the pews below them. Perhaps no scene has ever been more ill-used in the cause of redemption. It is always easy, of course, to scare people, to make them feel guilty, to manipulate them into false perceptions about God. Indeed, this panorama of judgment has been invoked to make people feel ashamed and guilty about themselves when, startlingly, its point is quite different.

The story holds the truth, as all great myths do, keeping it safe against the recurrent Pharisaism that outwits time like an innovative virus. And the truth is a humanly simple one. The most remarkable thing about the story of the judgment lies not in the grandeur of the scene but in the reactions of those who are called the inheritors of the eternal Kingdom. They are surprised by what the Son of Man says. They cannot even remember when they gave food to the hungry or clothes to the naked, or comforted those who were ill. When, they ask, did we do all this? The most characteristic thing about those blessed by the Father is that they cannot recall the very incidents which God seems to prize so much.

How can this be? The answer is simple and easily understood by people who, without counting the cost, give themselves away in love for others. The blessed cannot remember because in these crucial moments of their lives they forget themselves. That is why they cannot remember: they perceive human need and respond to others for their sake, ignoring their own needs, unworried about their own appearance, unconcerned about the impression they are making. The saved are the people who pay the price of loving others without keeping an account of it. They are amazed as good people are when we thank them for what they do for us. They smile, rejecting self-consciousness, and say, "Oh that, that's nothing more than any friend would do."

The citizens of Jesus' Kingdom are wonderfully free of concern about themselves. They are the genuinely religious people who do not consider themselves that way at all. Nothing special, they say, just what any good neighbor would do. How comforting to know that, despite the distortions of the hellfire preachers, the last judgment is a profoundly human experience, one in which we will be welcomed because of gifts given outright, risks taken and losses sustained for the sake of others. We become aware of our citizenship in the Kingdom through the fruits of love we cannot even remember.

EPILOGUE

Verses 1–2; 3–5

Jesus had now finished all he wanted to say, and he told his disciples, "It will be Passover, as you know, in two days' time, and the Son of Man will be handed over to be crucified."

Then the chief priests and the elders of the people assembled in the palace of the high priest, whose name was Caiaphas, and made plans to arrest Jesus by some trick and have him put to death. They said, however, "It must not be during the festivities; there must be no disturbance among the people."

———— ∞ ————

The beginning has ended as Jesus, aware as only a poet-prophet can be of the subtlest shifts and movements around him, understands that the end has indeed begun. Everyone's destiny is, in fact, at hand, and if some of his followers will sleep as he prays, another will betray their friendship while yet another will deny it. The climax of Jesus' life is reached through the sacrilege of a shattered trust, made doubly shameful by the signal of a kiss from a friend turned informer. Jesus is handed over as so many other good men and women have been in history because of a failure of the kind of friendship that defines his Kingdom.

Judas chooses his destiny by breaking out of the closeness that he somehow cannot abide, through a last-minute attempt to manipulate Jesus into initiating the earthly reign that he craves so deeply. He thinks, in this wild and extravagant plan, that he can bring Jesus to the point where he will have to use his power to save himself, that his act will be the occasion for the grand revelation of Jesus to the world, and that he will then have title to the first place of influence.

Jesus understands Judas's restlessness; he also knows that nothing can prevent a man like Judas from completing the design of his life, that it is cruelly fitting—and matches the mystery of evil that clouds the world—that he should be handed over by somebody he has loved and trusted. So, too, he senses the mood of the city and the uneasiness of Caiaphas, the high priest collaborator with the Romans, who wants to seize Jesus but, anguished by the terms of his deceit, hesitates to do anything while Jerusalem boils over with pilgrims home for Passover.

Caiaphas is a fitting counterpart for Judas. They wear a thousand different faces in the world around us as, for the sake of their careers rather than principle, they made their commitments of self-interest. Made for each other, they can be counted on not to be counted on when the time to stand up for truth or honor arrives. Jesus is hurried into the last days of his life by the kind of men whose weakness has served as the strength of evil throughout the centuries.

Verses 6–13

Jesus was at Bethany in the house of Simon the leper, when a woman came to him with an alabaster jar of the most expensive ointment, and poured it on his head as he was at table. When they saw this, the disciples were indignant. "Why this waste?" they said. "This could have been sold at a high price and the money given to the poor." Jesus noticed this. "Why are you upsetting the woman?" he said to them. "What she has done for me is one of the good works indeed! You have the poor with you always, but you will not always have me. When she poured this ointment on my body, she did it to prepare me for burial. I tell you solemnly, wherever in all the world this Good News is proclaimed, what she has done will be told also, in remembrance of her."

———⋙———

This extraordinary scene has been described and argued about for years by scholars seeking to harmonize various Gospel accounts and to identify the woman who, without a word, anoints Jesus' head with oil. The action is enough in itself for Jesus; seated in the midst of his garrulous disciples, he watches calmly as the woman approaches. While his closest friends draw back indignantly as she raises the jar, Jesus allows the woman to complete the gesture she has begun. Indeed, he seems for the moment lost in the fragrance and the sweet flow of the oil as if, in some way, he acknowledges and accepts the gift with a heart as full as that of the woman who now stands back, making no further claim, but sure that she has done the right thing.

There is a mystery in this loving exchange, a powerful transaction, a communication on an intimate level of the intensity of this woman's love for Jesus. And he loves her in return and proves it by accepting this bittersweet anointing because they both sense the same thing: Jesus is going to complete his work soon, and this action, too poetic for the disciples who are already arguing about its practicality, is the kind of tender gesture that bears the immense weight of feeling that people who love each other share as they face separation from each other. It is as touching as a person's last embrace of a dying spouse, as bittersweet as a farewell to a husband or son off to war, as rich in meaning as any of the thousand half-words and keepsakes by which we bind ourselves to our beloved across the rude joints of separation that fill our lives. It is the right *human* thing to do, it is the *only* human thing to do.

And this, we remember, is a story about human things illumined by Jesus' experience of them. He raises his hands against the protest of his followers and shakes his freshly anointed head. He has come to underscore the infinite tenderness and pain that are inescapably combined in the deepest and closest experiences of love. Cost is the least of considerations here because there is nothing efficient about love, and there is no way it can be understood economically. This is the right gesture, Jesus says, because it is the humanly loving gesture, the free gift of a heart as overflowing as the jar of oil, and this woman will always be remembered for it.

Verses 14–16

Then one of the Twelve, the man called Judas Iscariot, went to the chief priests and said, "What are you prepared to give me if I hand him over to you?" They paid him thirty silver pieces, and from that moment he looked for an opportunity to betray him.

———◅∞▻———

We focus on Judas, shaking his head free of this incomprehensible scene, as he hurries away. Jesus' other followers do not understand love or money, he thinks as he pounds along the great stones toward the temple. And Jesus himself does not seem to understand the opportunity he has at the time of this feast to show the whole world his extraordinary power.

I understand what he can do and I know, as well as the woman knew about the oil, that *this* is the time to bring about a situation in which Jesus will have to follow up on his claims to be the Messiah. Then *I* will be remembered as the one who brought it about, the link between his vision and the practical reality of establishing his Kingdom. The city is crowded with people who will acclaim him instantly if he only steps forward and shows them the powers that he possesses. Now, Judas thinks as he sees the heads of the chief priests bobbing beyond the grillwork of their court, *now* at the Passover is the time to bring this about!

Verses 17–19

Now on the first day of Unleavened Bread the disciples came to Jesus to say, "Where do you want us to make the preparations for you to eat the passover?" "Go to so-and-so in the city," he replied, "and say to him, 'The Master says: My time is near. It is at your house that I am keeping Passover with my disciples.' " The disciples did what Jesus told them and prepared the passover.

Verses 20–25

When evening came he was at table with the twelve disciples. And while they were eating he said, "I tell you solemnly, one of you is about to betray me." They were greatly distressed and started asking him in turn, "Not I, Lord, surely?" He answered, "Someone, who has dipped his hand into the dish with me, will betray me. The Son of Man is going to his fate, as the scriptures say he will, but alas for that man by whom the Son of Man is betrayed! Better for that man if he had never been born!" Judas, who was to betray him, asked in his turn, "Not I, Rabbi, surely?" "They are your own words," answered Jesus.

Almost every verse in this section bears an aura of the mystery of friendship and love that is the cornerstone of Jesus' spiritual Kingdom. For we begin with his closest friends asking where they will be together for the Passover meal, and we find that another friend has already made his house available. He will understand when the disciples pass Jesus' codeword-like message to him. It is a story of friends gathering at a table under a roof of welcome, a celebration of the faith and trust through which people become a family together. This is set against the starkness of the betrayal of Jesus and his community by one of its own members.

Jesus does not need to see into the future to sense what is happening in Judas's heart. He observes the slightest changes in this now restless disciple's attitude and behavior. Judas, his dream of forcing Jesus into the position of establishing a great Kingdom flashing crazily in his imagination, goes through the motions, his preoccupation unnoticed by the other disciples. They are caught up in the feast and are not good at noticing such things anyway. Judas avoids Jesus' glance. Can he read my mind? Does he know what I am thinking? Judas's hand shakes slightly as he dips it in the bowl with the others.

Jesus cannot mistake the tainted mood of the room. He looks at his friends who grow suddenly attentive. One of them will betray him, he says evenly, but this is beyond their imagining. No man could have traveled so far with Jesus into this Kingdom of trust with a heart set on destroying him. Beside themselves, they plead for forgiveness as Jesus' eyes shift gradually around the small circle of men. He pauses and speaks of the destiny that lies at the end of the path of betrayal. Then he looks deeply into the eyes of Judas. Jesus can feel his plan for power, a lizard thrashing inside Judas's soul.

Judas cannot help himself. Like every deceiver in history he reveals himself in his question, the desperate inquiry that rises up out of his unconscious to proclaim the truth of his betrayal even as his consciousness defends against it. "It isn't I, is it?" he asks anxiously, the betrayer betraying himself by inserting a negative that has no meaning in unconscious communication. Jesus understands this very well. Just as he has picked up Judas's jumbled inner conflict, so now he hears his public admission. He does not have to accuse him, for Judas has in every way made his intentions clear. This exchange takes only a few seconds and the other disciples do not pick up its significance. Jesus answers softly, speaking to Judas's heart. "They are your own words." ("It is you who have said it.")

Verses 26–30

Now as they were eating, Jesus took some bread, and when he had said the blessing he broke it and gave it to the disciples. "Take it and eat"; he said, "this is my body." Then he took a cup, and when he had returned thanks he gave it to them. "Drink all of you from this," he said, "for this is my blood, the blood of the covenant, which is to be poured out for many for the forgiveness of sins. From now on, I tell you, I shall not drink wine until the day I drink the new wine with you in the kingdom of my Father."

After psalms had been sung they left for the Mount of Olives.

We sit together at the feast of Passover which is here transformed by Jesus into the Eucharist of his new Kingdom. We are familiar with the preparation for Passover, the cleansing of the house of leaven to commemorate the hurried flight of deliverance from Egypt where the yeast was left behind, the purchase and sacrifice of the lamb whose blood is sprinkled on the doorposts so that the avenging angel would pass over the homes of the Jews. These are rings that lie deep in the heart of the ancient tree of salvation history that is in full bloom on this spring evening.

What strikes us is Jesus' directness, his sureness about his words and movements. There is nothing tentative to his placing himself at the center of this now fulfilled celebration of Israel's freedom from slavery. Jesus is the offering, it is his blood that saves us from sins rather than stays the blow of the angel. The waiting, Jesus tells us, is over, and the longing of all mankind is answered in my life and death. This is what makes you free now, this is what you will remember.

The mystery of the Eucharist speaks on its own to us. We must let it invade the pores of our being and hold off the rational analysis or the comparison with other Gospels that may interfere with this. And this mystery of mysteries, this extraordinary event that breaks the hold of time and provides the food that unites and nourishes us, does speak to our depths if we allow it to do this.

In the silence of our contemplation we recognize that the Eucharist is a mystery of separation in which all our separations and losses are understood and reconciled. Life may be best understood as a paradoxical feast in which we draw close together—in which, in other words, we learn of human love and, through that, receive our best revelation of God's love—only as we accept the seemingly contradictory and painful condition of our separateness. Togetherness, the easy love sought through tricks as treacherous as those of the Pharisees, the promises about how love can be trapped and taken captive: all these fall short of the tragic grandeur of the real love symbolized in the Eucharist. It is *the* mystery in which we live and move and have our being, and separation is the sharp and hazardous edge that we feel in every relationship of any depth.

Without separation no love possesses enough density to make an impression or to be remembered or to make any difference in people's lives. People who love each other are always letting each other go: parents must surrender their children to life, the family flowers and dies or fails of its purpose; husbands and wives never merge protoplasmically but, instead, reach continually across that filament of separation that is the medium of their love; men and women are forever giving up something of themselves for the sake of real love, emptying themselves and being refilled, accepting separation and loss as the very condition of their being filled and healed. No relationship of love or trust succeeds except it embrace this mysterious yielding up of the self as integral to its experience.

This Kingdom of relationships is here seen in miniature as friends gather around the table and as Jesus commits himself to take on sin and death, to transcend these most threatening instruments of separation, and to bring back the prize of life for all genuine lovers. We can only allow this to sink into our consciousness, to let its redeeming truth work its way through us as leaven in the dough, for we discover in the separation of the body and blood of Jesus the meaning of our lives. That is why Jesus faces his death speaking of the coming of His Kingdom and singing psalms of praise into the night.

Verses 31–35

Then Jesus said to them, "You will all lose faith in me this night, for the scripture says: *I shall strike the shepherd and the sheep of the flock will be scattered*, but after my resurrection I shall go before you to Galilee." At this, Peter said, "Though all lose faith in you, I will never lose faith." Jesus answered him, "I tell you solemnly, this very night, before the cock crows, you will have disowned me three times." Peter said to him, "Even if I have to die with you, I will never disown you." And all the disciples said the same.

Verses 36–46

Then Jesus came with them to a small estate called Gethsemane; and he said to his disciples, "Stay here while I go over there to pray." He took Peter and the two sons of Zebedee with him. And sadness came over him, and great distress. Then he said to them, "My soul is sorrowful to the point of death. Wait here and keep awake with me." And going on a little further he fell on his face and prayed. "My Father," he said, "if it is possible, let this cup pass me by. Nevertheless, let it be as you, not I, would have it." He came back to the disciples and found them sleeping, and he said to Peter, "So you had not the strength to keep awake with me one hour? You should be awake, and praying not to be put to the test. The spirit is willing, but the flesh is weak." Again, a second time, he went away and prayed: "My Father," he said, "if this cup cannot pass by without my drinking it, your will be done!" And he came back again and found them sleeping, their eyes were so heavy. Leaving them there, he went away again and prayed for the third time, repeating the same words. Then he came back to the disciples and said to them, "You can sleep on now and take your rest. Now the hour has come when the Son of Man is to be betrayed into the hands of sinners. Get up! Let us go! My betrayer is already close at hand."

Jesus looks at the men who have just sung the Hallel, the psalms of praise with him. They are exhilarated, profoundly moved by their Eucharistic celebration, certain that Jesus, despite his ominous words, will launch his Kingdom definitively in the festival city that seems to breathe with religious awareness on this mild evening.

Your ability to remain loyal to me, Jesus says softly, will be tested this very night. We are about to taste the first bitter sip of the cup of separation. This will strain your belief in me, as this mystery does for all men and women. Jesus tells them a truth too deep for them to bear, and Peter, eager, bear-like, certain of his strength, steps forward, claiming huskily that he will stick by Jesus no matter what happens.

Jesus sees as deeply into Peter as he has seen into Judas. Peter and the others will taste separation in a way they do not expect, they will feel it within themselves as their spirits sag under the impact of the night's occurrences. He smiles at their pledges of friendship but he knows the price they will finally have to pay to separate themselves from an imagined kingdom of glory and triumph. They will be a long time becoming wise in spiritual things. He gestures for them to follow him, aware of their ignorant eagerness, of their untried willingness, of their generous but profoundly human hearts. Jesus needs their companionship, he needs the strength that friends supply, as he enters Gethsemane to pray.

And here, as swift in its stroke as a scythe, we find Jesus crossing the border into the most savage and desolate of human experiences. Profoundly aware of the world around him, aware even that his well-meaning friends do not fully understand what he is talking about, Jesus feels suddenly the full weight of his isolation. He is a Messiah for a Kingdom that cannot be seen. His closest followers are looking the other way and one of them, pursuing a crazed design of his own, lends himself to those who wish to destroy his work and do away with him.

Jesus looks at Peter and the sons of Zebedee. They have argued about their places in the Kingdom, they have pledged to stay with him, but, in the feeling that streaks a fissure in his heart, he knows that they have not yet grasped the point, that they are already prey to their distractions, that in this terrible moment he will feel utterly alone. He falls into that deep and muddy trench of the spirit in which he must wrestle, as Jacob once did with the angel, with the work whose nature comes clearer to him as he loses himself in prayer. Jesus feels at a distance from everyone, alone in agonized communion with the Father, lonely for the affection of his friends. He enters more deeply each time he returns to prayer into the mystery of separation which runs like a royal highway through his Kingdom. It is only as he tastes the dregs of abandonment and takes the true measure of his journey to the uttermost provinces of spiritual devastation that he can conquer and redeem the long, sad experience of all mankind.

Jesus must battle with the desolating angel as his disciples, awash in dreams of glory, sleep on, outside his struggle, unable as yet to comprehend it, innocent as drowsy children of the decisive hour—that of a separation so radical that they will despair of seeing him again—arriving now for all of them. And Judas, as Jesus can sense, is moving closer to him at this very moment.

Verses 47–56

He was still speaking when Judas, one of the Twelve, appeared, and with him a large number of men armed with swords and clubs, sent by the chief priests and elders of the people. Now the traitor had arranged a sign with them. "The one I kiss," he had said, "he is the man. Take him in charge." So he went straight up to Jesus and said, "Greetings, Rabbi," and kissed him. Jesus said to him, "My friend, do what you are here for." Then they came forward, seized Jesus and took him in charge. At that, one of the followers of Jesus grasped his sword and drew it; he struck out at the high priest's servant, and cut off his ear. Jesus then said, "Put your sword back, for all who draw the sword will die by the sword. Or do you think that I cannot appeal to my Father who would promptly send more than twelve legions of angels to my defense? But then, how would the scriptures be fulfilled that say this is the way it must be?" It was at this time that Jesus said to the crowds, "Am I a brigand, that you had to set out to capture me with swords and clubs? I sat teaching in the Temple day after day and you never laid hands on me." Now all this happened to fulfill the prophecies in scripture. Then all the disciples deserted him and ran away.

———⦾———

Judas heads into the garden, more cunning in his own way than his just waking friends: for he, at least, understands the high stakes of the game he is playing. The darkness is filled with the noise of the moving crowd —its members, sniffing danger and excitement, having been transformed dangerously by the possibilities of the evening. Judas makes his way directly to Jesus, who waits for his embrace as he waited for the woman to anoint his head with oil.

Madness and evil enfold each other like the many-limbed gods of paganism, for there is calculation in Judas's move. Why does Jesus need to be pointed out to these people who have seen him teaching daily in the temple? It is part of Judas's strategy not only to identify Jesus but, by his action, to offer Jesus, as the tempter in the cave once did, another chance to claim the kingdoms of earth. Judas puts his arms around Jesus and kisses him. Here, he suggests with his glance, here is the moment you need, Rabbi, seize it as I know you can and confound the crowds with a wonder. You will forgive and embrace me as the one who has made this moment possible. He kisses Jesus again. Surely, Rabbi, you will snatch this moment. Now, now, for a kingdom such as the world has never seen . . .

Jesus looks into Judas's twitching face. Do what you came here for, he says firmly as he pulls away from the stunned betrayer. Judas gapes at Jesus as the guards step forward to arrest him. Judas's insane vision that Jesus could be provoked in one last, well-mounted moment is shattered as he is shoved aside. The cry of a wounded guard fills his ears as Judas sees clearly what he has been blind to until he was roughly separated from Jesus. He has not manipulated Jesus into a show of cosmic power, but into a kind of spiritual authority that Judas does not understand. Used by those he would use, he is nobody, just one of the crowd, a man lost who can only stumble awkwardly as the crowds pull Jesus away and his own disciples flee under a blood-filled moon into the night.

Verses 57–68

The men who had arrested Jesus led him off to Caiaphas the high priest, where the scribes and the elders were assembled. Peter followed him at a distance, and when he reached the high priest's palace, he went in and sat down with the attendants to see what the end would be.

The chief priests and the whole Sanhedrin were looking for evidence against Jesus, however false, on which they might pass the death sentence. But they could not find any, though several lying witnesses came forward. Eventually two stepped forward and made a statement, "This man said, 'I have power to destroy the Temple of God and in three days build it up.'" The high priest then stood up and said to him, "Have you no answer to that? What is this evidence these men are bringing against you?" But Jesus was silent. And the high priest said to him, "I put you on oath by the living God to tell us if you are the

Christ, the Son of God." "The words are your own," answered Jesus. "Moreover, I tell you that from this time onward you will see the *Son of Man seated at the right hand of the Power and coming on the clouds of heaven.*" At this, the high priest tore his clothes and said, "He has blasphemed. What need of witnesses have we now? There! You have just heard the blasphemy. What is your opinion?" They answered, "He deserves to die."

Then they spat in his face and hit him with their fists; others said as they struck him, "Play the prophet, Christ! Who hit you then?"

Verses 69–75

Meanwhile Peter was sitting outside in the courtyard, and a servant girl came up to him and said, "You too were with Jesus the Galilean." But he denied it in front of them all. "I do not know what you are talking about," he said. When he went out to the gateway another servant girl saw him and said to the people there, "This man was with Jesus the Nazarene." And again, with an oath, he denied it, "I do not know the man." A little later the bystanders came up and said to Peter, "You are one of them for sure! Why, your accent gives you away." Then he started calling down curses on himself and swearing, "I do not know the man." At that moment the cock crew, and Peter remembered what Jesus had said, "Before the cock crows you will have disowned me three times." And he went outside and wept bitterly.

———————∞———————

Peter hurries through the night, catching his breath as he contemplates the foundered wreckage of the Kingdom that, just a few hours before, seemed as secure as a fishermen's fleet sailing for home. The sounds of the crowds chanting their welcomes to Jesus a few days ago have turned into the taunting of bullies as Jesus—Peter cannot really make him out—is proffered by the crowd like a present to the high priest Caiaphas. Peter waits a moment, then enters the residence, sitting among the guards as the chief priests noisily summon what witnesses they can against Jesus.

This is a blur, distant sound and fury. The stunned Peter watches Jesus as, after the arguing about the contradictory testimony dies down, the chief priest steps toward him. Caiaphas studies this prophet who has caused so much trouble. He has questioned many prisoners. What, he asks, confident of his powers, does Jesus have to say about these charges that he has claimed to be able to destroy the temple and rebuild it in three days?

Caiaphas seems to be the captive of the silent prisoner. He will make the issue plain enough so that everyone will understand what this man has been claiming. Like Judas's, the question that Caiaphas asks is an affirmation of what he fears, and what he must stamp out if he is to preserve his good favor with Rome. People speak of Caiaphas as a survivor, a wily man who has been able to hold his post much longer than many of his predecessors. The fullness of his consciousness speaks for him as he demands that Jesus tell him if he is the Messiah, the Son of God. The question form does not change the validation that the chief priest's unconscious self has given to Jesus as Messiah. "It is you who say it," Jesus replies, adding a prophecy about the coming manifestation of his power.

Caiaphas is as angry at himself as he is with Jesus. He has given this prophet an opportunity to twist his own statement and to threaten him with his power. There is no need for anything further, he cries, tearing at his robes in mock horror at the blasphemy. Caiaphas must make short work of this calm, unsettling man. What do the people want, he asks, knowing that a crowd, possessed by a seething spirit that stirs to life as it draws itself together, always wants blood, that in its savage soul it will do what none of its members would do individually. The beast of the crowd surges forward with shaming words and cowards' blows as it closes its spittle-covered jaws on Jesus.

The world seems ended for Peter as he sits shivering in the now subdued courtyard. The big man cannot sort out what has happened. He had seen the power of Jesus, had seen it again in the garden of his capture when Jesus healed the soldier whom Peter himself had wounded. What has happened to all the promises and expectations, to that great world in which Peter would fill such a glorious role? Had not Jesus promised that he would be one of the judges of the tribes of Israel?

He barely sees the questioner, this young servant girl who accuses him of having been with the Galilean. Peter grunts a denial as the people moving through the yard pause and listen curiously to him. He feels the pressure of their skeptical gazes, rises and hurries to the gate.

Another servant girl looks suspiciously at him. Yes, yes, you were with him, she says mockingly. Peter cannot escape these women who have so stirred the bystanders' interest in him. They are coalescing into a crowd, forming a semicircle around him. Yes, they saw him, yes, of course you were with him. You give yourself away with your accent!

Peter pulls farther away, and we move with him as he curses the idea that he has ever known Jesus. All over, just like that, all those years, those dreams and promises. Peter too has tasted this gagging brew of separation. Everything he had gained through his friendship with Jesus has been torn cruelly away from him. There is only emptiness now and perhaps, with luck, a chance still to get away.

And as the cock crows against the distant rim of dawn, Peter suddenly sees himself as he is, a betrayer of his friend as much as and more than Judas, a failure as a companion in those long hours of prayer in the garden, and a coward in his soul in this courtyard ablaze with the eyes of accusers. In an instant he sees the emptiness of his bluff, boasting self and begins, choking with sobs, to make his way, through a cleft of sorrow, back into the Kingdom.

CHAPTER 27

Verses 1–2

When morning came, all the chief priests and the elders of the people met in council to bring about the death of Jesus. They had him bound, and led him away to hand him over to Pilate the governor.

Verses 3–10

When he found that Jesus had been condemned, Judas his betrayer was filled with remorse and took the thirty silver pieces back to the chief priests and elders. "I have sinned," he said; "I have betrayed innocent blood." "What is that to us?" they replied. "That is your concern." And flinging down the silver pieces in the sanctuary he made off, and went and hanged himself. The chief priests picked up the silver pieces and said, "It is against the Law to put this into the treasury; it is blood money." So they discussed the matter and bought the potter's field with it as a graveyard for foreigners, and this is why the field is called the Field of Blood today. The words of the prophet Jeremiah were then fulfilled: *And they took the thirty silver pieces, the sum at which the precious One was priced by the children of Israel, and they gave them for the potter's field, just as the Lord directed me.*

Judas watches as Jesus, made more powerless by the thongs of his binding, is led away to the Roman governor, Pilate, for the next step in fashioning the death sentence on which the chief priests and their henchmen have decided. They can leave nothing to chance now. Crowds must be coached, guards must be bribed, the straight ways of Jesus' truth must be forced out of shape, for this is a day on which everyone's destiny takes final shape. Peter will weep for Jesus, Judas will groan for himself, and Pilate will pragmatically wash his hands while the men who followed Jesus will hang back and the women who love him will see him to his death.

As the light spreads across the land the meaning of Jesus' work, the central thrust of his teaching, can be seen more clearly. He has come to bring illumination to the darkness, to speak for the truth in a world bewildered by the distortions by which it chooses to live. Jesus preaches as he lives, openly and without affectation, a man who is seen as dangerous because he sees and describes men and events with an unshakable bias toward truth. His trial is built on testimony that is made to appear true by leaders of a religion that is a facade for their own corrupt uses of power.

Jesus has challenged the demon of hypocrisy that breathes smokily in every fix and crooked deal, in every lie and deception, in each false word spoken and every pretended act of fidelity, in all contrived religious postures and insincere prayer. Jesus has shaken the foundations of a temple in which the truth was long ago made into the devil's own grinding mill of falsehood. Jesus, in himself and in his faith, is too healthy for this world: he must be destroyed, but only after he is first disfigured, raised up for the world's derision. The tree of Jesus' passion and death grows out of that murky chasm that splits truth from falsehood in the world. Jesus conquers this divisive power of sin by entering the mystery of separation that is his own death.

Judas can only see the void. He cannot weep, he can only attempt to take back what he has done, to recant, to sweep the desert sands over his betrayer's footprints. His desperate dream now is to put the appearance of order back into the universe by returning the silver to the chief priests, to undo what is irrevocably done. I have, he tells them urgently, delivered up an innocent man. This is no time for truth, their harsh glances say, your problem has nothing to do with us.

Now the dry-throated Judas understands that there is no way to restore the world; he has helped shatter its wholeness for good. The shower of coins scatters and rolls on the temple floor as he turns toward the darkness of his own death. The elders nod as they retrieve the coins. Judas is gone from their thoughts as soon as he is gone from their sight. But this silver, that is another matter, there must be a distinction of the law by which we can retain it. And so the price of lies is recalculated by men wise in the ways of distortion. They will purchase an unclean field in which to bury unclean strangers, a field to soak up the blood of all the lies of history.

Verses 11–19

Jesus, then, was brought before the governor, and the governor put to him this question, "Are you the king of the Jews?" Jesus replied, "It is you who say it." But when he was accused by the chief priests and the elders he refused to answer at all. Pilate then said to him, "Do you not hear how many charges they have brought against you?" But to the governor's complete amazement, he offered no reply to any of the charges.

At festival time it was the governor's practice to release a prisoner for the people, anyone they chose. Now there was at that time a notorious prisoner whose name was Barabbas. So when the crowd gathered, Pilate said to them, "Which do you want me to release for you: Barabbas, or Jesus who is called Christ?" For Pilate knew it was out of jealousy that they had handed him over.

Now as he was seated in the chair of judgment, his wife sent him a message, "Have nothing to do with that man; I have been upset all day by a dream I had about him."

Verses 20–26

The chief priests and the elders, however, had persuaded the crowd to demand the release of Barabbas and the execution of Jesus. So when the governor spoke and asked them, "Which of the two do you want me to release for you?" they said, "Barabbas." "But in that case," Pilate said to them, "what am I to do with Jesus who is called Christ?" They all said, "Let him be crucified!" "Why?" he asked. "What harm has he done?" But they shouted all the louder, "Let him be crucified!" Then Pilate saw that he was making no impression, that in fact a riot was imminent. So he took some water, washed his hands in front of the crowd and said, "I am innocent of this man's blood. It is your concern." And the people to a man, shouted back, "His blood be on us and on our children!" Then he released Barabbas for them. He ordered Jesus to be first scourged and then handed over to be crucified.

It is as if Jesus, roped roughly with lies, so burns with the power of truth that he lights up the shadowed figures enlisted in the cause of convicting him falsely. Peter has seen himself as anything but strong, Judas has glimpsed the blind maze of his own soul, and now the urbane and uncertain Pilate must confront the truth about himself. The intensity of Jesus' personality affects the deepest levels of the souls of the men and women who now circle around him. Pilate's wife watches from a distance and pulls back; this man is not like the ruffians and lawbreakers usually brought before her husband. She paces as if in a dream, shakes her head to clear it of the impression this good man has made on her. She returns to see her husband cocking his head skeptically at Jesus.

Pilate is uncomfortable with this man who, held by others, seems strangely free. The procurator feels drawn into his claims to be the King of the Jews. If you won't say anything about yourself, what of these charges? Pilate, holding the scroll of charges, blinks expectantly. The accusations seem weak, ill-founded, not well supported. Surely, Jesus can respond to this indictment. It seems to smell of the jealousy that inspired those who drew it up. Pilate shifts position, lets the scroll slip into his lap. Silence is the last thing he anticipated from this prophet. Yet the silence is haunting, disquieting, filled with more truth than the crowd's shouts that he should release the thief Barabbas instead of the obviously innocent Jesus.

Pilate glances at a message from his wife, looks up at Jesus, searches himself for some way to resolve the situation. His skill at handling just such pesky provincial difficulties has won him the confidence of Rome. Why can't he settle this one? There is *always* a way to solve such problems; but he needs cooperation from the accused, some word of defense he can seize on so that he can use a technicality against the Pharisaic masters of technicalities. The crowd, incited by the chief priest, is growing noisier, its members are clamoring for Jesus. It is the moment in which Pilate, filled with apprehension and foreboding, must confront the inventory of his own character, must face, if he can, the design in the tiles that he has been laying down, judgment by judgment, for a lifetime.

The people demand Barabbas from the now visibly anxious procurator. And their innocent Messiah, what of him? Crucify him, the shouts roll back, crucify him. These people are not only impossible, they are becoming dangerous. And Pilate, stationed as far on the fringes of the empire as he can tolerate, cannot allow that to happen. It is a day for truths to emerge, and the truth about Pilate is discovered in his life of compromise, in his willingness, when the chips are down, to save himself by doing what he must do. He is a politician and he must live by the versions of truth that work.

It is a day filled with decisions made, in the perverse strategies of mistruth, to look good on the surface, their wickedness transformed into a blessing by words, their deadliness purified by the water tumbling over Pilate's hands. It is a triumphant high noon for the Father of Lies.

Verses 27–31

The governor's soldiers took Jesus with them into the Praetorium and collected the whole cohort around him. Then they stripped him and made him wear a scarlet cloak, and having twisted some thorns into a crown they put this on his head and placed a reed in his right hand. To make fun of him they knelt to him saying, "Hail, king of the Jews!" And they spat on him and took the reed and struck him on the head with it. And when they had finished making fun of him, they took off the cloak and dressed him in his own clothes and led him away to crucify him.

Verses 32–34

On their way out, they came across a man from Cyrene, Simon by name, and enlisted him to carry his cross. When they had reached a place called Golgotha, that is, the place of the skull, they gave him wine to drink mixed with gall, which he tasted but refused to drink.

We follow as cautiously as Peter did last evening, for we sense the power that radiates from the truthful Jesus as he is pushed forward into the praetorium. If the demon's main work is deception, the mockery now heaped on Jesus ironically authenticates his Kingship of the universe. Jesus is never more transcendentally king than in his acceptance of this debasement and ridicule, for he feels and understands the fragility and smallness of the men who taunt him, these poor, half-grown men who will not even have a thought tomorrow about the man they shame tonight. Thinking to make a fool of him they make fools only of themselves, revealing their weakness in the face of his strength. Jesus knows that they are victims of the darkness that is unable to stand the light, that, strangers to love, they bind their miserable lives together out of fear. He cannot be overcome by a world whose love of the easy way of lies he understands so well.

The question, as it has been for Peter and Pilate, is how much of our own truth we comprehend and how well we live by it. Have we added or subtracted to the sum total of truth? Or have we, by every finely rationalized compromise, by every exception claimed for ourselves, somehow failed the truth, eaten away at its underpinnings, made it weaker, less recognizable, less available as the binding fundament of the universe? Is the derisive praetorium laughter louder in this very moment, is it just one of the imbalances in the cosmos to which we have contributed because we have not loved the truth enough?

We cannot stand outside the double mystery of this day, that of the apparent victory of falsehood and that of the separation of the body and blood of Jesus, for they are intimately related in all of our lives. The more we try to live by truth, the more we encounter the unexpected demands of separation—the thousand small ways in which we must give up ourselves in order to lead loving lives. The truth makes us free because it affords us a demanding but ultimately safe passage into the Kingdom of loving relationships over which Jesus reigns. Lies lock us on the outside because no relationship with either God or other persons can be successfully rooted in distortion. The unforgivable sin remains hypocrisy—to live by appearances—because it hopelessly clogs the conduits of the heart. Strangers to truth never really love anybody.

Simon of Cyrene waits in the crowd assembling along the route of crucifixion, little suspecting that truth will take hold of him this very day. He is a freer man for picking up the crossbar of Jesus, not because the wood is miraculous but because it is so undeniably real, because its rough surface draws him into the aura of truth that rises from the intensity of Jesus' giving himself over so unreservedly to his sufferings. The Cyrenian senses confusedly that, in pilgrimage to the place of skulls with Jesus, he walks in a powerful field of truth.

There is a compelling wholeness to Jesus' embrace of his death. He vanquishes death by entering its heart, tasting it as it is, by feeling keenly throughout his being the full range of pain the prince of lies has inflicted on the world. Jesus, therefore, will not take the drugged wine as he is raised above the crowd. He battles death, purifying it of deceit through his own consciousness of it, setting its cowardly ghosts to flight by his courage. Death's corrosive falseness is drained from it as cancer might be leached out of a bone, to be absorbed and cleansed through the suffering and death of Jesus. He breaks death's back and sets us free. The truth of Jesus, hanging under a placard deriding his kingship, becomes clear at last.

Verses 35–44

When they had finished crucifying him they shared out his clothing by casting lots, and then sat down and stayed there keeping guard over him.

Above his head was placed the charge against him; it read: "This is Jesus, the King of the Jews." At the same time two robbers were crucified with him, one on the right and one on the left.

The passers-by jeered at him; they shook their heads and said, "So you would destroy the Temple and rebuild it in three days! Then save yourself! If you are God's son, come down from the cross!" The chief priests with the scribes and elders mocked him in the same way. "He saved others," they said, "he cannot save himself. He is the king of Israel; let him come down from the cross now, and we will believe in him. He puts his trust in God; now let God rescue him if he wants him. For he did say, 'I am the son of God.' " Even the robbers who were crucified with him taunted him in the same way.

Verses 45–50

From the sixth hour there was darkness over all the land until the ninth hour. And about the ninth hour, Jesus cried out in a loud voice, "Eli, Eli, lama sabachthani?" that is, *"My God, my God, why have you deserted me?"* When some of those who stood there heard this, they said, "The man is calling on Elijah," and one of them quickly ran to get a sponge which he dipped in vinegar and, putting it on a reed, gave it him to drink. "Wait!" said the rest of them, "and see if Elijah will come to save him." But Jesus, again crying out in a loud voice, yielded up his spirit.

———————◦◦◦———————

Jesus completes this Eucharist through enduring and giving meaning to the rift of separation that runs, sometimes a hairline crack and sometimes a ragged gash, through all human experience. He journeys on the cross to the far reaches of loneliness, feeling in himself a concentration of the pain of all generations, taking our woe into his own outstretched hands and shaping it with meaning, breaking forever the deadman's grip of hypocrisy on the human soul. Jesus drinks the cup of all our sorrow, taking away its killing power through feeling it himself.

He is separated from his family, for many of them had doubted him. He is separated from his closest disciples, for one betrayed him out of a dream of power, and the others scattered out of the reality of fear. The people who waved branches of welcome just a few days ago now stand below him as if on a lime-scalded shore, within shouting distance far enough to claim later that they had nothing to do with his death, close enough to challenge him to display one last wonder, to give in to the temptation to dazzle the world into submission by freeing himself from the cross. Give him something to drink. No, wait, he's calling on Elijah. Wait, let us see if Elijah comes to save him . . .

There is nothing that Jesus does not understand about the pain that hangs like the darkening sky over the valley of history. Jesus is making it sacred through his death, feeling throughout his being every separation and loss, everything that will seem incomplete or wrong, the suddenness and the wrongness of the separations wrought by fate, the families shattered, the children parted from their mothers and fathers, the gulfs of suffering brought on by wars and their evil harvests of separations of all kinds, the people dispersed like seeds in the wind, hearts broken, wounds of the spirit that will not close, all the riven experience of every man, woman, and child down through all the generations of time.

As his own clothing is divided, as he groans in a spasm of feeling cut off from every source of comfort, Jesus forces the mined-out universe of human suffering, the sulphur-and-ash pain of our souls, to be plunged into the renewing waters of his own soul. Prisoner of pain, he imprisons it forever through his own sacrifice. No longer will it be meaningless, the harsh jest and hollow laugh of creation, for it is transformed permanently in the Eucharist Jesus now celebrates. Nothing is lost and everything is found in this death that defeats death to break open a source of unending life, in this suffering that brings healing to all human brokenness. Jesus takes us all with him as he tears away the veil of death once and for all.

Verses 51–56

At that, the veil of the Temple was torn in two from top to bottom; the earth quaked; the rocks were split; the tombs opened and the bodies of many holy men rose from the dead, and these, after his resurrection, came out of the tombs, entered the Holy City and appeared to a number of people. Meanwhile the centurion, together with the others guarding Jesus, had seen the earthquake and all that was taking place, and they were terrified and said, "In truth this was a son of God."

And many women were there, watching from a distance, the same women who had followed Jesus from Galilee and looked after him. Among them were Mary of Magdala, Mary the mother of James and Joseph, and the mother of Zebedee's sons.

Verses 57–61

When it was evening, there came a rich man of Arimathaea, called Joseph, who had himself become a disciple of Jesus. This man went to Pilate and asked for the body of Jesus. Pilate thereupon ordered it to be handed over. So Joseph took the body, wrapped it in a clean shroud and put it in his own new tomb which he had hewn out of the rock. He then rolled a large stone across the entrance of the tomb and went away. Now Mary of Magdala and the other Mary were there, sitting opposite the sepulcher.

Verses 62–66

The next day, the one following the Day of Preparation, the chief priests and the Pharisees called at Pilate's residence. "Sir," they said, "we have recalled that that impostor while he was still alive made the claim, 'After three days I will rise.' You should issue an order having the

257

tomb kept under surveillance until the third day. Otherwise his disciples may go and steal him and tell the people, 'He has been raised from the dead!' This final imposture would be worse than the first." Pilate told them, "You have a guard. Go and secure the tomb as best you can." So they went and kept it under surveillance of the guard, after fixing a seal to the stone. (NAB)

Now we enter the language of the dream again, of symbols that roll out of the narrative like the broken boulders of Matthew's imagery. Exhausted by memory, Matthew offers an apocalyptic scene to join imaginatively the resurrection of Christ with his death. Everything is made new as creation breaks open and everyone and everything that was in bondage to death is set gloriously free. Matthew sings a hymn to the achievement of Jesus, reminding us, from his end-of-the-century viewpoint, that, just as at the desolate place of skulls, the Gentiles will recognize that Jesus is the Son of God.

It is as if the telling of the tale this one last time, this great effort to balance its facts and its symbols, and then entrust it to the still young Church, has worn Matthew out. He must, however, get in these last incidents, for they complete the story, and, like hard-rubbed silver coins, they gleam in the lowering darkness. Yes, Matthew says to the eager young men helping him, we must remember the women because they were faithful to Jesus while we men were not. Everyone must know that they would not leave or shield their eyes, that they knew the full measure of pain and loss, and that they did not desert Jesus, even after his body, lovingly bathed and wrapped in the softest linen, was laid in the gouge of rock that belonged to Joseph.

The women remain there in that awful silence after the great stone is pushed thunderously and sadly into place. They remain near Jesus during that time when falsehood feasts on itself again as the Pharisees attempt to manipulate the appearances of history once more. Pilate regards them coldly. Jesus alive was problem enough, he will not deal with him dead. Jesus, whoever he was, is their business now.

Matthew rolls these last bright stones, their facets catching the final fixed truths of the central characters of his narrative, the fearful men and the faithful women, the good friend Joseph, the Pharisees bent under their crusted robes and their hypocrisy, and Pilate washing his hands forever of the blood of Jesus. Yes, Matthew says, you could see us all plainly in that last interlude before the Sabbath ended and history had its new start.

CHAPTER 28

Verses 1–7

After the sabbath, and toward dawn on the first day of the week, Mary of Magdala and the other Mary went to visit the sepulcher. And all at once there was a violent earthquake, for the angel of the Lord, descending from heaven, came and rolled away the stone and sat on it. His face was like lightning, his robe white as snow. The guards were so shaken, so frightened of him, that they were like dead men. But the angel spoke; and he said to the women, "There is no need for you to be afraid. I know you are looking for Jesus, who was crucified. He is not here, for he has risen, as he said he would. Come and see the piace where he lay,·then go quickly and tell his disciples, 'He has risen from the dead and now he is going before you to Galilee; it is there you will see him.' Now I have told you."

Verses 8–10

Filled with awe and great joy the women came quickly away from the tomb and ran to tell the disciples.

And there, coming to meet them, was Jesus. "Greetings," he said. And the women came up to him and, falling down before him, clasped his feet. Then Jesus said to them, "Do not be afraid; go and tell my brothers that they must leave for Galilee; they will see me there."

Verses 11–15

While they were on their way, some of the guards went off into the city to tell the chief priests all that had happened. These held a meeting with the elders and, after some discussion, handed a considerable sum of money to the soldiers with these instructions, "This is what you must say, 'His disciples came during the night and stole him away while we were asleep.' And should the governor come to hear of this, we undertake to put things right with him ourselves and to see that you do not get into trouble." The soldiers took the money and carried out their instructions, and to this day that is the story among the Jews.

Verses 16–20

Meanwhile the eleven disciples set out for Galilee, to the mountain where Jesus had arranged to meet them. When they saw him they fell down before him, though some hesitated. Jesus came up and spoke to them. He said, "All authority in heaven and on earth has been given to me. Go, therefore, make disciples of all the nations; baptize them in the name of the Father and of the Son and of the Holy Spirit, and teach them to observe all the commands I gave you. And know that I am with you always; yes, to the end of time."

———— ∽ ————

The landscape of the dream once more floats about us. What other language could Matthew use to describe this event which made so much difference and reveals as unchanged so many of the people we have been living so closely with in this long meditation? These paragraphs, as familiar as the long litany of names with which Matthew began, are, nonetheless, profoundly human, for they resound with the joy of resurrection, with that deep peace of reunion, with that rich sense of friends coming together again that holds the gift of love safe against the ravages of pain and time. Resurrection is more than survival, just as the truth is more than the absence of lies.

We have passed through death and live in a new way, with a better sense that the Kingdom of Jesus is one of truth and love that spreads across the world not by force, harangue, or scolding, or by any of the crafts of manipulation characteristic of and dear to Pharisaic forms of religion. This Kingdom lives, as a family does, in and through its members. It responds not to worldly temptations to power but to human needs for service. Wherever we find that kind of Church, we discover the unmistakable Kingdom of Jesus.

It is a clear morning in the spring and we stand at the edge of the world together. It is a moment to inhabit silently, hand in hand, at peace in our understanding that nothing of loss of falsehood or fear can rob us of the victory Jesus has decisively won for us over death and that ravaging temptation of the spirit: that history lacks meaning, that it is a tale of the madness of accidental beings on a planet drifting like a mote on a tide of light through the endless vastness of space.

Jesus emphasizes unfeigned love as the quality of life by which his followers may be identified. It is the lifeblood of the Kingdom whose central and unifying relationship is with Jesus himself. Fidelity is, then, of no small consequence, as it must match in depth and breadth the great edifice of love which it supports in our individual and community lives. Jesus finds it easy to forgive sins of the flesh in the lives of loving people who do not deceive themselves or others about their actions. What he cannot forgive is the pretense to goodness, the acid of hypocrisy that eats away the fabric of every relationship. What inserts the real evil in any behavior, whether a fall of the flesh or a pompous sigh of the spirit, is falsehood, the rottenness like that inside whitewashed tombs. Infidelity is fundamentally wrong because it is rooted in falseness and lies, in the desecration of a relationship whose worth is measured in the truthfulness with which it is lived. Religion is meaningless when it is a contrivance that sucks the spiritual energy out of men and women by misleading them about what God expects of them.

Jesus' battle was against the fixers, the self-invested who claim exemptions from the demands of honesty as they brutally pursue their own interests, always at the expense of others. No greater sinners exist than those who falsify the idea of God into that of an eternal and small-minded bookkeeper whose favor can only be won by keeping rules and regulations. Jesus speaks, above all, to the healthy instincts of people, affirming these and underscoring the sacramental moments of life, such as birth and marriage, in which the countless ordinary days of love and devotion are drawn together, recognized as the fields from which the harvest of real religion is finally taken. Jesus talks often of plantings, of seeds good and bad, of their time of flowering when their true nature will be recognized. He has, in a challenge that confounds modern distorters of faith as much as it did the Pharisees, given us a simple message that truthful people already understand and that hypocrites never will.

We cannot have a relationship with Jesus and falsehood, for Jesus is truth and in his Kingdom we discover our truest selves. Many Gospel incidents offer us examples of people coming to terms with the real truth about themselves in the presence of Jesus. He seems to smelt the truth out of men and women, freeing them from the dross that cripples them physically and spiritually. They admit some truth of themselves—that they are sinners, that their children are in need, that they have acted falsely in some way or other—and they discover the deepest truth about themselves. The power of truth is the energy of the long miracle of faith; that is what makes us free. To be perfect does not mean to follow ensnaring rules but to be whole, to live the fullest truth of our existence.

Jesus is the opponent of the lie, that sweat of demons that blurs our perception of ourselves and the universe. That philosophers and theologians have wrangled endlessly over a proper definition of lying illustrates its fascinating and convoluted nature. It is the seed and fruit of a culture which values appearances over reality, which distorts religion for the furtherance of power, which ultimately estranges people from knowing and being themselves.

With the great coda of Matthew's writing, the commission to carry Jesus' teachings into the depths of the universe, we reflect on the central points of the meaning of his life. Jesus challenges the world's bias in favor of falsehood, its enchantment with the counterfeit even in those grave and constant experiences that define us as human, its flirtation even in the heart of organized religions with the tempting power of deceit. Our meditation on Matthew comes to an end, but our relationship with Jesus, who is truth, continues. His Kingdom of friendship will forever stand out, brightly lighted in a darkened world, often under siege, sometimes ignored, but always true to itself. It remains the only environment in which men and women ever flourish.